D1321182

KAW VALLEY
LANDSCAPES

KAW VALLEY LANDSCAPES

A Traveler's Guide to Northeastern Kansas

JAMES R. SHORTRIDGE

UNIVERSITY PRESS OF KANSAS

Second edition, revised
© 1977 by James R. Shortridge
© 1988 by the University Press of Kansas

Illustrations by Antoinette Cook Smith
Maps by Norman Carpenter
and the Kansas University Cartographic Service

Published by the University Press of Kansas (Lawrence, Kansas
66045), which was organized by the Kansas Board of Regents and is
operated and funded by Emporia State University, Fort Hays State
University, Kansas State University, Pittsburg State University, the
University of Kansas, and Wichita State University

Library of Congress Cataloging-in-Publication Data

Shortridge, James R., 1944–
Kaw Valley landscapes.
Bibliography: p.
Includes index.
1. Automobiles—Road guides—Kansas—Kansas
River Valley.   2. Kansas River Valley (Kan.)—
Description and travel—Guide-books.   I. Title.
GV1024.S44   1988   917.81   88-17167
ISBN 0-7006-0382-4
ISBN 0-7006-0383-2 (pbk.)

Printed in the United States of America
10 9 8 7 6 5 4 3 2 1

TO

Walter M. Kollmorgen,

who taught me the

value of local studies

PREFACE

People are innately curious about places, and Americans in particular have always longed to explore and experience what lies just beyond the horizon. Newspapers, recognizing this trait, issue weekly travel sections to cater to it; but geographers, the professionals who specialize in the study of places, have seldom provided material to aid in the exploration process. This book represents an attempt to rectify the situation by presenting what one geographer sees in his local surroundings.

Kansas, perhaps more than many other places, needs a tour guide because the state is more generally viewed as a place to escape from rather than as a place to visit. An Alaska state promotional piece in the 1970s, for example, carried the caption "Once you've seen Alaska everything else looks like Kansas." And I once found graffiti on a university library wall that said, "Living in Kansas is a contradiction." Another example of the prevailing image of Kansas comes from television's M*A*S*H series, when Major Winchester's displeasure over the possibility of spending time in the Leavenworth Disciplinary Barracks changes to horror with his realization "Oh, my God, that's in Kansas."

Although it is true that Kansas cannot offer a traveler Colorado's mountains or California's beaches, there is much that is interesting in the state. Kansas' beauty is perhaps more subtle than that of other places, but it is certainly present in abundance. One who travels exclusively by the bland interstate highways misses a fascinating local panorama of land and life. How many Kansans have stopped to look at the red boulders brought to the area by ancient ice sheets, for example, or have noticed the other striking differences in the appearance of land that underwent glaciation? How many know that there are Indian reservations in this area or concentrated settlements of Slavic or German peoples?

The list is long: coal-mining towns, new types of agriculture that cater to leisure-minded urbanites, the serene majesty of the Flint Hills grazing area, the impact of reservoirs on sleepy rural towns, the variety of folk architecture. These and countless other things make up the Kaw Valley landscape.

The rural areas and small towns of northeast Kansas are the focus of this tour, and an attempt has been made to sample the full physical and cultural variety of the region. Lawrence, Topeka, and Kansas City, Missouri, are purposely not included, because even cursory discussions of them would make the book impossibly long. These cities are dealt with indirectly, however, through their impact on the land-use and settlement patterns of their hinterlands. Kansas City, Kansas, and Leavenworth are the only large cities that are toured in detail. As described in the following pages, these are two very special places, quite different from the "textbook" cities familiar to most Americans. They deserve more attention than they have heretofore received.

The body of this guide endeavors to interpret the visible landscapes that exist in northeast Kansas, but it barely touches on what many observers feel is the very essence of local life—the weather and the climate. If Kansas land forms are rather subtle, Kansas weather provides a spectacular counterbalance. A big sky, tremendous sunsets, violent storms, and extremes of temperature—all are important components of the regional personality, and these phenomena should be kept in mind while making the tour. Those who travel only by "armchair" may wish to sample works of artist John Steuart Curry, a native of Jefferson County, especially *The Line Storm* and *The Tornado*. The general feeling is also well expressed by another native, playwright William Inge. The following paragraphs are from his introduction to *The Plains States*, a 1968 publication of Time-Life Books, which has kindly granted permission to reproduce them here:

A person lives in this mid-country with an inherent consciousness of the sky. One is always aware of the sky in these states, because one sees so much more of it than in the mountainous regions where the horizons are blocked and the heavens are trimmed down like a painting, to fit a smaller frame. And human life on the prairie is more dependent upon and influenced by the sky and its constant maneuverings than in other regions. Men here look at the sky each morning as soon as they get out of bed, to see what kind of a day is indicated. Life and prosperity depend upon the sky, which can destroy a season's crops in a few hours, by hail or blizzards or tornadoes or a relentlessly burning sun that can desiccate the land like an Old Testament curse.

During my growing years in Kansas, I witnessed every extreme of weather and learned that it is as unpredictable in all the Plains States as the pictures that show up on a slot machine. I attended the University of Kansas, at Lawrence, in the early 1930's, when dust storms were periodically enveloping the land. The dust darkened the sun and filled the atmosphere, seeping into houses and stores. There was no way of escaping it. It discolored all the air and made the necessary act of breathing a hazard and a discomfort.

The spring when I graduated from the university, there was a deluge. Between mid-April and early June there were but three days when there was no rain at all. Graduating seniors had to march in the rain to the vast Hoch Auditorium, where we sat in moist attendance in our damp caps and gowns, smelling of wet wool. All the rivers and streams overflowed their banks and the entire eastern half of the state was flooded. Train and bus service was either stopped or rerouted. When the rains finally ceased, the sun came out in full force, creating a steamy heat that lasted the summer. The following spring and summer there was a tragic drought. The rivers and streams withered dry, livestock died on the plains with parched throats, and the record-breaking heat (for two weeks temperatures reached 118 degrees in my own section of Kansas) kept people closed up inside their homes, hanging wet sheets over electric fans to create a semblance of air and refreshment. The entire earth looked as if blasted in a furnace. The Plains States were a partition of hell.

In April of 1938, when I was teaching high school in a small mining town close to my home, I experienced my first tornado. It struck unexpectedly at noon after a still and sunny morning when students and faculty had walked to school with no anticipation whatever of the freakish violence that the elements were preparing for them. About one third of the town, as I remember, was leveled.

But of course there is beautiful weather on the plains. Nowhere in the world is the morning sky such an innocent blue. And nowhere is the sunset more awesome; a burning globe covers the land with a phosphorescent glow before it sinks into the far horizon. When spring comes early, the month of April can be joyous with bright green grass, budding leaves and yellow daffodils. And sometimes the sun is gentle to the summer months, providing days of pleasant warmth and nights that are cool and sweet with the smell of honeysuckle. In October there is a quickening of life when the trees turn orange and yellow and red, and the harvest brings apples, melons and pumpkins to the markets. The new school year is begun by now, and the daytime world is left to the elders, while the young attend classes and cheer at football games. And there is always good hope for a mild winter.

This book owes its direct inspiration to E. Cotton Mather, professor emeritus at the University of Minnesota, who has written a similar guide to the vicinity of Minneapolis–St. Paul. Indirectly, I am indebted to the anonymous writers of the 1930s who composed the remarkable American Guide Series to the individual states of the country. These books are well worn in the libraries I have visited, a testimony to their popularity and utility. They are still valuable today as gauges on which to measure the pace of change in recent decades. Work on the original edition of this Kaw Valley guidebook began in a 1972 seminar on local geography at the University of Kansas, and the enthusiasm of my students provided the impetus to complete the research. Thanks are therefore due to Richard Groop, Steve Lavin, and Charles Wendt and, especially, to Kevin Condon, Jay Farrell, and Joseph Manzo for their strong initial forays into Jefferson County, Wabaunsee County, and Jackson County, respectively. Later field assistance to complete the book was provided by Joseph Manzo, again, on the Strawberry Hill area, Debora Field on Leavenworth, and Harold MacDowell on Johnson County. Antoinette Cook Smith fashioned graceful line drawings for the text, and the Kansas University Cartographic Service drafted the maps and diagrams. I am also grateful to the late John Longhurst at the Coronado Press, who took the risk of publishing the first edition of this somewhat unusual book.

The possibility of a second edition for the guide was initiated by the enthusiasm of staff members at the University Press of Kansas and the cooperation of Bonnie Kounas at Coronado Press. New data were provided by the Leavenworth Chamber of Commerce, the Lenexa city-planning office, and the Kansas City, Kansas, Information and Research Department. Many residents along the tour route shared their time and insights with me; they made the work of revision both stimulating and enjoyable.

The last detailed field reconnaissance of the route was conducted during the fall of 1987. Changes have occurred in the landscape since then, of course, sometimes predictably, as in the expansion of Lenexa, but sometimes not. The tour book is like a photograph, capturing the Kansas scene at a particular point in time. I hope it will be useful, not only now, but in the future as well. Understanding changes in the landscape can be as interesting as observing current conditions.

The starting point of the tour is easy to find, at the Kansas-Missouri border on Interstate Highway 70. It is an appropriate place, because the Kansas River, whose valley is our subject, here empties into the Missouri River. The spot has added significance, because the viaduct over the Kaw—Kansans' familiar name for their river—is dedicated to Lewis and Clark. What better place for a modern exploring expedition to begin?

Directional information is set in italic type throughout the guide for easy reference. Mileages are indicated in two ways: as a cumulative figure and then, in parenthesis, by the distance from the last notation. The latter figure is especially important, for with side trips and detours, not to mention faulty odometers, the cumulative mileage often becomes of limited value.

One final piece of advice—the more slowly you go, the more you will see. A three-hundred-and-fifty-mile tour is far too long to be attempted in a single outing; in order to know an area, one must stop frequently, talk to people, and explore on foot. The mileages in the guide are cumulative, but it is perhaps better to think of the route as consisting of a number of trips, each convenient for a day. One may join the route at any point. Interstate Highway 70, which bisects the tour area, provides easy access to its various sections. Have a pleasant journey.

KAW VALLEY
LANDSCAPES

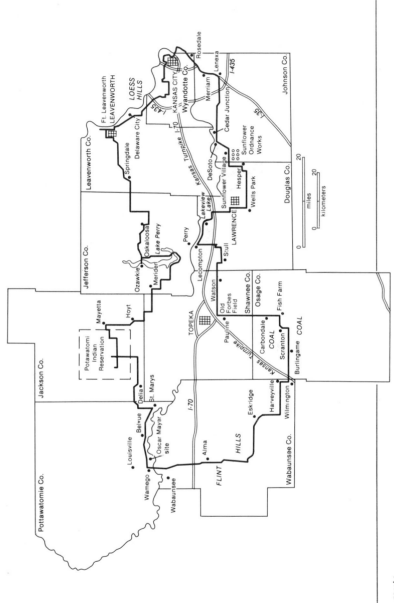

Trip route

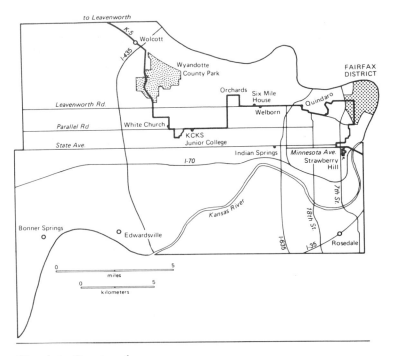

Wyandotte County reference map

» *Mile 0.0 (0.0) Begin on the Lewis and Clark Viaduct at the Kansas-Missouri Border. Proceed west on Interstate 70, following the signs to Minnesota Avenue and downtown Kansas City, Kansas.*

Kawsmouth. The smoky, odorous lowland that lies beneath the roadway was the commercial heart of nineteenth-century Kansas City. Immediately on the left is a warehouse district, which is served by innumerable railroad spurs; but the traditional focus of the area is several blocks south, where the Kansas City Stockyards span the state line. In the past, the stockyard area was ringed by Armour, Swift, Cudahy, and other major meat packers; but today, both industries have all but vanished from the Kansas City scene. Feed lots located in smaller Kansas towns furnish the market for more and more cattle producers, and the packers have followed along, replacing the antiquated plants they had in Kansas City with new facilities (see discussion on the proposed Oscar-Mayer operation in Wamego, mile 185.65).

Several legacies of the meat-packing industry remain with Kansas City. For example, a choice steak carries the city's name, and the American Royal livestock show still draws a crowd annually into these river bottoms. Armourdale, the portion of the lowland west of the Kansas River, perpetuates the past era with its name.

0.6 (0.6) *The Kansas River.*

0.8 (0.2) *Gateway Center.* This impressive entrance to Kansas City, Kansas, resplendent with a flagpoled mall, a bank, office buildings, and a shopping center, is a recent product of urban renewal. It is also a symbolic attempt to deal with an inferiority complex that has haunted this city for a century. Stemming originally from the greater development on the Missouri side of the line, the problem has been compounded by the emergence of Johnson County, to the south, as a prestigious residential area. Wyandotte County thus sees itself as second-rate in regard both to housing and to business. As one observer has noted: "The legend is told—and with a good deal of truth—that those from the Missouri side invariably state that they are from Kansas City, Missouri, while persons living on the Kansas side report that they are from Kansas City. The implication is clear."[1]

It seems as if Kansas City, Kansas, has turned inward on itself. Local realtors rarely advertise in the *Kansas City* (Mo.) *Star* and *Times*, for example, thus making it highly unlikely that newcomers to the Kansas City area will locate in Wyandotte County. Partly because of this, the population here is more stable than in most other cities of comparable size, and the residents have deeper historical roots in the area. Kansas City Kansans like their town for the most part and do not see why outsiders should hold unfavorable opinions about it. Yet such opinions are general. One wonders if the situation is not caused primarily by a cultural isolation of the area. Wyandotte County is very different from its surrounding counties in basic things such as ethnic background, type of labor force, general industrial structure, and political loyalties. Taken together, these factors may have turned Wyandotte County into a cultural island on the Kansas scene, and cultural islands are commonly misunderstood by outsiders.

» *Mile 1.0 (0.2) Turn left onto Fifth Street, then left again in two blocks onto Ann Street.*

Strawberry Hill. You are now entering an older residential section of the city called Strawberry Hill. The name, now boldly announced on a new billboard at Fifth and Armstrong, comes from the wild strawberries that used to grow in the area, but today it is synonymous with peoples of Slavic heritage. These people came to Kansas City in large numbers between 1890 and World War I to work in the Armourdale packing plants. The move to Strawberry Hill began in 1903, after a major flood forced them out of the bottom lands. Today the neighborhood occupies the upland area south of Armstrong and east of Seventh Street. The first landmark is St. Mary's Church, a massive limestone building at Fifth and Ann, which was the first Catholic parish in Kansas City (1858).

The block between Fifth and Fourth streets on Ann is typical of the area. Note that the houses, though old, are well maintained. This area is one of the most stable in the city; few houses come on the real-estate market, and many have known only one family in their sixty or so years of existence. Several things strike the eye of someone who is used to seeing only suburban residential areas. The houses front on 25-foot lots, which gives the impression of crowding, even though the actual distance between the houses may not be much less than that found in new subdivisions. Garages are scarce here, and the sidewalks are made of brick. One looks in vain, however, for evidence of traditional Slavic architectural styles. The houses were built by American contractors and were then sold to the immigrant peoples.

» *Mile 1.3 (0.3) Turn right at Fourth Street, then right again in two blocks onto Sandusky as Fourth Street turns west.*

St. John's. Along the west side of Fourth Street is St. John's parish, the social and religious center for the Croatian families in the area. Old World customs are encouraged here. Older people can still confess in their native tongue on Saturday afternoons, and the Tamburitzans, a singing and dancing group, keeps traditional culture alive for young people.

Across Fourth Street are the remnants of St. John's Park. This former playground for Ray Evans, the Kansas University football All-American, and Andrew and Edward Skradski, of Kansas State basketball fame, was largely appropriated for the expressway you see below. The park still provides an excellent view of the Kawsmouth industrial area that is well worth the short walk from your car.

Residential scenes in Strawberry Hill

» *Mile 1.5 (0.2) Turn left onto Thompson. After one block, turn right onto Orville.*

» *Mile 1.6 (0.1) Intersect Fifth Street. Continue straight ahead on Orville after looking at Fifth Street.*

Neighborhood Center. Along the west side of Fifth Street there are several small businesses that serve the Strawberry Hill area. Two small neighborhood grocery stores survived here until recently; they provided specialty items and local news. Today, the popular information exchanges are Rose's Beauty Salon and Jennie's Restaurant. Another, and even more obvious, neighborhood symbol is just north of Jennie's: a brick building with a large concrete sign that reads Croatian-Slovene National Home.

As you drive through Strawberry Hill, it is interesting to observe the street names. You have already intersected Barnett, and coming up is Elizabeth Avenue. These and other streets in the area, such as Splitlog, Tauromee, Northrup, and Armstrong, take their names from Wyandotte Indians who owned this land prior to white settlement. (Many Wyandottes acquired English names via white contact in their earlier Ohio reservation.)

» *Mile 1.7 (0.1) Turn right onto Sixth Street.*

Near the intersection of Sixth and Orville are two prominent local businesses. Just south on Sixth is the headquarters of the Darby Corporation, a large producer of structural steel, which was founded by former U.S. Senator Harry Darby. The unlikely location is explained by the Strawberry Hill origins of Darby, and the building's existence is visible testimony to the loyalty that people feel for their area. Also note the modern Skradski Funeral Home with its red-tile roof. Is this Mediterranean architectural touch more than just a coincidence?

Church Density and Community Vitality. From the corner of Sixth and Orville two additional Strawberry Hill churches are visible. Two blocks south is Holy Family Church, of massive Romanesque construction, which features another suggestive tile roof. The ministry here is to a largely Slovene congregation. On a hill about a mile south of Holy Family stands still another ethnic church. Its distinctive steeple marks it as Eastern Orthodox, in this case Russian Orthodox. The density of churches in this area is amazing, as is their vitality. All have sizable congregations that include many families from outside the neighborhood who could not find housing within the limited confines of Strawberry Hill but who choose to keep ties here.

The combination of well-kept homes, active local businesses and churches, and the desire of young families to stay in the Strawberry Hill area is rare in other American ethnic communities today. The local vitality may be related to the peculiar isolated nature of Kansas City, Kansas, as we noted earlier. In such a setting it should be easier for minority groups to maintain their identity.[2]

1.8 (0.1) On the right, at 417 North Fifth Street, is the Strawberry Hill Memorial V.F.W., one of a few establishments that have incorporated the community's name into their titles. North of this point, the Strawberry Hill neighborhood becomes increasingly diluted by the commercial developments of downtown Kansas City. A final hurrah is the strawberry design incorporated into the sign for Joe's Auto Body Works in the 500 block on the left.

2.0 (0.2) The modernistic white buildings on the left house the police and county health departments and various municipal offices. In front of the Seventh Street main entrance, ethnic flags have been raised to symbolize the pride the city takes in its diverse origins. This unusual procedure is further testimony to the cultural uniqueness of Kansas City, Kansas.

2.1 (0.1) On your left is a municipal rose garden; just beyond it, on the hilltop, is a two-acre cemetery, which is still owned by the Wyandotte Indians. Its survival in the midst of downtown Kansas City is a historical anomaly. The cemetery was to have been turned over to the city for business purposes in 1906, but three local women, the Conley sisters, took up the Indian cause. They entered the cemetery and erected a small shelter, which was quickly dubbed Fort Conley. By this maneuver and by later arguing the case personally, though unsuccessfully, before the U.S. Supreme Court, the sisters succeeded in winning public support for their cause. Today the cemetery has been declared a National Historic Site, and the Conley sisters rest there, alongside the Wyandottes.

» *Mile 2.1 (0.0) Turn right onto Armstrong Street. In one block, turn left onto Fifth Street and then, in another block, turn left onto Minnesota Avenue.*

The block that you have just circled is a no man's land between urban-renewal projects. The Gateway Center project extends west to Fifth Street, but the Center City project, which we are approaching, does not begin until Sixth Street. After those projects were completed, this block stood vacant for some time before it became a municipal parking lot.

2.5 (0.4) *Downtown Kansas City.* The Minnesota Avenue shopping district has suffered from competition with the larger Kansas City, Missouri, downtown ever since the completion of the intercity viaduct in 1907. The problem became acute during the 1960s. Retail sales in the county actually fell between 1966 and 1967, and most of the overall growth during the decade was offset by inflation.[3] The Center City urban-renewal project that you see before you was an attempt at revival. In the words of the mayor who pushed the project through: "The goal is to make our Center City so attractive that people for miles around will come to look and shop, and merchants will be attracted to bid for space in the project."[4]

Center City has never fulfilled its promise; in fact, it was generally regarded as a waste of money even before it was completed. The project probably cost the former mayor his reelection, and business disruption caused by the construction of Center City was a deciding factor in the move of major stores, such as Adler's, Montgomery Ward, and Helzberg's, from their locations on Minnesota Avenue.

What caused the problem for Minnesota Avenue? Many residents feel it was precipitated by the opening of the Indian Springs shopping center about three miles west at Forty-fifth and State Avenue, but this seems unlikely, because business was bad long before that shopping area opened in 1971. The real culprits were probably the earlier shopping centers in neighboring counties and, especially, the increasing suburbanization of Wyandotte County itself. Fewer affluent families live near Minnesota Avenue each year. The money that is now being spent at Indian Springs is not being diverted there from Minnesota Avenue; rather, it represents a retention for Wyandotte County of dollars that otherwise would have been spent in Missouri or in Johnson County, Kansas.

The economic structure of Minnesota Avenue is in a state of flux. ABC Furniture, in the 700 block, is one of the few remaining examples of the old class of general merchants. Vacant stores in this block once housed similar enterprises. Newer businesses that cater to a neighborhood, rather than to a larger municipal clientele, are represented by a café, a jeweler, and two savings-and-loan offices. A market exists for more businesses of this type. The big growth industry on Minnesota Avenue is offices, however, particularly governmental offices. Headquarters for two large banks are in the 600 block, along with the Board of Public Utilities building and the municipal library. The 700 block contains the local Chamber of Commerce office and headquarters for region 7 of the Environmental Protection Agency, which recently relocated here from Missouri after some prodding by Robert Dole, the influential Kansas senator. Conversion to governmental offices is a common fate for old central-city shopping areas. Cynics say the trend represents still more subsidy by taxpayers, but it is also an appropriate way to utilize an area that has good access to transportation and a central location but a declining density of population.

Symbolic Kansas. Most Kansas City Kansans feel that the $20 million spent on Center City could better have been invested elsewhere, but given the reality of the mall area, their assessments vary from bombastic approval to chagrin. The original design was supposed to reflect the Kansas landscape with, in the words of the local Urban Renewal Agency, "the horizontality of the western prairie, the protective intimacy of the Flint Hills, the grandeur of the eastern river country, [and] the strong vertical way man has dealt with the rural and urban environment."[5] Given both horizontal and vertical components, as well as grandeur and intimacy, it is clear that the designers of the mall could do anything they chose. The Kansas inspiration was a ruse, and the extreme elements in the design have now been modified. Stainless-steel pylons once stood near the intersection of Seventh Street, symbolizing, according to the designers, either city skyscrapers or Kansas grain elevators. The memory of them is recalled by the Pylon

Plaza office building at 710 Minnesota. Midway between Seventh and Eighth streets was a split hemisphere, which supposedly represented either an Indian mound or a Kansas hill penetrated by a highway cut.

The principal visual impression that one gets from the new mall is that of a clean, stylized look with few soft lines. This contrasts sharply with the hodgepodge façades of the existing buildings and their typically garish signs. Some find this vivid juxtaposition unbearable; others regard it as pleasing or see the mall as an incentive to upgrade the downtown buildings.

» *Mile 2.8 (0.3) Turn right onto Eighth Street, then, after three blocks, turn right again, onto Washington Boulevard.*

The Brotherhood Block. The impressive building at the northeast corner of Eighth and Minnesota takes its name from the International Brotherhood of Boilermakers, Iron Ship Builders, Blacksmiths, Forgers, and Helpers. This union, which figures prominently in the nation's shipbuilding industry, has its headquarters in landlocked Kansas City for historical reasons. It came in 1893, when a Topeka man was president and when railroads provided the bulk of union employment. The older part of the building was constructed in 1920, and a nine-story tower was added on the north in 1948. A variety of retailers and professional people fill the building, including the Brotherhood Bank and Trust Company.

3.4 (0.6) *Gateway Revisited.* Crossing Fifth Street you reenter the Gateway renewal project. On the right is a small shopping center and a good view of the ten-story office building called Two Gateway Center. These developments appear to be a boon to Wyandotte County until one makes a closer examination. Cars from Missouri and Johnson County dominate the office building's parking lots, and the shopping center is filled primarily with bureaucratic institutions, such as an Armed Forces Recruiting Center and a Selective Service Office. The most successful appearing of the enterprises is Pitko's, a Slavic restaurant, which is obviously more in harmony with the surrounding residential neighborhood than are the other stores. Here, Wyandotte County license tags predominate.

» *Mile 3.6 (0.2) Turn left onto Fourth Street.*

The Gateway Plaza apartment complex on the right is a low-income housing project sponsored by the Baptist Church as part of the overall Gateway renewal. Note the currently popular "French-style" mansard roof, which covers most of the second-story walls.

3.8 (0.2) Jersey Creek. This open sewer used to be an engaging, if not particularly sanitary, play area for local children. A cyclone fence now prevents access to it.

» *Mile 3.9 (0.1) Turn right onto Walker Street.*

Walker Street. Here is another type of low-income housing. One could make remarks about small houses and lots, but these features are much the same as the ones seen previously on Strawberry Hill. The main difference between here and there is upkeep. Weediness is the rule on Walker Street; it is the exception on Strawberry Hill.

It is also interesting to compare Walker Street with the Gateway Plaza apartments. Is living that much better in the new apartments? The advantage of Gateway in regard to such basic items as heating efficiency and plumbing is clear-cut; but does this fully compensate for the loss of less obvious features such as a front sitting porch and a private yard and garden? Many people say no and therefore remain on Walker Street. They carry a clear message to planners and architects to become more involved with cultural values.

» *Mile 4.05 (0.15) Turn left onto Third Street. After one block, turn right onto Richmond Street and proceed two blocks east. Turn left onto First Street.*

Juniper Gardens. This 400-unit public-housing project was built during the late 1950s and is now beginning to show its age. Aluminum doors have been kicked in, and the wood trim needs paint. Note the number of people on the street who are tinkering with their cars. This formerly universal American custom seems to be localized today in urban low-income areas and in small towns.

Juniper Gardens is the largest of Kansas City's public-housing complexes, and its condition may have been influential in a 1965 decision to build no more units of this size. The city views concentrating the poor as undesirable. Future projects will be smaller and will be dispersed throughout the city, which may lead to a more economically and socially integrated community.

» *Mile 4.4 (0.35) Turn left onto Edgerton Street, then right after two blocks onto Third Street.*

» *Mile 4.55 (0.15) Turn right onto Quindaro Boulevard.*

Fairfax. In 1920 the flat lowland area that you see ahead was a marsh known as the North Bottoms. By 1931 it had been transformed into one of the nation's first planned industrial parks, and today its payroll and taxes form the mainstay of the economy of Kansas City, Kansas. The 170 or so industries here employ some 13,500 workers and generate 18 percent of the city's assessed valuation. Without Fairfax the local area would have been plunged into deep depression by the closing of the Armourdale packing houses.

The possibility of an industrial park here was dependent on levee construction to keep out the Missouri River floods. When this was accomplished in the early 1920s, the Union Pacific Railroad was induced to spend $1 million to develop the park. The result was highly successful. Industry liked the flat land, the plentiful water supplies that the flood-plain location provided, and, especially, the idea of an area that was specifically designed for their needs. They could have transportation facilities and did not have to worry that nearby residential and shopping areas would complain about noise and the number of local trucks and railroad crossings. Moreover, as Fairfax was not inside the city limits of Kansas City, there were substantial savings in school and property taxes. When one realizes how rare this combination of advantages was in the early 1930s, it is easy to understand the rapid growth of the area. Fairfax had a head start on other industrial parks, and it profited from this.

» *Mile 4.8 (0.25) Turn left on Fairfax Trafficway.*

The name Fairfax was taken from Fairfax County, Virginia, where bottom-land development along the Potomac River provided the inspiration for Kansas City entrepreneurs.

5.2 (0.4) Intersect Stanley Road. This street honors Guy Stanley, the founder of Fairfax, who bought the land and interested Union Pacific in developing it. On the right is the Sealright Company, the first plant to locate in the district in 1931. The list of corporations that flank this section of the trafficway is impressive: Massey-Ferguson, Firestone, Simmons, Certainteed, Pacific Chloride, and Sealy.

5.4 (0.2) *General Motors.* Before 1985, Fairfax Trafficway from here northward marked the border between the industrial park and a municipal airport. The airport was used extensively by Fairfax business people, but it became expendable after the construction of the mammoth Kansas City International complex completely freed the old regional airport, just across the Missouri River channel, for smaller business planes (see mile 357.3). City officials decided to open the Fairfax airport site to industry and were delighted when General Motors agreed to replace its aging automobile assembly plant here with a new facility. This state-of-the-art complex is visible on the right for the next half mile. It cost approximately $750 million to construct and is controlled by the Chevrolet-Pontiac-Canada group. Its five thousand workers make it the third-largest industrial employer in the state, after Boeing Aircraft in Wichita and Southwestern Bell statewide.

» *Mile 5.95 (0.55) Turn left onto Sunshine Road.*

At the intersection of Fairfax Trafficway and Sunshine Road stands a Kansas City fire station, mute evidence that Fairfax has been annexed by the city. The event occurred in 1964, after nearly twenty years of bitter debate. The city claimed that it needed tax money to finance its development programs, and it argued that Fairfax had been given a "free ride" long enough. Industrialists said they didn't need city services and accused the city of going back on its original promises. The citizenry, wanting tax relief but fearing a loss of jobs should the plants relocate, were split on the issue.

6.05 (0.1) Junction of Chrysler Road. The majority of the roads in Fairfax have been named after local industries. Here is Chrysler, and coming up in the next two miles are Fiberglas (after Owen-Corning Fiberglas), Dodge, Harvester (International Harvester), and McCormick. These street names are evidence that Fairfax was planned especially for industry; moreover, by comparing the street names with a list of corporations that are currently operating here, one can demonstrate the long tenure of the companies.

6.6 (0.55) *Access and the Future of Fairfax.* The Seventh Street Trafficway here is one of the two original highway transportation lifelines for Fairfax. Both it and Fairfax Trafficway, which connects Fairfax with the Lewis and Clark Viaduct and Interstate 70, had become increasingly inadequate by the 1970s. To alleviate the situation, the city has recently completed a new highway, Kansas 5, which links the district with Interstate 635. This new road has invigorated the district by helping commuters and suppliers alike.

On the southwest corner of Sunshine and Seventh Street Trafficway is the mammoth Sunshine Biscuit Company, the obvious namesake of Sunshine Road.

7.0 (0.4) The new highway link, noted above, joins Sunshine Road on the left.

» *Mile 7.1 (0.1) Fork in the road. Keep left, leaving Sunshine Road and joining Tenth Street.*

7.25 (0.15) Esplanade Street, branching off to the right, approximates the boundary between the upland and the Missouri River flood plain. Note the Board of Public Utilities (BPU) light plant on the right. Its location is excellent: isolated from residential areas yet close to the city and with good access to a railroad (for coal) and water (for cooling).

Rolling Hills. A quarter of a mile up Esplanade is the entrance to a Georgian-style brick apartment complex built by the Fairfax

Sunshine Biscuit Company in Fairfax

visionary Guy Stanley. Stanley's ingenuity is apparent in the units' heating system. By simply arranging to pipe in waste heat produced by the nearby BPU plant, he saved both his tenants and BPU considerable money.

7.55 (0.3) Underpass for the new extension of Kansas Highway 5.

» *Mile 7.7 (0.15) Turn right onto Roswell for one block, then turn left onto Baltimore. Merge onto Parkwood Boulevard in one and one-half blocks.*

7.9 (0.2) *Parkwood.* The appearance of lampposts along the road marks the beginning of Parkwood subdivision. Plotted in 1908, its curved streets were far ahead of their time. The area has been well maintained, and was even more beautiful before Dutch elm disease claimed most of the large roadside trees. Note the near universality of the front porch. America lost this comfortable feature when it adopted the ranch-style house and air conditioning everywhere after World War II.[6]

» *Mile 8.0 (0.1) Turn right onto Laurel. After one block, turn left onto Eleventh Street.*

» *Mile 8.1 (0.1) Turn right onto Quindaro Boulevard.*

8.4 (0.3) *J. C. Nichols.* Five blocks north of Quindaro on Thirteenth Street is the old subdivision of California Park. Most of the original homes are gone now, and the area is somewhat blighted, but California Park is important because of what might have been. This was the first project (1905) undertaken by J. C. Nichols.

Nichols was undoubtedly the man who was most responsible for the emergence of Johnson County and the Country Club Plaza area of Kansas City, Missouri, as prestigious residential areas. His luxurious Mission Hills development in the former and his exquisite pioneer shopping center in the latter have been acclaimed nationwide. Local stories persist that Nichols originally wished to build the Plaza in Wyandotte County. What would the area have been like had Nichols remained? It is interesting food for thought.

8.75 (0.35) This area has one of the highest crime rates in Kansas City. Note the protective iron bars on the window fronts of L. A. Furniture, Rucker Shoe Repair, and A and M Records and Tapes. German shepherd dogs are numerous in this neighborhood.

» *Mile 9.1 (0.35) The road jogs to the north. Stay on Quindaro Boulevard.*

Iron bars are present even on several of the well-maintained bungalows on the left. Note also the high frequency of storefront churches along Quindaro. Almost all are conservative independent groups that offer the economically disadvantaged in this area an alternative to the religions of mainstream America.

» *Mile 9.4 (0.3) Turn right onto Twenty-seventh Street.*

» *Mile 9.6 (0.2) Turn left onto Brown Avenue, whose name changes to Leavenworth Road at Thirty-fourth Street.*

Old Quindaro. The intersection of Twenty-seventh Street and Brown Avenue marks the heart of the modern Quindaro neighborhood. Quindaro was originally an independent town, located a mile north on Twenty-seventh Street, whose history is related to the slavery controversy in territorial Kansas. Quindaro was founded in 1856 to provide Free State forces with a Missouri River port, because existing towns were generally controlled by proslavery Missourians. The city grew rapidly for a few years but then began to fade. After Free Staters gained control of Kansas politics, Quindaro's special need for existence disappeared.[7]

Today, evidence of old Quindaro is almost gone. Its principal legacy is the concentration here of a sizable percentage of Kansas City's black population. This came about in 1879, when the county received an influx of nearly a thousand Negroes from the lower Mississippi Valley in the space of two weeks! These Exodusters, as they were called, came to Kansas because of its Free State reputation; they concentrated in the early Kawsmouth town of Wyandotte, because it was the first river port they encountered. Wyandotte's forty-six hundred citizens were sympathetic, but they could hardly absorb so many people so quickly. Therefore, many Exodusters were sent to old Quindaro, where a black university, Freedmen's, was still in existence. These people furnished the core of a permanent black community.[8]

Freedmen's University eventually became Western University, a respected institution that was active until 1933. Its site, 1.4 miles north on Twenty-seventh Street, is now deserted, but a monument has been erected at the corner of Twenty-seventh and Sewell. It features a statue of the abolitionist leader John Brown.

10.2 (0.6) *I-635.* Construction work for Interstate 635 was completed in 1975. The road traverses Wyandotte County from north to south and provides a new bridge across the Missouri River. Officials see much of the future economic development of the area as being tied to this route. The connector link to Fairfax is one benefit. Moreover, by providing the county with direct access to the massive Kansas City International Airport, just across the river, it could generate general business activity on a significant scale.

It is historically ironic that the new interstate bridge is at Quindaro. The airport and the highway combined have made this a principal entrance into the county at the same time as the Kawsmouth area is having its troubles. There may be some chuckling in the old Quindaro cemetery!

Vegetable Stands. Thirty-fourth Street marked the western boundary of Kansas City from 1939 until a large-scale annexation program was begun in 1966. The area you will now be traversing was thus settled in a more haphazard manner than would have been allowed by city zoning laws. There is very uneven development, especially off the main thoroughfares, and large areas of vacant land are still common. House lots tend to be large, a reflection of the cheaper land costs outside the city and of the initial absence of sewer taxes and similar assessments. Given this background, it is not surprising to observe the numerous vegetable stands that spring up seasonally along Leavenworth Road.

11.5 (1.3) On the left is tiny Welborn Lake, an early developer's attempt to sell homesites by providing water amenities.

11.7 (0.2) *Six Mile House.* The route of Leavenworth Road approximates the upland divide, which separates streams flowing southward into the Kaw from these emptying directly into the Missouri River. Divides were usually favored as pioneer transportation routes because there were no bridges to build or maintain, and this one has long been in use. On the right, at 4960 Leavenworth Road, is the site of old Six Mile House, which was built as a tavern along the stage route from Kansas City to Leavenworth. It was constructed in 1860, and it took its name from the distance to the Kansas City ferry. The house was recently razed, but the front yard is still intact, complete with concrete steps, driveway, and large trees.

11.75 (0.05) On the left, note the intersection of Welborn Lane with Leavenworth Road. The odd angle of the junction is explained by the former presence of a railroad line that ran parallel to Welborn Lane.

12.0 (0.25) *Little Strawberry Hill.* Christ the King Church, on the left, is the religious focus for many Slavic families that have historical connections to Strawberry Hill (see mile 1.0). Some people moved here because they could not find housing in the old neighborhood, but more were drawn by the suburban amenities of large yards and good shopping centers. Several families have a double allegiance, maintaining membership at St. John's but attending most services at Christ the King. Christ the King offers religious inspiration but, because it is a diverse congregation, only modest ethnic support.

» *Mile 12.8 (0.8) Turn right onto Fifty-ninth Street.*

The next several blocks provide a good illustration of the urban settlement method in much of Wyandotte County. The houses are of many different architectural styles, indicating a prolonged, irregular settlement process that is very much in contrast to modern suburban tract developments. Lot sizes also vary considerably.

» *Mile 13.3 (0.5) Turn left onto Cernech Road.*

13.45 (0.15) *Orchards and Slopes.* After intersecting Sixtieth Street, look to your right, beyond the single tier of houses. The orchards you see are part of a sizable complex that extends to the north and west. The location here is classic. The soil is good, but the land slopes so much that it could not be plowed for conventional crops. In addition, the sloping land is actually an advantage for the orchardist. Cold air, which might injure the fruit with frost in either spring or fall, does not collect here. Instead, its weight carries it into the valley below. The moving air on the slope acts as an additional frost retardant. The microclimate that the slope thus creates can be the difference between success and failure in certain seasons. It is especially important here with peaches, a much more tender crop than apples.

» *Mile 13.8 (0.35) Turn left onto Sixty-third Street.*

If the season is right, you may wish to take a brief side trip one-half mile north on Sixty-third Street to visit the headquarters of Sigler's Orchards. Apples, peaches, and sweet cider are their specialties.

» *Mile 15.35 (1.55) Turn right onto Parallel Parkway.*

At the northeast corner of Sixty-third Street and Parallel Parkway, note the remnants of a farm. Until recently, a second farm occupied the site of the Butler Funeral Home on the north-west corner. This area has been inside the city limits for only about seventeen years.

Parallel Parkway. This is one of the most interesting roads in Wyandotte County; it is also one of the most frustrating for planners and developers. To understand the problem, however, some background information is necessary.

Unlike the Eastern Seaboard, midwestern America came under governmental control before there was pressure to settle it. This gave the government time to survey the land in order to provide a regular, easily understood system of subdivision. The procedure, believed to have been proposed by Thomas Jefferson, was to lay out carefully an east-west and a north-south line and then use these to survey a smaller grid, consisting of squares six miles by six miles (see diagram). A problem was in the meridional north-south lines. Because meridians converge as they extend poleward, the surveyed squares would become progressively deformed. It was therefore necessary to correct for this by having supplementary east-west survey lines at intervals paralleling the original base line. These are known as standard parallels.

To return to Wyandotte County, Parallel Parkway, as its name suggests, is one of these standard parallels. The problem that it creates for planners and developers is clear, both on the diagram and from observing the next mile or so of the roadway. The roads that come from the south do not match up with the ones from the north, because of the adjustment for converging meridians, which was made long ago.

15.5 (0.15) Note the jog in Sixty-fourth Street Terrace. This reflects the old surveying adjustment, even though Sixty-fourth Street Terrace was not one of the original meridional lines. It is a result of having the original road skeleton faithfully reproduce the surveyed lines and of having subsequent roads regularly spaced within the grid.

15.6 (0.1) Sixty-sixth Street enters from the south, but there is no northern continuation.

15.7 (0.1) Note here, and at the next two tenth-mile intervals, that streets enter Parallel Parkway from the north but have no southern continuation.

The township and range survey system

16.25 (0.55) Victory Hills Country Club on the left is one of many examples of low-intensity uses of the land along Parallel Parkway. Several factors are responsible for this, including the recentness of city annexation and the higher traffic count found on competing State Avenue, one mile to the south. The problem of the old land-survey system is also important, however, because it is expensive for developers to establish the good access roads that they deem necessary.

16.6 (0.35) The new campus of Kansas City, Kansas, Community College is on the left. The availability of space within the city for large land users like this is a positive legacy of the Parallel Parkway phenomenon.

» *Mile 17.1 (0.5) Turn left onto Seventy-seventh Street.*

Note the sweeping curve you negotiate just after turning. The curve transforms Seventy-seventh Street into Seventy-eighth Street; it is yet another reminder of the special status of Parallel Parkway.

» *Mile 17.5 (0.4) Turn right onto Walker Avenue.*

Prestige Housing. One of the most striking aspects of Wyandotte is the scarcity of high-income housing. Since leaving the

Fairfax district, the trip route has traversed an area of typical homes, whose mean family incomes in 1980 fell between $12,000 and $18,000. This reflects the blue-collar core of the Kansas City population. Wealthy families have traditionally chosen to live in the luxurious developments of northeast Johnson County and the Country Club Plaza, but some have remained loyal to Wyandotte County. The old prestigious area is centered on Washington Boulevard at Twenty-second Street, in the vicinity of Wyandotte High School, while the newer one stands directly before you. This development extends from Seventy-eighth to Eighty-second streets and from State Avenue north to our present location. Net family income in 1980 was more than $32,000.

As you drive along Walker, note the trappings that currently signify a "premier subdivision," such as this Normandy West. White paint is definitely out as a dominant color; it has been replaced by a variety of earthy, natural tones. The natural idea is further reflected in the roofs, with wood shingles being almost universal. Current taste is also clear in the endless repetition of formal evergreen plantings (especially yews) and the use of rock beds as a base for much of the landscaping. Less indicative of the times, but a sure sign of prestige homes in general, is the liberal use of brick and stone.

» *Mile 17.7 (0.2) Turn left one-half block on Seventy-ninth Street and then right onto New Jersey.*

The houses on New Jersey are part of the Westborough subdivision. It is a little older and less luxurious than Normandy West, but it still ranks as one of the best neighborhoods in the city. The lots here are smaller than in Normandy West, and the roofs are not shingled with wood, but the other ideas just discussed hold true, especially the emphasis on brick.

» *Mile 18.0 (0.3) Turn right onto Eighty-second Street.*

» *Mile 18.4 (0.4) Turn left onto Parallel Parkway.*

Note once again the road displacement at Parallel Parkway. The northern continuation of Eighty-second Street is Eighty-third Street.

» *Mile 18.7 (0.3) Turn right onto Eighty-fifth Street.*

White Church. The area centered on Eighty-fifth Street and Parallel is one of the oldest permanent settlements in Kansas, having been established as a Delaware village in the early 1830s. The name White Church comes from the Baptist mission that was set up amongst the Indians shortly thereafter.

18.8 (0.1) On the left is the site of the original White Church. The older stone part of the building carries a plaque stating that the mission was built in 1832, was destroyed in 1886, and was rebuilt in 1904.

» *Mile 19.2 (0.4) Turn left onto Georgia Avenue.*

The area to the north and west of the intersection of Eighty-fifth Street and Georgia Avenue was outside the city limits of Kansas City until recently, and open spaces, such as those visible coming north on Eighty-fifth, now become the rule, rather than the exception. New houses line Georgia for the first 0.4 mile, but cows and small older barns dominate the rest of the distance.

» *Mile 20.0 (0.8) Turn right onto Ninety-first Street.*

Note the widely varying quality of the houses near this intersection. An absence of city regulations has made it difficult to control blighting.

20.2 (0.2) A large pumpkin field on the left is well situated to take advantage of both bottom-land soil and the nearby urban jack-o-lantern market.

» *Mile 20.5 (0.3) Intersect Leavenworth Road. Proceed straight ahead on Ninety-first Street.*

Race Tracks. An automobile track, Lakeside Speedway, is located 0.4 mile west on Leavenworth Road. Another 0.6 mile beyond, at Ninety-ninth and Leavenworth, is the proposed site for a major horse and greyhound racing track. Parimutuel wagering was approved by Kansas voters in 1986, but licenses have not yet been issued. Experts predict that the state can support two major tracks, and this Leavenworth Road plan is one of two proposed for the Kansas City area. The site is adjacent to I-435, for easy access, and the proximity of Lakeside Speedway suggests that local residents will not be hostile to this land use.

Horse racing is now the third-largest spectator sport in the nation, and the greyhounds are right behind, at number six. Promoters say a major facility that would feature both animals would add $10-20 million annually to the local economy. Such a track would require fifteen hundred horses per season, which would use some 210,000 bales of straw for bedding and would eat two million pounds of grain and six million pounds of hay.[9] The greyhound business, though generating fewer dollars than the horses, is appealing for Kansas, because the state is already a breeding center for the animals and is home to the Greyhound Hall of Fame at Abilene.

20.8 (0.3) *Wyandotte County Lake.* Wyandotte County Lake is easily the best of its genre in Kansas. It combines a beautiful setting in a hardwood forest with a development plan that enhances rather than subjugates the natural beauty. The park was the idea of a local banker, Willard J. Breidenthal, who bought up fifteen hundred acres of the Marshall Creek watershed and donated it to the county.[10] Actual development was done in large part as WPA and PWA projects during the 1930s, and the area shows abundant evidence of the many hours of hand labor put in under these programs.

The substantial wooden entrance signs, with their sunken letters and stone bases, are reminiscent of those found in National Parks. The similarity is more than coincidental, because the whole system of roads, picnic areas, and shelter houses around the lake was designed in cooperation with the National Park Service. As is easily seen, the plan is admirable and still functions efficiently after fifty some years.

» *Mile 21.0 (0.2) "T" in the road; turn left and proceed along west side of the Lake.*

21.05 (0.05) Observe the bridge you are crossing. Constructed of hand-laid stone, it features three arches to handle the water flow. The amount of labor that went into this was very large, but the bridge is beautiful and is typical of the quality of Wyandotte County Lake.

21.3 (0.25) One of many local picnic areas. Again note the quality evident in the heavy wood construction.

21.4 (0.1) A nice overlook to the lake on the right.

» *Mile 22.0 (0.6) Road to Shelter House number 4: turn right and proceed to the shelter.*

Although broken glass and carved initials mar the picture to a degree, the shelter areas are still things of beauty. They are isolated from road noise, yet have nice views of the water. Enough trees have been left so that the tables seem to be nestled in their places. Observe more quality in the wooden shingle roof of the shelter and the stone fireplace.

» *Mile 22.15 (0.15) Turn around and return to the main park road; then turn right.*

22.5 (0.35) The massive, skillfully constructed rock retaining wall on the left was another WPA project.

» *Mile 23.0 (0.5) Turn left at intersection and follow the sign to Ninety-third Street—Nelson Lane.*

» *Mile 23.5 (0.5) Keep right, turning onto Ninety-third Street.*

23.8 (0.3) *Pleasant Countryside and the Absence of Suburbia.* This area contains some of the most beautiful undeveloped acreage in the metropolitan area. It has the hill-and-dale and the partially wooded setting that currently appeals to home buyers and contains many ideal sites for small lakes. When one adds the proximity of Wyandotte County Lake Park to these assets and when one notes that the area is only ninety-three blocks from downtown Kansas City, the anomaly seems strange indeed. Why is this land left idle while developers are busy on the flat, unappetizing plains of Johnson County, some forty blocks farther from the urban center?

There are about as many opinions on this question as there are people in the county. Some point to a traditional conservative attitude toward growth by Wyandotte County politicians; others, to the high property taxes of the county; still others, to the need for excessive numbers of expensive sewer-lift stations in this vicinity. Two factors, however, seem especially significant: inadequate transportation and the image of Kansas City, Kansas, as being a laboring person's town.

Northwest Wyandotte County has no equivalent of I-35, which daily speeds Johnson County's commuters to their jobs. Moreover, an important transportation barrier is posed by the Kansas River. The collector roads of Kansas City, Kansas, must funnel traffic to a very few bridges, and the resultant bottlenecks are tremendous. The image problem is harder to evaluate, but its importance is obvious. Developers of modestly priced housing, such as is demanded by many Fairfax workers, cannot easily take advantage of the local hill sites and lake possibilities because of the expenses involved. Developers of higher-priced tracts, on the other hand, are hesitant to step in because of the risk of building in a traditional blue-collar area. Johnson County, with its upper-middle-class reputation, simply provides a safer investment. This process has evolved to the point that high-income Wyandotte County people are almost being forced to reside in Johnson County; they find only a very limited choice of housing at home.[11]

» *Mile 24.4 (0.6) Underpass I-435. Proceed straight ahead on Ninety-third Street (Kansas 5).*

» *Mile 24.9 (0.5) Stop Sign. Turn right, following Kansas 5.*

» *Mile 25.1 (0.2) Junction on the flood plain and the upland. Turn left, still following Kansas 5.*

Wolcott. Wolcott has always been small. Unlike many towns of similar size today, there are no large old houses here to recall days of brighter hope. The urban growth patterns had already been determined when the town was plotted in 1868 as Connor City. A chance to grow came at the turn of the century, however, when an interurban railroad was being constructed between Kansas City and Leavenworth. In 1902 Connor City changed its name to Wolcott, to honor the general manager of the line, and thus secured the company headquarters. A measure of prosperity resulted, but the flurry lasted only until the 1930s, when the automobile forced the interurban from the scene.

Today, Wolcott's residents sense that they may be able to capitalize on another transportation development. Interstate 435, the outer loop around Kansas City, has recently bridged the Missouri River here. New dreams have emerged, yet one cannot help but wonder if the automobile age will last much longer than the thirty-year span of the interurban.

25.3 (0.2) The contrast in land use between the upland and the flood plain is almost too striking to need mention. Pasture was the rule on the thin-soiled, easily eroded upland, whereas lush corn crops are ubiquitous on the rich bottoms across the Missouri Pacific tracks. The Missouri River flows near the far line of bluffs here, giving Kansas the lion's share of these rich agricultural lowlands.

Note the long, low building across the tracks to the right, with a loading dock running its entire length. It currently houses the Tri-County Concrete Company. It was originally built to serve a large truck-farming industry, which existed in the Wolcott bottom lands until about seventeen years ago but has now transferred its operations to the Kansas River plain near DeSoto.

On the left is evidence of another bygone era. The three-story brick structure was formerly the power station for the interurban railroad. Adjacent to it is a long stucco building, whose fluting marks it as originally something more than a stock barn. This was the "car shed" for the interurban, where excess units were stored and where repairs were made.

26.3 (1.0) As the road begins to climb out of the flood plain, look to the right about a quarter-mile across the corn. The group of busses visible there combines two of Wolcott's former industries. The busses are an interurban legacy; they were used to house Mexican labor that came to work on the vegetable farms.

27.05 (0.75) Leavenworth County line.

27.5 (0.45) *Loess Hills.* On the right is an exposure of about six feet of soil made by the roadcut. The uniform buff color and the fine texture of this soil, as well as its ability to stand verti-

Landscape in the loess hills

cally without slumping, mark it as something special. It is known as loess; it probably had its origins during the glaciation of the upper Midwest more than 750,000 years ago. The theory is that near the front of the ice sheet, land was left unprotected by a cover of vegetation. Winds could thus pick up and carry large amounts of small soil particles. This phenomenon would be especially active in river valleys during the time of glacial retreat. The rivers would be choked with soil and other glacial debris, and as their volume decreased with the ice recession, there would be much material for wind removal.

Today, significant deposits of loess occur in the valleys of the Mississippi and the lower Missouri rivers. In Kansas, the thickest and most extensive deposits are in Doniphan County, in the state's northeast corner, where a depth of 195 feet has been recorded. Locally, the thickness is much less, and the deposits are not continuous, but exposures of some thirty feet are visible along I-70 between I-435 and I-635.

Loess normally develops into a very good agricultural soil, but here erosion has created a largely uncultivatable hill country. Observe that the local hilltops are all about the same height. This probably represents the original loess surface before erosion.

27.9 (0.4) A ten-foot loess exposure on the right. Note the absence of any visible rock outcrops, as the loess masks the older land forms.

28.3 (0.4) Snell Creek. Rock outcrops reappear in the valley, where the stream has cut through the loess mantle.

» *Mile 29.5 (1.2) Junction with County Route 22; turn right, staying on Kansas 5.*

29.55 (0.05) Another small loess exposure on the right.

30.2 (0.65) Any departure of fence lines or roads from the cardinal directions in the Midwest is usually worth investigating. The strange angle taken here by the utility poles and fence posts on the left is accounted for by our previous acquaintance, the interurban railway that once connected Kansas City and Leavenworth. The posts mark its old right of way. This particular intersection was known as Ettenson.

31.2 (1.0) On the right is a very hilly field that has been cleared for cultivation. This practice would be ruinous for most soils; even the loess will not long stand such obvious abuse.

31.3 (0.1) If one looks off to the right down the small stream valley, the Missouri River is visible. The water used to flow much closer to the Kansas bluffs than it does at present (see map). Shifts in channels are a normal part of the life cycle of a river, but they can spell disaster for a river town, when its "main street" suddenly migrates several miles across the flood plain. An example of this phenomenon is coming up.

31.5 (0.2) *Delaware City.* The grey frame building on the left functioned as Delaware School until recently. It carries the same name as this township. The two together are about the only remaining evidence of old Delaware City. The townsite extended for about a mile northwest and a half mile northeast of here, along the bluff. Its location on the river, its proximity to Fort Leavenworth, and its early start (1855) all boded well for the city; but because there were two other towns nearby that had identical assets—Leavenworth, five miles upstream, and Kickapoo, another seven miles beyond—the future was uncertain. Securing the seat of county government loomed as crucial. The struggle that resulted became almost a model for later counties across the West.

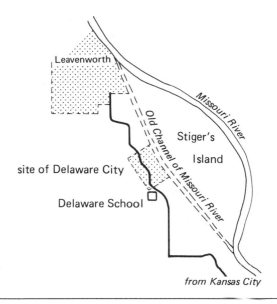

Townsite of Delaware City

Kickapoo won an 8 October 1855 election, but Delaware City, protesting that all its citizens had not had a chance to vote, succeeded in keeping the polls open on 9 October and thus emerged victorious. Delaware City prospered for two years, until the opposing towns got new elections declared in 1857. Kickapoo won again, but this time Leavenworth objected. Fraud was proved, and in a final election, Leavenworth won.

After losing the county seat, Delaware City quickly declined. Residents moved either to Leavenworth or a mile east, where a settlement called Lansing was growing along the overland route that connected Forts Leavenworth and Scott. The town had not existed long enough for community loyalty to grow up and thus keep people there. Buildings were moved wholesale, and foundation stones were appropriated for use in farm structures. When the river finally shifted its channel, Delaware City had no objection. It had already disappeared.

» *Mile 31.9 (0.4) Junction with County Route 24. Keep straight ahead on Kansas 5.*

Kansas State Penitentiary. The green "K.S.P." sign at the junction of routes 5 and 24 announces the presence of the Kansas State Penitentiary. For the next mile, Kansas 5 cuts across some of the twenty-five hundred acres of prison land. This land serves a double purpose: it insulates area residents from the real and imagined dangers of the actual prison buildings, and it provides a large portion of the food supplies used by the institution, including all of the dairy products. Stigers Island (see map) constitutes a large part of the prison acreage, and its alluvial soils usually produce a rich harvest.

The location of prisons is an interesting geographical phenomenon. Remote areas, far from population centers, come immediately to mind, but the one here is adjacent to a city of thirty-five thousand people. One might assume that the city's growth was recent and that there was no local population cluster when the prison was originally located, but this is not the case. Prison construction began in 1861, at a time when Leavenworth was far and away the largest and most influential city in Kansas. Leavenworth obviously wanted the facility and had the political clout to get it. Why was this? Why wouldn't the largest city in the state choose to have some other public institution, such as the capitol or the state university, instead of the lowly prison?

The capitol probably had to be given to a spot that was more centrally located in the state, but the choice between a prison and university was definitely Leavenworth's, and it was made, from the mid-nineteenth-century view, quite logically. The deciding factor was the relative size of the two institutions. The prison was considerably larger, and this meant more construction money for Leavenworth, as well as a bigger payroll when the facility was completed. No one could have foreseen the growth of universities during the twentieth century. The then-governor of the state, Charles Robinson of Lawrence, was livid at the decision about the prison. He had tried long and hard to get it for Lawrence, and he was dismayed to have to settle for the humble one-building university.

32.5 (0.6) The main prison complex is located a mile west of here. The assemblage on the right is a branch operation, the Kansas State Correctional Institution for Women. The power plant on the right and the soap factory and the orchard on the left are visible signs of self-sufficiency, an ideal sought partly by necessity (e.g., the control of electric power) and partly by convenience (e.g., a way to utilize the abundant prison labor).

32.95 (0.45) Cross Ninemile Creek. The stream was named, not for its length, but for its distance from the flagpole on the Fort Leavenworth Main Parade. The flagpole was used as the base point for distances in all directions; this particular route was the military road south to Fort Scott. Three-tenths of a mile ahead, just beyond the railroad crossing, is Sevenmile Creek. The distance discrepancy is because the military road was located west of here, where the streams are farther apart.

34.1 (1.15) *Leavenworth and Its Institutions.* Leavenworth is one of the most interesting cities in Kansas. It has a population of only about 35,000, yet it contains three major federal institutions, a private college, and the headquarters of an order of Catholic nuns. A major state institution (the prison just passed) adjoins the city on the south. Together, these institutions employ 4,345 civilian personnel, about 40 percent of the city's total. When one adds to this some 250 nuns, 1,270 college students, 3,800 active military personnel, and 10,000 military retirees from the above places, the institutional dominance of Leavenworth becomes obvious. In a real sense, the institutions *are* Leavenworth (see map).

Because of the institutions, Leavenworth has a special flavor about it that you will sample in the ensuing miles. One overriding theme is conservatism, which stems jointly from the military people, the Catholic sisters, and the elderly residents of a large Veterans Administration Center that lies directly ahead. One can see it in hair and clothing styles, in voting behavior, in recreational choices, and even in radio programming.

Past Glories. Obsession with the past is a second trait of Leavenworth. Some of this is caused simply by age, for Leavenworth is one of the oldest cities in the state, and Fort Leavenworth, which dates back to 1827, was the only white settlement in Kansas for some fifteen years after its founding. Leavenworth High School's athletic teams are appropriately known as "Pioneers." The historical passion has deeper roots than these, however, and probably springs from the abrupt truncation of Leavenworth's dream to be a major metropolis. The dream had seemed well within the grasp of the city, indeed almost inevitable, from its

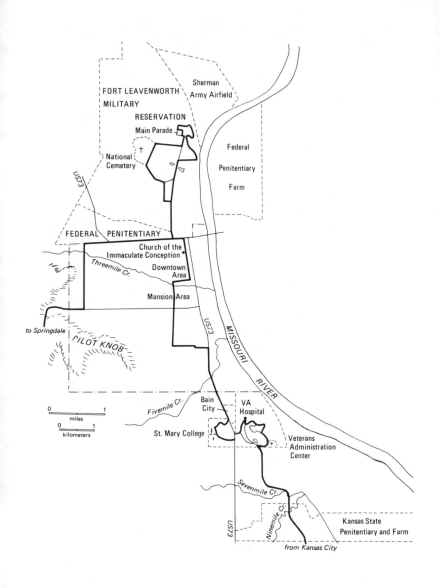

Leavenworth County reference map

founding in 1854 until the early 1870s, when Kansas City firmly established itself in the metropolitan position. An understanding of this shattered vision is essential to the understanding of present-day Leavenworth.

No one ever doubted that a major city would evolve on the "elbow" of the Missouri River. From St. Louis westward to the Kansas border the river was a natural route for migrants and trade, but at the Kansas line the stream bent northward, away from the traditional trading destination of Santa Fe and the mid-nineteenth-century lures of Colorado gold and central-Kansas grain. Somewhere on this "elbow" a city was needed to link the two markets of Chicago and St. Louis with the West and the Southwest. By the late 1850s there were four rivals for the position: St. Joseph, Atchison, Leavenworth, and Kansas City. All had their positive attributes. St. Joseph was the western terminus of the Hannibal and St. Joseph Railroad, the first track across Missouri, which connected directly with Chicago. Atchison's claim was based on its location on the westernmost bend of the Missouri River, the backing of Kansas' powerful Senator Samuel Pomeroy, and an early ferry connection to a spur line of the Hannibal and St. Joseph, built to the river opposite Atchison. Both towns were poorly located to make the St. Louis connection, however, for a railroad that followed the river would have to swing far north out of its way to reach these towns.

The Rise and Decline of a City. Leavenworth and Kansas City were much more favorably located. As the diagrams show, both were far enough south to be on the St. Louis route, and both could easily tap the Chicago market with a short spur line north to the Hannibal and St. Joseph. Each city time and again trumpeted its site advantages in its efforts to interest eastern capitalists in building their railroads to it and to construct the all-important first bridge across the river.

Kansas City's obvious asset was its location below the mouth of the Kaw, which enabled it to tap southwestern trade without a second bridge. The Kaw valley also provided an ideal track bed. These were impressive facts, but the case for Leavenworth appeared to be even stronger. It was by far the larger city (7,500 versus 4,500 in 1860), and it enjoyed many benefits from its proximity to Fort Leavenworth. Overland transportation was focused here via the military roads and the efforts of Russell, Majors, and Waddell, the

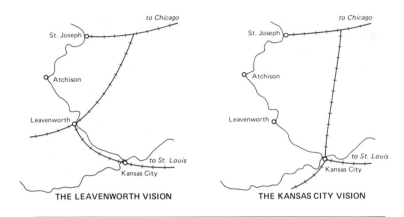

Railroad visions of Leavenworth and Kansas City

famous freighting firm, which came to Leavenworth in 1855.[12] The town was also aided by the Civil War. Missouri towns, given the proslavery leaning of their state, fell into disfavor as investment outlets for eastern capital, and Kansas ones rose accordingly.

Given the above considerations, the dominance that Kansas City assumed over Leavenworth during the 1870s is difficult to explain. In retrospect it appears that the large size and the previous success of Leavenworth worked to its disadvantage in two important ways. It probably created overconfidence. The city assumed that the railroads would have to come to it, and it was therefore not as active in its promotion as it might have been. The large population also encouraged factionalism. Some interests wanted to concentrate on railroad routes west, others on connecting lines to the east. Another sizable group, composed of freighters and cattlemen, was against all railroads. Its members saw their livelihood being threatened by the new transportation development and its importation of cheap Texas cattle.

Kansas City, as a smaller town than Leavenworth, had fewer of the above problems. Vested-interest groups were less developed, and the city knew it would have to be united and fight hard if it were to overcome Leavenworth's advantages. It time and again voted railroad bonds, whereas Leavenworth voters would frequently turn them down. Eventually, Kansas City's maneuvering paid off. In 1869 it got the coveted Missouri River bridge and soon became

Cemetery at the Veterans Administration Center

the regional metropolis. Leavenworth, with the institutions it had acquired during the previous decades, did not fade completely, but its grandiose dreams had ended. Like a dowager, it began to live partially in the past.[13]

» *Mile 34.5 (0.4) Turn right off Kansas 5 onto the grounds of the Veterans Administration Center. Just inside the grounds, turn right onto Cemetery Road.*

Veterans Administration Center. The Veterans Administration Center is the newest of Leavenworth's major institutions; it was established in 1884 as a home for disabled soldiers. Its beautiful site on the river bluff was donated by the city, but the gift has been returned many times over through the citizens' enjoyment of the well-landscaped, meticulously maintained grounds. The $20-million annual payroll of the center has also endeared it to the city.

On your left, immediately after you turn onto Cemetery Road, is a twenty-foot cut in the hillside. This marks the former path of a railroad spur which once brought supplies to the center.

34.6 (0.1) The cemetery ahead is available to any veteran who dies in a V.A. facility, and funerals are conducted with full military honors. To the outsider the most striking feature of this cemetery is how it contrasts with public ones, such as Leavenworth's Mount Muncie, which is visible to the south. In Mount Muncie a rich variety in gravestones bespeaks the income and personality traits of its inhabitants, and the organization of the stones into family plots tells of basic societal beliefs. In the V.A. and other military cemeteries, however, as in those of a few communal societies, such as Iowa's Amana Colonies, the individuality of the person is suppressed. Stones are all alike, rows are uniformly spaced, and the particular burial site is determined, not by family, but by time of death. Military discipline and orderliness thus endure even to the grave.

» *Mile 34.8 (0.2) Turn left onto Cooke Drive at the cemetery chapel.*

» *Mile 35.1 (0.3) Turn left onto Riverview Avenue.*

35.2 (0.1) Note the small brick mason's shop on the left. Like other Leavenworth institutions, the V.A. Center is partially self-sufficient. It has its own power plant, fire station, library, theater, laundry, and chapel. Until recently it even had its own railroad station and post office, both named Wadsworth.

» *Mile 35.3 (0.1) Intersection with Water Street. Keep left on an unnamed paved road.*

» *Mile 35.4 (0.1) Fork in the road. Turn right, then sharply to the left, rejoining Riverview Avenue.*

Domiciliaries. The four large barrackslike buildings on either side of the road were the traditional focus of the V.A. Center. These are some of the original living quarters erected in 1885/86 for the veterans. In its early days the center had a formal military atmosphere about it; the residents wore uniforms, and strict discipline was enforced. This aura is reflected in the domiciliary architecture. After World War I the character of the institution began to change. Attention was focused more on medical care, and the formal rules were relaxed. Although the "home" aspect of the center is now less important than its hospital, there is still space for nearly one thousand veterans in these and other living quarters.

» *Mile 35.5 (0.1) Turn right onto Franklin Avenue.*

Directly ahead on Franklin Avenue is the hospital, the modern focus of the center. It was constructed between 1930 and 1933; it has a capacity of 741 patients. The staff is outstanding, in part because of its affiliation with the University of Kansas Medical Center in nearby Kansas City.

» *Mile 35.6 (0.1) Turn left onto Rowland and descend the hill to the main entrance.*

35.8 (0.2) On the hill to your left stands Immanuel Church, the most famous building at the center. Its interesting mixture of Gothic and Romanesque architecture is part of the reason, but the inclusion of the building in *Ripley's Believe It or Not* undoubtedly brought it more visitors. The uniqueness lay in having both Protestant and Catholic services under the same roof, though on separate floors.

» *Mile 35.85 (0.05) Turn right onto South Drive and leave the center. Turn left onto U.S. 73.*

Note the old Wadsworth railroad station on the right, just as you leave the center.

» *Mile 36.0 (0.15) Turn right into the arched entrance marked Sisters of Charity of Leavenworth.*

The Sisters of Charity. Visitors who enter Leavenworth from the south on U.S. 73 have an impressive greeting: the immaculate V.A. grounds on the right and, on the left, this equally impressive 240-acre tract occupied by the Sisters of Charity and their St. Mary College and St. John Hospital. The sisters came to Leavenworth in 1858 at the request of Bishop Jean Miege, who had established in Leavenworth a diocese that stretched westward to the Rocky Mountains. Although Leavenworth's central role in the West soon faded, the sisters kept their order here to teach and care for the sick and the orphaned. There are currently some nine hundred members who serve society in Kansas and elsewhere with branch houses scattered over nine states.

» *Mile 36.2 (0.2) Fork in the road; keep right.*

36.3 (0.1) The sisters moved to this hilltop site in 1868 from downtown Leavenworth, and many of the plantings date from that time. The buildings directly ahead and on the left are the focus of the convent. Some two hundred retired nuns reside here along with the active members.

36.4 (0.1) The beautiful Chapel of the Annunciation is on the left. It is modeled after an Italian chapel; its elegant interior is well worth a visit.

» *Mile 36.4 (0.0) Turn right and continue along the circle drive.*

36.45 (0.05) *St. Mary College.* The buildings around the circle drive are the core of St. Mary College, a school of some four hundred students that is run by the sisters. It has evolved through the years from an academy for girls to a junior college and, in 1930, to a four-year liberal-arts institution. More recently it has become coeducational. Its strengths and weaknesses are those of many small private schools. Its excellent student-faculty ratio—9 to 1—permits individual attention, but financial limitations restrict library acquisitions and hinder the hiring of quality teachers. The future viability of such schools is threatened as the spiraling costs of education almost necessitate public funding.[14] For example, a semester's tuition at St. Mary was $2,435 in 1987, compared to $662.50 for Kansas residents at the University of Kansas. St. Mary appears to be faring better than many other private colleges, however. It enjoys good church support, the nuns on its staff work for minimal wages, and the college administration seems flexible. Part-time students from the city and the fort are encouraged to enroll, and so far this has compensated for a slight decline in the full-time student count.

The college has fairly strict rules. Two courses in theology are required and, for freshmen, so is class attendance. Students must be in their dormitories by certain hours, although each living group is allowed some latitude in setting its own specific rules. Such restrictions are rather rare in American colleges today, but because some students and parents prefer them, St. Mary can serve a certain market. Approximately half of the students attended parochial schools during their childhood, and the college provides these people with a similar type of cultural atmosphere. Students come predominately from Kansas, Missouri, Nebraska, and Iowa, as one would expect, but there are surprisingly large contingents from Colorado and Montana. This is because of the branch houses that the Sisters of Charity operate in these states.

The buildings around the campus are heterogeneous, reflecting the architectural styles that were popular when each was built. Berchmans Hall (1930) on the west side of the circle, for example, is classic university Georgian, whereas St. Joseph Hall (1963) on the southwest corner is quite modernistic. The newest building is DePaul Library on the north side, which was completed in 1981. All of the buildings are connected by underground tunnels, an expensive but pleasant convenience in winter.

Note the wide variety of plantings within the circle. The bald cypress, one of the few needle-leaf trees that annually sheds its leaves, is especially interesting.

» *Mile 36.5 (0.05) Turn right off the circle and proceed down the hill toward the highway.*

36.55 (0.05) The pavement changes here to brick, hand-laid by the sisters shortly after their arrival in 1868. The trees—maples on the right, pines on the left—were also set out at this time.

36.7 (0.15) On the left is St. John Hospital, originally founded in 1864. It is run by the Sisters of Charity and is one of five hospitals in the curious town of Leavenworth. A small cemetery for the convent lies between the road and St. John. Its arrangement echoes that of the V.A. cemetery: uniform, orderly stones. The similarity suggests that many parallels exist between life in the military and life in a convent.

» *Mile 36.9 (0.2) Turn left onto U.S. 73.*

Bain City. The site of the new Best Western motel and the AMC/Jeep dealership on the right was a residential neighborhood before 1975. Bain City was its name; it was one of Leavenworth's slum areas. The striking visual contrast between it and the lush estates of St. Mary and the V.A. Center was a factor in prompting city officials to take action.

37.2 (0.3) The Leavenworth Plaza shopping center on the left is on land owned by the Sisters of Charity. The rents help them considerably with their programs.

37.5 (0.3) Intersect Limit Street. This road long served as the southern boundary of Leavenworth and thus acquired its name. Settlements south of here therefore had separate identities and names: namely, Bain City, Wadsworth (V.A. Center), and Xavier (Sisters of Charity).

Two blocks to the right on Limit Street are the Valley View Apartments, a new low-income housing area where many Bain City residents have relocated. Its streets are called M. L. King Drive and Ralph Bunche Drive. One wonders whether people will long remember who these men were or whether Bunche Drive will soon be as meaningless a name to its residents as Jackson Street or Washington Avenue are to the many who live along such streets across the country.

37.85 (0.35) Cross Fivemile Creek, which is also named for its distance from the Fort Leavenworth flagpole.

38.2 (0.35) The two-story brick Gould Battery building on the right has a venerable history. It was once the "largest manufacturer of (automobile) batteries in the world,"[15] and before that, it was occupied by the nationally famous Parker Amusement Company. Parker made carnival equipment, including circus wagons and merry-go-rounds, when such entertainment was in its heyday. One can see a sample carousel horse on the coffee-shop wall of the Cody Hotel in downtown Leavenworth.

» *Mile 38.4 (0.2) Turn left onto Pennsylvania Street.*

» *Mile 38.65 (0.25) Road jogs to the right, then back left; stay on Pennsylvania.*

39.0 (0.35) The church and school on the left are named Casimir, after the Polish patron saint. They were built, fittingly, by Polish immigrants who came in the last century as coal miners.

The church building was constructed in 1893/94 and the school in 1908. The school has recently been converted into a day-care center.

» *Mile 39.05 (0.05) Turn right onto Broadway Street.*

Nineteenth-Century Mansions. Nowhere is the past glory of Leavenworth better reflected than in its old homes, and Broadway Street is the setting for many of them. The extraordinary width of the street suggests the grandeur that lies ahead, although the subdividing of many of the large old lots has subdued the effect somewhat.

39.3 (0.25) The home at 1215 South Broadway is one of the newest of Leavenworth's mansions; it was built in 1883 for H. D. Rush, a local miller. Its complex roof line and heavy dark appearance are characteristic of some Victorian-era architecture. Like several of the old homes, this one is currently occupied by a Fort Leavenworth officer.

39.4 (0.1) There are many examples in this neighborhood of an architectural technique called half-timbering. The houses at 1206 and 1204 South Broadway are typical; they have exposed, heavy-appearing framing timbers, filled interstitially with stucco. This old technique arose in Europe as a practical measure to conserve wood; various materials were used to "nog" between the supporting beams of the house. Today the origin of the practice is not generally known, and the exposed "timbers" are, of course, all for show. The whole image now often goes by the name English Manor.

39.5 (0.1) Two blocks east on James Street is the Leavenworth Historical Society Museum, at 334 Fifth Avenue. Located in another old mansion (1898), the principal attraction is its collection of nineteenth-century furnishings. Its hours are 1–4:30 Tuesday through Sunday.

39.7 (0.2) Intersect Spruce Street.

39.8 (0.1) Olive Street. The former home of Fred Harvey is located three blocks east of here at the Seventh Street intersection. The man who provided quality food for railroad passengers across the country with his Harvey Restaurants and Lunch Counters was one of Leavenworth's most famous citizens. Both the material (limestone) and the style (French Empire) are unusual in the city.

Broadway Ridge. The ridge that parallels Broadway on the left for the next four blocks contains some of the best mansions in Leavenworth. The natural setting is impressive—a high overlook northeast to the business district and the river beyond. Before the recent elm blight the area was even more beautiful, as trees canopied the street. These homes would not exist today if the local economic history had been any different from what it was. An early period of great success and optimism was necessary to build them, of course, but their permanence was contingent on the city's rapid, though not complete, decline. If the decline had been total, the homes would naturally have been destroyed, but paradoxically, continued rapid growth would have had the same effect. A new highway, a warehousing district, or even a slum would have claimed precedence in an area this close to a booming city center.

These homes were built mostly during the 1860s and 1870s. Their widely varying styles—everything from bright Greek Revival (500 South Broadway) to somber Romanesque (420) to Spanish Mission (508)—are typical of the times. The Greek Revival era was just at its end, and architects were turning to other cultures for inspiration. Clients thus could and did decide whether their "personalities" were more Roman, Spanish, or whatever. There is more uniformity in the choice of trees here. Maples were as popular in the 1860s as they are now, but the large ginkgoes that you see at the 410, 500, and 600 addresses have since passed out of style. These oriental trees were new to the country then, however, and were symbolic of wealth and status. Their fan-shaped leaves make them easy to identify.

The Broadway Apartments sign at 420 and the YWCA one at 520 South Broadway reveal the fate of some of the old homes, but such uses are not yet very common. A few of the houses still remain with their original families, and more have been lovingly taken over by retired military people and other Leavenworth citizens. So far there has been no influx of Kansas Citians, but with the quickening of activity at the international airport, just across the river, this may soon change.

40.0 (0.2) Cross Threemile Creek, still another in the military sequence. This valley was the original townsite for Leavenworth.

» *Mile 40.1 (0.1) Turn right onto Delaware Street.*

Downtown Leavenworth. Delaware is Leavenworth's principal business street. Like Kansas City, it has experienced urban renewal, but on a less drastic scale. The canopied sidewalks and planters constitute only a superficial face-lift, but most residents feel it has given their downtown a boost.

If one were to survey the goods and services available in Leavenworth, several interesting variations from the norm would appear. The town is a bit short on food stores and recreational facilities, but it is somewhat long on clothing shops and ones that sell general luxury items. Selective competition from the institutions, particularly Fort Leavenworth, is the reason. The commissary at the fort, for example, is one of the better ones in the country, and by offering military people quality food at low prices, it hurts local supermarkets. Nonfood items are also available at the fort, but customers complain about the inadequate variety and size selection. Many mothers will thus buy their children's underwear at the Post Exchange and their other clothes in downtown Leavenworth. Downtown has a monopoly on some items, such as large appliances and furniture.

Merchants have long since adjusted to the above facts and think little about them. The merchants are, however, cognizant of the stabilizing effect of the governmental payrolls on their business. Leavenworth has always suffered less than other communities in times of depression.[16]

» *Mile 40.45 (0.35) Turn left onto Fifth Street.*

Note the distinctive marqueed building at the northwest corner of Fifth and Delaware. It is the old Hollywood Theater, built in the early 1950s, just before television began to cut into the movie market. The 750-seat theater had become an anachronism by the 1970s, like the musical opera houses of a generation ago. Community action saved the structure, now the Leavenworth Performing Arts Center.

40.5 (0.05) Another ginkgo tree stands on the northwest corner of the City Hall lot, on your right.

Indian Street Names. As you drive north on Fifth Street, note the names of the streets being intersected. North of the downtown area, they are all named for Indian tribes. These were predominantly not tribes native to Kansas but those eastern peoples who were placed here briefly between the 1830s and the 1860s, before the land hunger of the white settlers caused a wholesale Indian removal to Oklahoma. Because the tribes were here during the initial period of white settlement, many places in eastern Kansas commemorate them. The street roster here is (south to north): Choctaw, Cherokee, Delaware, Shawnee, Seneca, Miami, Osage, Pottawatomie, Ottawa, Kickapoo, Kiowa, Dakota, Pawnee, and Cheyenne.

40.9 (0.4) *Cathedral of the Immaculate Conception.* The church at the corner of Kiowa and Fifth is not particularly grand, but before a disastrous fire in 1961, a magnificent edifice stood on this site. Its history is a miniature of Leavenworth as a whole. The Cathedral of the Immaculate Conception was its name, and under Bishop Jean Baptiste Miege it once had authority all the way to the Rockies. Gradually its power waned. First, the diocese's area was decreased, and in 1891 the bishop began to live in Kansas City. Finally, in 1947 it lost its cathedral status to St. Peters in Kansas City. The bell you see on the tower above was about the only thing saved from the 1961 conflagration.

» *Mile 41.2 (0.3) Turn left onto Metropolitan Avenue.*

» *Mile 41.4 (0.2) Turn right onto Grant Avenue and enter the Fort Leavenworth Military Reservation.*

41.55 (0.15) Entrance Booth. Stop here to obtain a free "Self-Guided Tour" booklet to the fort; it contains a brief history, a map, and data on various historical sites. The comments that follow here will focus on other aspects of the area, as a supplement to the information in the booklet. For a more complete historical account you may wish to read George Walton's book *Fort Leavenworth: Sentinel of the Plains* (Englewood Cliffs, N.J.: Prentice-Hall, 1973). Copies are available at the Post Museum on Reynolds Avenue.

Command and General Staff College. Fort Leavenworth is the home of the Army's Command and General Staff College, which teaches officers the principles of strategy and command. Because of this educational emphasis, Leavenworth is definitely *not* a typical military base. There are more officers than enlisted personnel on the post, the average age is higher than normal, and a large percentage of the soldiers have families. Because many officers from allied countries also receive training here, there is a definite international flavor. Although the military image is very strong here, the above factors have also created a certain country-club atmosphere. Amenities abound, and one can easily sense that Fort Leavenworth people enjoy the good life.

Note the meticulous grounds keeping and the regularly spaced trees along Grant Avenue. Attention to detail and love of symmetry are two important attributes of institutional environments.

41.8 (0.25) *A Cultural Island.* The George S. Patton, Jr., School on the right is one of two on the base. As the name suggests, it is owned by the military, although the teachers are civilian. The school is only one of many indicators that Fort Leavenworth operates as a nearly self-contained unit. Its personnel do not just work here; most of them live, bank, and shop here. The base offers medical and dental care, religious services, a library, and almost limitless recreational opportunities. The schools just make it complete. Since the quality of most of the goods and services is high and the prices are low, personnel on the base are constantly tempted to isolate themselves from the town of Leavenworth.

Military bases constitute one of the most significant subcultures that exist in America today. The isolation discussed above is important in their formation, but in addition, they are composed of a particular type of people. Neither army officers nor enlistees are random samples of Americans. Those who chose this life must be somewhat like-minded, sharing similar drives, ambitions, and feelings. Although this phenomenon has not yet been thoroughly studied by cultural geographers, it appears that military bases are only one of a number of new, self-sorted, or voluntary culture regions that exist in America.[17] Other examples are the retirement meccas in Florida and the Southwest, educational centers, and latter-day Bohemias, such as the communes in the Ozarks.

» *Mile 42.1 (0.3) Turn left onto Kansas Avenue.*

42.2 (0.1) This area is one of the fort's main shopping centers. On the left are a credit union, a large gasoline station, and a Burger King; on the right are the Army National Bank and a mammoth new commissary.

» *Mile 42.25 (0.05) Turn right onto Third Street and continue straight ahead through the parking lot.*

42.3 (0.05) The main post exchange is on the left. In addition to the principal store, the building houses beauty, barber, tailor, and optical shops, a snack bar, a coin-operated laundry, and a special order service. As was discussed earlier, however, users are not totally satisfied with the PX (see mile 40.1).

» *Mile 42.4 (0.1) Jog left on Iowa Avenue to Fourth Street, then turn right.*

42.5 (0.1) The red-brick buildings on the right are barracks. Their uninspired architecture marks them as "real Army," one of the few such examples visible at elitist Fort Leavenworth.

» *Mile 42.65 (0.15) Turn left onto Cody Road.*

The spacious grounds on either side of Cody belong to the base's country club. A nine-hole golf course is on the left, and an eighteen-hole one is on the right, along with the clubhouse. It was at Leavenworth that Maj. Dwight D. Eisenhower first took up the game in 1926.

» *Mile 43.1 (0.45) Turn right onto Biddle Boulevard.*

43.2 (0.1) The Fort Leavenworth National Cemetery is on the left, its uniform white stones looking like a replica of the V.A. Cemetery. Burials began here in 1846, and the site became a National Cemetery in 1862.

43.35 (0.15) The drive on the right leads to the main officers' club. Reputedly one of the best in the nation, it serves as the social center of the fort. Attractions include a swimming pool, excellent food, and, traditionally, open bars. Before 1986, Kansas law forbade liquor to be sold by the drink, but federal installations were exempted from the ruling.

» *Mile 43.5 (0.15) Turn right onto Pope Avenue.*

Pope is another focus of community services. The post hospital, the dental clinic, and a church are on the left. Three services are held at the chapel each week: Jewish, Catholic, and general Protestant. For those people who wish a less institutionalized religious experience, two other churches are also available on the reservation (see miles 43.9 and 45.2). The Georgian buildings on the right are residences for majors and lieutenant colonels.

43.9 (0.4) St. Ignatius Church on the left, with its traditional Gothic styling, is the Catholic alternative to the Post Chapel. It was built as a gift to the soldiers; it is the only nongovernmental structure on the fort.

» *Mile 44.0 (0.1) Turn left onto Grant Avenue.*

Centrality and Colonels. You are now near the heart of the post. The large homes on the left, thoroughly imbued with nineteenth-century grandeur, are some of the best at Leavenworth. Fittingly, they are occupied by full colonels, the highest rank present here in any quantity. The location of the elite at the center of the post stands in contrast to the homesites that are chosen by the wealthy in civilian society. In the latter situation, the accessibility advantages of center-city location have been overcome by the rapid encroachment of industrialization and its traditional accompaniments of noise, traffic, and general blight. The rich, whose former home locations were typified by Leavenworth's Broadway mansions (mile 39.8), have been forced farther out. An analogous change has not been necessary at the fort, of course, and the colonels thus still enjoy the pleasure of being able to walk to work.

The houses on Grant Avenue are also good illustrations of the formality and the austerity that characterize landscapes at the fort. Only an occasional flower bed gives a hint into the personal tastes of individual occupants.

» *Mile 44.2 (0.2) Turn left onto Kearney Avenue.*

Housing for colonels at Fort Leavenworth

The statue at the intersection is of Ulysses S. Grant. Its prominence and the naming of the main post thoroughfare after him suggest that Grant was especially influential in Leavenworth affairs. As president, it was he who ordered a reorganization of the army to put more emphasis on military education. The location of a school here in 1881 gave new vigor to a place that was about to die with the end of the western frontier. Fort Leavenworth thus literally owes its life to Grant.

» *Mile 44.25 (0.05) Turn right onto Sumner Place.*

Main Parade. This area was once the center of post activities, and the oldest buildings at the fort are here. The Rookery, at 12–14 Sumner Place, was constructed in 1832; it is the oldest house in the state. Its famous occupants have included Douglas MacArthur and the first territorial governor of Kansas, Andrew H. Reeder. The individuality of many of the houses on Sumner is unique at the fort. Most later housing was built in homogeneous batches, such as the quarters that you just saw on Grant Avenue.

The open area to the left is the old Main Parade. It has been many decades since the last military review was held here, however, for the grounds are covered with large trees. The famous flagpole used in reckoning distance from the fort is located near the northwest corner of the Parade.

» *Mile 44.45 (0.2) Turn right onto McClellan Avenue.*

» *Mile 44.5 (0.05) Turn right onto McPherson Drive.*

44.6 (0.1) The United States Disciplinary Barracks, on the left, is one of four prison facilities in the Leavenworth area. It is currently the only military prison in the country for the army and the air force, which jointly administer it.

» *Mile 44.7 (0.1) Turn sharply left onto Riverside Avenue and descend to the flood plain.*

45.0 (0.3) *The Oregon and Santa Fe Trails.* Seldom can one "see" history on the landscape as vividly as here. Behind the marker on the right the river bluff has been deeply scarred by the passing of literally thousands of heavily laden wagons that carried families westward. Segments of both the Oregon and the Santa Fe trails began at Leavenworth, for during the second quarter of the nineteenth century, when movements to the Far West got under way, the fort was one of the few places in the area to offer dock facilities and reliable information about the western country. By docking here instead of at Kansas City, Oregon migrants avoided a crossing of the Kansas River.

An excellent collection of animal-drawn vehicles, including a Prairie Schooner and a Conestoga Wagon, like those used on the early westward treks, is on display nearby, at the Fort Leavenworth Museum (see mile 45.8). Its hours are 10–4 Mondays through Saturdays and 12–4 on Sundays and holidays.

» *Mile 45.2 (0.2) Turn very sharply left onto Scott Avenue.*

The stone chapel on the left is used for individual Protestant services. Methodists, Lutherans, and others each have an hour reserved on Sundays.

45.4 (0.2) The home of the commanding general is on the right at 1 Scott Avenue.

» *Mile 45.45 (0.05) Turn left onto Sherman Avenue.*

The impressive complex at the junction of Scott and Sherman Avenues is the post headquarters. The building names (Grant, Sherman, and Sheridan) commemorate the persons who were responsible for bringing the precursor of the Command and General Staff College to Leavenworth. Grant, as president, ordered the new emphasis on military education; Gen. William T. Sherman was in charge of the army program; and Gen. Philip H. Sheridan was the one who actually selected this site for the school.

» *Mile 45.7 (0.25) Stop at the river overlook near the benches and old cannons.*

Erosion and Jetties. The Missouri River, below, is tight against its bluff on the Kansas side, leaving only a narrow path for the Missouri Pacific Railroad tracks. Across the channel and occupying much of the vast flood plain is the Federal Penitentiary Farm. Its main buildings are directly opposite you.

The river has been in its present channel since before the fort was established in 1827, a rather long period of quiescence. There has been a constant erosion of the near shore, however, from the centrifugal force of the water as it flows around the bend. The process has been slowed by constructing stone jetties out into the river, to divert the force of the current. Several of these are visible just downstream to the right.

» *Mile 45.75 (0.05) Turn right onto Reynolds Avenue.*

The large modern building on the left is Bell Hall, seat of the Command and General Staff College.

45.8 (0.05) The excellent post museum, referred to at mile 45.0, is on the right.

» *Mile 46.1 (0.3) Turn left onto Grant Avenue.*

46.2 (0.1) The small valley now occupied by Lake Smith and Lake Merritt, on the left and right respectively, was cut by Onemile Creek, the first in the series of streams that are numbered from the fort.

46.5 (0.3) *"Peasant Housing."* The East Normandy housing complex on the left is occupied primarily by lieutenant colonels; it ranks intermediate on the local quality scale. The duplexes are modern and clean, but their boxy style has none of the appeal of the older, more centrally located quarters that you have already seen. Four-tenths of a mile farther down Grant Avenue is another housing group, Pershing Park. As one could predict from the quarters sampled thus far, Pershing Park is a step down from East Normandy, both in quality and in the rank of the people who live there. In a maze of tightly spaced matchboxes that lack both garages and genuine porches live the Fort Leavenworth "peasants": majors, captains, and a few lieutenants. Surely, status is all relative.

» *Mile 47.5 (1.0) Leave Fort Leavenworth. Turn right onto Metropolitan Avenue.*

47.6 (0.1) *Prison Surroundings.* Metropolitan here divides the town of Leavenworth, on the left, from the grounds of the United States Penitentiary, on the right. The attitude of the city toward the prison can be seen in the developments built along the roadway: a power relay station, a run-down doughnut shop, and a cheap motel. Clearly, Leavenworth wants to have a buffer zone between itself and the "pen," although one seldom hears citizens openly condemn the institution. Some of the moderate-income housing in this area is occupied by families of prisoners.

Cows are usually visible in the fields on the right. They are a reminder that the prison, like Leavenworth's other institutions, tries to be self-sufficient. Indeed, given the special nature of this particular institution (i.e., a retention facility for the nation's more hardened criminals), it is not surprising that the self-sufficient ideal is carried farther here than in the other facilities toured. As a prison brochure states: "Every facility needed for the daily operation of a fair sized town must be contained within the confines of these walls." On the agricultural side, the prison keeps some

90 dairy cattle and 4,000 chickens, and it annually raises for slaughter 1,500 hogs and 300 beef cattle. Most of this is done on the 1,600-acre farm located on the Missouri River flood plain (mile 45.7).

47.8 (0.2) The houses to the right on the circle drive and for the next quarter mile are plainly institutionally owned, even though they vary somewhat in individual design. Their colors give them away: the limited range has to be the result of governmental paint and painters. Administrative personnel at the penitentiary live in the homes.

48.1 (0.3) *The "Big Top."* The prison itself is now visible ahead on the right. The Big Top, as the facility is familiarly known in reference to its central dome, is truly an awesome sight. The 22-acre enclosure is red brick on three sides but is steel gray on the front. This lifeless color has a very somber effect on the visitor; one wonders why it was chosen, instead of a continuation of the brick. Would the red brick have projected too warm and too inviting an image to be proper for a prison?

This complex was built with inmate labor on land that was formerly a part of the military reservation; it was completed in 1927. After Alcatraz it has probably been the best known of American penitentiaries. Some one thousand primarily long-term and potentially dangerous offenders are held here for an average sentence of eleven years.

Rehabilitation programs are active, of course; these include vocational training in many fields and academic programs, from elementary-school work through an Associate of Arts degree. More factual information is available in a brochure that is available at the entrance just ahead.

» *Mile 48.6 (0.5) Fork in the road; keep left on County Route 20.*

The land on the right is still prison property. Ahead is Pilot Knob, a prominent limestone ridge that was a tremendous handicap to the development of overland commerce out of nineteenth-century Leavenworth. Horace Greeley, the famous New York newspaperman who visited the area in 1859, claimed it was an obstacle "which Leavenworth must soon cut down or it will cut her down materially."[18] The exact role of the ridge in decisions about the location of the railroad in the 1860s is not known.

A mile north of here, on an eastward projection of the ridge called Government Hill, is a former site of a Nike missile base. Four of these were built during the Cold War of the 1950s to protect Kansas City, but the pace of technological change quickly rendered them obsolete, and the sites were all abandoned.

» *Mile 49.1 (0.5) Turn left onto Twentieth Street.*

Twentieth Street is bordered by the ranch-style split-level homes that typify modern suburban developments. In Leavenworth, such activity has been heavily concentrated in this area, for the city has no other direction in which to expand. The river blocks the eastern side, whereas large institutional land holdings stand to the north and south.

49.35 (0.25) Another crossing of Threemile Creek.

» *Mile 50.3 (0.95) Turn right onto Kansas Route 92 (Spruce Street).*

50.6 (0.3) *Quarry Hill Farm.* Operations like Quarry Hill Farm are found on the fringes of most midwestern cities. It is a horse farm, and as such, it proudly displays two cherished symbols of its status: a white board fence and a name sign. Both are practices adopted from the famous horse country of the Kentucky bluegrass. Why horse farms should be named is not known. Perhaps it is an attempt of the basically urban, leisure-minded people who own these operations to re-create the romantic, disciplined landscape of the old European landed gentry. Certainly the European holdings bore names similar to those given to American horse farms.

The board fences have a more practical origin. They are considered the best fences for valuable stock, because they will not nick, as barbed wire does, or entangle hoofs, as conventional wire mesh does. Some persons even claim that the visibility of the white boards helps to prevent injury. All this is not without its price, however. In the Kentucky bluegrass, such fences cost about

$9,000 per mile, not including maintenance. No wonder many small operations have not been able to keep up appearances and have seen their showpiece fences fall into disrepair. Rising costs have even affected the bluegrass fences, where many operations are shifting from white painted boards to cheaper unpainted ones treated with dark wood preservative. These are changing the whole appearance of the area.[19]

50.9 (0.3) Begin ascent of Pilot Knob Ridge.

51.4 (0.5) The narrow top of Pilot Knob Ridge has excellent air drainage, and the Burre Fruit Farm on the left takes advantage of it (see mile 13.45 for details on this climatic phenomenon). Melons and tomatoes are also available in season.

51.7 (0.3) *Ridge Top Activity.* Kansans crave places with a view. Give them this and a paved road, and they will produce a minor housing development. From Pilot Knob the view northwestward, into the Salt Creek Valley, is as impressive as the one eastward, back to Leavenworth. Houses therefore line the road for several miles.

Another practically ubiquitous member of ridge-top society is the cemetery. The rationale for this is apparent: hill tops are obviously "above" the turmoil of everyday human affairs and are "closer" to God and to heaven. Sunset Memory Gardens on the left is unusual only bcause it is in the modern genre, with bronze surface markers instead of tombstones. The seeming nccd for burial ornament has not been totally ignored, however, for several statues and a patriotic flagpole display are located around the edge of the cemetery.

Stop to examine the large red boulder incorporated into the flagpole display. It is a piece of Sioux quartzite, a rather common sight in northeastern Kansas. The rock is not native to the area; it was carried here from the northern plains by glaciers some 750,000 or more years ago. Pieces like this (termed erratics) were scattered in an area north of the Kaw and east of the Big Blue River, where the ice had been. Recently they have become so popular as lawn ornaments that they are now rare sights in the countryside.

51.8 (0.1) The beautiful Salt Creek Valley is on the right. This is locally famous as the boyhood home of William F. ("Buffalo

Bill") Cody. He soon left the area to become a Pony Express rider, but his name was perpetuated by the Leavenworth citizenry in the 1950s when they named their new hotel after him.

The headwaters of Fivemile Creek are on the left. They have been dammed to form a series of small lakes.

53.6 (1.8) The farmstead on the left features a tank house, one of the few surviving buildings of its kind in eastern Kansas. The tall, square-based white structure, which has a pyramid roof, houses a small water tower. The tank's holding capacity is unneeded in an era of powerful electric pumps, but it was important when pumping was done with limited capacity and necessarily unreliable windmills. Tank houses (and windmills) survive in the more isolated parts of the western range country.

54.2 (0.6) *High Prairie.* For several miles, Kansas Route 92 has been following the divide between the Kansas and the Missouri River systems. This is productive upland country but is rather monotonous to the eyes of most travelers. Horace Greeley, who passed near here, called it "a gently heaving sea of grass" but didn't like the region "so well as the more rolling country south of Olathe and Prairie City" (about forty miles south of here).[20] There is indeed a certain loneliness about high prairies such as this one, and being here, one can understand even now a little of the torment that the open, flat grassland gave to many pioneer settlers.[21] The wind seems to blow constantly, and there is no place to escape from the elements. Significantly, no town sites were ever established in this vicinity.

55.9 (1.7) The quarry on the left is one of many in the region operated by the Hamm family of Williamstown and Perry. Limestone is nearly ubiquitous in eastern Kansas, so the location of quarries is determined by the proximity of markets. Ideally, this one should be much closer to Leavenworth than it is, but in recent years there have been increasing numbers of complaints about noise and dust from the exurbanites whose homes dot the countryside for a considerable distance around most cities. Leavenworth customers, of course, must pay for the longer hauls the quarry trucks now have to make.

56.6 (0.7) The numerous white plastic structures scattered

about the Edward Bott, Jr., farm on the left are modern versions of McLean hog sheds. The main virtue of these buildings, developed in McLean County, Illinois, is their portability. The occasional movement of hog facilities is helpful in controlling worms, and because the McLean sheds are small and are built on skids, this operation is easily accomplished. The substitution of molded plastic for the original triangular faceted wooden structures increases this advantage.

57.5 (0.9) The turn in the highway marks the end of this section of upland prairie. The road now slowly descends into the Stranger Creek Valley.

57.6 (0.1) *Southern Barns.* Stop to observe the barn on the left. Its color and general shape are nothing extraordinary, but it possesses a hay hood that is very unusual locally. The hay hood is the roof projection visible over the gable end of the barn. Its purpose was to protect a beam, pulley, and rope system that was used to pick up and lift loose hay into the barn loft. Since hay is now put up exclusively in bales, hay hoods have become archaic and will gradually disappear from the landscape. While they last, however, they may be used to indicate the background of the barn builders.

The common hood in Kansas is a simple peak (see sketch), but occasionally a more elaborate form appears, such as the one here. The enclosed form you see is characteristic of barns in Appalachia; therefore, this barn was probably built by a southerner. Several miles ahead the Appalachian form becomes dominant over a considerable area. Although it has not yet been established that this region has a definite southern heritage, local place names such as Kentucky and Alexandria townships and the city of Winchester (from Virginia) suggest that such a finding is likely.

57.9 (0.3) Another board fence on the left marks the local residents as atypical farmers.

58.6 (0.7) *Bethel.* The abandoned Bethel Church and weed-choked cemetery are ghostly reminders of the changes that have occurred in rural America over the last century. Bethel served as a community focus for a considerable group of people after the

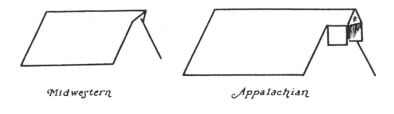

Midwestern   *Appalachian*

Hay hoods

church was built in 1870, but urban opportunities and easy transportation have gradually eroded its clientele. A few years ago an annual homecoming for former area residents was started, but even this was short-lived. When the church falls down shortly, there will be very few left to mourn. The presence of new houses along the highway, such as the A-frame structure on the right just beyond the cemetery, would seem to belie the demise of Bethel. The new population is different from the old one, however. Modern life has encouraged people to spread their allegiances thinly over a wide area; usually not enough time and energy remain to sustain a sense of rural neighborhood.

Note the old cedar trees in the cemetery. Their evergreen symbolism of life everlasting has made them standard items in nearly all burial grounds in the area.

59.1 (0.5) Several glacial erratics are clustered in the yard on the left; several more lie 0.2 mile ahead (see mile 51.7).

59.8 (0.7) *Springdale Covered Bridge.* Stranger Creek lies directly ahead. The private road that branches off to the left was the main thoroughfare across the valley until 1943, and from then until 1958 it was the road to the last covered bridge in Kansas. A lightning fire destroyed the structure on 21 September 1958. Nothing now remains except some stone pilings.

Kansas never had many of these quaint bridges, for the state was settled after steel had replaced wood as the primary bridge-building material. Although stories circulate that the bridge covers were to keep horses from shying at the sight of water and to keep ice off the bridge surface, the primary reason for their construction was simply protection from the elements. Covered bridges lasted approximately three times longer than uncovered ones, a savings factor that more than offset their additional construction costs.[22]

60.3 (0.5) Stranger Creek. The path just beyond the bridge also leads to the site of the old covered bridge, a quarter-mile downstream.

60.5 (0.2) *Risky Acres.* The flood plain is about a mile wide at this point. Its fertility and flatness make it valuable for agriculture, but one who farms here must always be aware of the danger of flooding. Water can delay field operations at crucial times and can quickly suffocate a crop. In recognition of this double-edged nature of flood plains, W. W. Schwinn, who farms this land, has appropriately named his farm "Risky Acres." Schwinn is probably even more aware of the capriciousness of farming here than his neighbors are, for his house, as well as his land, used to be in the "bottoms." His old house is on the right.

» *Mile 60.8 (0.3) Junction with County Route 21. Keep left, staying on Kansas Route 92.*

61.1 (0.3) W. W. Schwinn's new mobile home is on the left as you ascend from the lowland. Note the "Risky Acres" sign on the mailbox. Note also the conventional midwestern hay hood on the adjacent Danny Schwinn farm.

62.3 (1.2) *Springdale.* In the territorial days, when Kansans were to decide by popular vote whether they would be admitted as a free or as a slave state, many types of people rushed into the region. Among these were the Quaker founders of Springdale. These people were adamantly Free State, but they could not fight or send military aid because of their faith. They could help with their vote, however, so several groups moved west in the late 1850s. The first group, from Indiana, founded Springdale in 1855.

The Quaker meeting house and cemetery, which lie one-half mile to the south, are well worth a visit. The Quaker faith stresses an individual relationship with God, and adherents thus studiously avoid ecclesiastical bureaucracy and terminology. The "church" building is usually called a meeting house, and the whole organization is called the Society of Friends. Another distinguishing trait is their simplicity of manner. The best-known expression of this is the traditional "plain language," whereby "thee" and "thou" are substituted for the pronoun "you," but the unassuming gravestones and the steepleless clapboard meeting house at Springdale express it as well. The present meeting house was erected in 1883.[23]

63.0 (0.7) A small red quartzite erratic is on the right in the corner of the field.

Terracing. Note the graceful terrace series in the pastures on both sides of the road. They were expensive to plan and construct, but they are requirements for cropping the narrow uplands of eastern Kansas. Westward across the state terraces disappear, because streams have not dissected the land surface so much. This phenomenon is caused partly by the lesser rainfall to the west and partly by the relative newness of the land surface there. Quite recently, in a geological sense, the area between the Rockies and the Flint Hills was mantled with stream-deposited material. This filled in an older, cut-up land surface and created the flat High Plains. Although streams have been eroding this new surface for several million years, this is only about one-hundredth of the time they have been active on the lands of eastern Kansas.[24]

The natural curving lines of the terraces stand in contrast to the appearance of the rest of the human landscape of rural Kansas. The roads are straight, the old farmhouses and barns are boxy, and the orientations of nearly everything are limited to the cardinal directions. Recently this has been changing. The terraces themselves are new, being built mostly since the 1950s, after erosion had stripped so much topsoil from the fields that yields were declining. Other manifestations are the curved streets of suburban and ex-urban tracts and the gentle bends of interstate highways. Some of these changes are products of America's new ecological concern; others (such as suburban streets) may be no more than temporary fads.

63.6 (0.6) In the 1970s, the property on the right displayed the sign "Heavenworth Acres." This interesting wordplay revealed that the people here look eastward to Leavenworth as their trading center, rather than westward to McLouth, Oskaloosa, or Lawrence.

65.0 (1.4) A barn with a "southern" hay hood is on the left; it is the second one on the route (see mile 57.6). From this point on, southern hoods become more numerous than the conventional midwestern ones.[25]

65.4 (0.4) Jefferson County Line.

66.2 (0.8) *McLouth Gas Storage Field.* Notice the small silver pipe apparatus in the field on the right. These usually signal a natural-gas field, but in this case the pipe marks the beginning of the McLouth underground gas-storage area, the "largest in Kansas," according to the welcoming signs of that community, five miles ahead on Kansas Route 92.

The McLouth field, which extends south for about four miles, was a viable oil and gas producer during the 1940s, but its small reserves had been depleted by the early 1950s. Cities Service Company then decided to convert it to a storage area. The need for gas storage is based on seasonal demand for the product in combination with the continuous supply coming from the wells. McLouth was in an ideal position to serve this need, because it is one of the few oil fields located between the major producing regions of southwestern Kansas, Oklahoma, and Texas and the big consuming areas to the east. Generally, gas is accumulated here during the spring and fall seasons and is piped out at other times.

66.55 (0.35) Another "southern" barn appears on the left; a "midwestern" one stands 0.15 mile ahead.

» *Mile 66.8 (0.25) Kansas Route 92 turns left; keep straight ahead on paved road.*

The Edmonds Evangelical United Brethren Church once stood at this intersection; two miles north was the Hebron Baptist Church. Both were casualties of improved rural transportation, but the Edmonds building, at least, has been preserved (see mile 77.4).

67.1 (0.3) *Barns.* A large, nicely preserved "southern" barn is near the road on the right. Other than its hay hood, it is typical of the general-purpose structures erected throughout the Midwest

A Jefferson County barn

between the Civil War and World War II. Most were framed with heavy timbers, which were obtained locally, and were covered with vertical planks of rough-sawn lumber. Originally, many of the barns had their principal entrance on the eave side, but often, as here, spatial needs led to shed additions on either side of the main structure and a consequent reorientation of the building. Roofs also underwent changes throughout the period. Early barns had simple gable arrangements, but two-pitched gambrel designs, such as on this example, gradually became more common on stock farms. They provided additional storage capacity in the hay loft.

Color is where this barn deviates most from the midwestern norm, because it is not the familiar red. The color red and barns are inextricably linked in American culture. Children's farm books always display barns of this color, suburban tool sheds are so painted to produce the "rustic" look, and even a restaurant chain calls itself "The Red Barn," presumably to suggest that it serves wholesome "country" food. Why Americans have traditionally painted their barns red is not known, but the custom probably began in colonial Pennsylvania. One theory is that the color evolved as poorer farmers tried to make their wooden barns resemble the red brick ones of their wealthy neighbors. The original color came from the iron ore, hematite; so other theories have suggested that the explanation may be nothing more complicated than the availability of hematite in Pennsylvania.

Large wooden barns have become relics on the landscape. Out-buildings are now being constructed of corrugated steel and are usually smaller, more specialized structures (see miles 68.2 and 70.0). The old barns were ideal when general, diversified farming was the rule, but they are mostly anachronisms today. Judging from the rate of decay in this area, the majority will not last for another generation.[26]

67.95 (0.85) More board fencing is on the right, but this time there is a practical reason for it. The structure is a corral and loading chute for cattle, and since large numbers of frightened animals are placed here, the strength and safety of boards is needed. The chute is elevated and positioned so that a truck can easily back up to it.

68.2 (0.25) Note the corrugated steel structure on the Chase property to the left. It is a pole barn, one of a new species that has rapidly replaced the rambling wood outbuildings. The substitution has been caused mainly by rising lumber prices and carpenters' wages. Farmers can erect pole barns virtually by themselves; one just sets up a skeleton of poles and then nails on precut sheets of steel. Plans are available from dealers, or they can be improvised on the spot.

68.4 (0.2) The traditional red paint covers the "southern" barn on the left.

» *Mile 69.3 (0.9) "T" in the road; turn left.*

Hay Economics and Rural Change. The field on the southeast corner of this intersection is blanketed for much of each year with huge cylindrical bales of hay. Their presence suggests that the summer ritual of "putting up" hay into barn lofts may be coming to an end. Not only are the barns in disrepair, wages are becoming so high as to prohibit the practice. The giant bales are a labor-saving solution. They can be left in the field because, with their size and shape, rain spoils only a small portion of each bale. A tractor that is equipped with a "fork" attachment moves individual bales to where feed is needed.

The substitution of machinery for labor, and then larger machinery for existing equipment, has been a fact of midwestern life for a century. The causes of the cycle are complex, but a nagging shortage of farm labor is partly responsible. Young people head for the cities, so the farmers have been forced to go with more machinery and economies of scale. The results are $30,000 tractors and 600-acre midwestern farms, accompanied by a rural landscape that is dotted with abandoned houses, obsolete outbuildings, and rusting equipment. The pace of change has been incredible. Those who can remember the area even a decade ago find many things totally different and feel tinges of nostalgia, in spite of the obvious advantages of the present situation in production efficiency. Farming as a "way of life" is about gone in the United States.[27]

69.6 (0.3) A nice example of rural decay appears on the right. Both the house and the barn have been abandoned and probably will not survive the decade.

70.0 (0.4) It is difficult to make generalizations about rural America. Ten years ago the farmstead on the left was abandoned. Today it has been completely rebuilt, with only the windmill remaining from the old scene. Abandonments are more common than renovations in this area, but sites along paved roads are exceptions.

Note the horse barn. The color is traditional red, and the white Xs on the doors imitate old wooden bracing; but all other aspects are new. It is a prefabricated steel structure, the third stage of modern barn evolution after wooden and pole structures (see miles 67.1 and 68.2). The change has been caused by convenience and by labor costs. Mass production keeps prices low for prefabricated models, and the quality control is excellent. This example even has guttering.

70.3 (0.3) The long trench in the pasture on the left is called a pit silo. This form is not nearly so attractive as the familiar vertical silo, but it is fairly efficient to operate and very economical to construct. It is easy to fill, and none of the silage spoils except for a thin surface layer. Access is the principal problem, especially in deep mud or snow. This example has been abandoned and is now half-filled with trash.

70.9 (0.6) The farm on the right used to be quite unusual in raising both cattle and sheep. From several perspectives, raising two kinds of livestock seems to make sense: it should provide a shield against market-price fluctuations in each, and it might allow better utilization of the various types of pasture on a farm. These advantages, however, have nearly always been overcome by two other factors: a deep-seated cultural antagonism between raisers of the two animals, and the growing need to specialize in one product in order to gain enough size to be able to afford specialized equipment. Here a beef herd provides the economic basis of the farm; the sheep used to be kept as a hobby.

71.1 (0.2) *Glacial Till.* To one who is familiar with the landscape south of the Kansas River, a striking feature of the tour route since Springdale has been the near absence of rock outcrops. Only in the deepest stream valleys have any of the familiar limestone ledges appeared. This is not because limestone is uncommon in northeast Kansas, but because the rock is covered with a thick blanket of unconsolidated material known as glacial drift or till (see map).[28] Although loess bluffs and quartzite erratics are perhaps more spectacular local remnants of glaciation (see miles 27.5 and 51.7), till has wrought far-greater changes on the land. As the ice sheet began to recede, large amounts of material that were dragged along within and beneath it were laid down. This filled in previously eroded areas and mantled the bedrock, thus smoothing the topography. Thin layers of loess were then deposited over most of the area, creating a landscape that is generally quite favorable for agriculture.

Till deposits over a hundred feet thick occur in Brown County to the north, but here, toward the extreme limit of glaciation, the layer is thinner. Streams have cut through it in many places, leaving only the uplands still covered. Excellent exposures are visible on both sides of this road cut. A stone-free loess layer lies at the surface, but most of the cut is through the unsorted mixture of sand, rocks, clay, and boulders that constitutes till. Many pieces of reddish Sioux quartzite and dark igneous rocks from far to the north are present, along with limestone fragments that originated closer at hand.

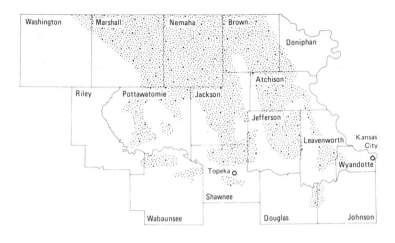

Glacial drift deposits in Kansas

71.2 (0.1) The new Countryside Baptist Church on the left brings to mind another paradox of rural America. Improved transportation brought about the demise of many rural churches (see miles 58.6 and 66.8), but recently this same force has prompted new building. The Countryside congregation found land prices cheaper here than in town, and its members have no access problems because of modern roads and automobiles.

71.4 (0.2) Note the old fence line that intersects the road just before the stream crossing. It is in a abnormal position because it divides the land into something other than 40-acre plots; it also violates another midwestern rule by trending in a noncardinal direction. This strange fence line is the old boundary of the nineteenth-century Delaware Indian Reservation. Land on either side of the border was settled at different times by different people, of course, and the real-estate transactions of the past hundred years have not erased the line. The boundary can easily be traced across two counties on land-ownership maps.

More till can be seen on the left. Beyond, young Christmas trees are growing, but they are not yet of marketable size.

72.0 (0.6) Another small till exposure is on the left.

72.1 (0.1) The mysterious huge white sphere to the left, a quarter mile from the road, is a radome. Inside is a radar screen, which is used to help establish flight paths for planes approaching and leaving Kansas City International Airport. This site, which is directly west of the airport, plays a crucial role in regulating the increasingly heavy east-west traffic across mid-America.

72.5 (0.4) On the left is old Hinton School, which has been converted into a house. With new siding and garage, the traditional exterior entry hall is the only clue to the building's schoolhouse past.

» *Mile 73.5 (1.0) Turn right onto the highway (Kansas Routes 92 and 16).*

Two Transitions. The next three miles form a transition zone between the barns with Appalachian hay hoods and those with midwestern ones. It is interesting that this transition occurs as one approaches Oskaloosa, because Oskaloosa was a strong Free-State center in territorial Kansas, and it attracted settlers from the northern states. This is further evidence that the barns may be significant indicators of population origins.

This same general area represents a transition in another sense too. The density of rather new ranch houses built by urban commuters is the lowest it has been since leaving Leavenworth, but it increases again a few miles ahead near Oskaloosa. You are driving along an urban "divide," a small area between the influence of Leavenworth to the east and Topeka-Lawrence to the south and west.

73.8 (0.3) *Dairy Farms.* On the left is the first of a small cluster of dairy operations along Kansas Route 92. To many urban eyes, dairy farms are the stereotype of American agriculture. This image is probably caused by the several ways in which modern dairies resemble the general farms of the last generation. They are smaller than the average farming operation today, and they have more and better-maintained outbuildings. The casual observer fails to see that such farms are a special case in modern agriculture.

Silos are a good indicator of the size of the dairy operation. The small-scale farm on the left has only one silo, a traditional structure of poured concrete. Farther ahead on the left, in contrast, stands the multispired agglomeration of the Houk farm. Note the large blue Harvestore silos rising above the rest, the crowning symbol of big-time dairying today. These units are very expensive, but they are spreading rapidly over the midwestern countryside because of their ability to receive, store, and dispense high-moisture silage more efficiently and in greater quantities than traditional silos.

74.1 (0.3) *The Houk farm.* Count the farmstead structures: a wooden barn, a pole barn, a new prefabricated steel barn, a concrete-block milk house, three smaller sheds, and two storage bins, not including the silos and the main house. The recent evolution of barns can all be seen in one glance.

74.85 (0.75) The last Appalachian hay hood is on the left.

75.2 (0.35) A nice view of Oskaloosa ahead and to the right. Note the unusual design of the water tower.

75.45 (0.25) The first midwestern hay hood is on the left.

75 6 (0.15) Robbins Salvage on the right shows the effects of Ladybird Johnson's campaign during the 1960s to beautify American roadsides. The existing cyclone fence left too much of the automobile wreckage visible, so pink and green lathes were inserted diagonally in the wire mesh. It looked a little garish until sunfading muted the impact. A much more pleasing touch is the extensive landscaping in front of the fence. A combination of redbud and Russian olive trees, spreading junipers, and other species creates a nice display and, in summer, an effective screen.

76.4 (0.8) Observe the beautiful red barn on the Bess Sharkey farm. The hay hood is familiar, but the rest of the design is unique in the area.

» *Mile 76.5 (0.1) Turn right, staying on Kansas Route 92.*

The lake on the left, immediately after turning, is the former water source for Oskaloosa; it was built in the 1930s as a W.P.A.

project. The city is now supplied by a Rural Water District from wells in the Kansas River flood plain some ten miles to the south. This was done partially as an aid to the area's rural population, to ensure that there would be enough customers to merit a water district, but Oskaloosa also had its own motives. As will be discussed below, the town is expecting some growth as a result of the construction of Perry Reservoir, and it wants to be ready with adequate water.

76.7 (0.2) The farmer on the left raises jackasses.

77.05 (0.35) *Oskaloosa's* city limit.

Jefferson County Towns. A century ago, midwestern counties featured a scattering of small rural service centers, with no unusually large town. Gradually this changed, typically with a centrally located county-seat town draining off much of the rural population and becoming the business and social center for the entire area. In Jefferson County this did not occur. Oskaloosa, the county seat, has only about one thousand people, a figure that is exceeded by Valley Falls and is nearly matched by Meriden and Perry. Winchester and Nortonville are other viable communities.

Why has Jefferson County kept a nineteenth-century urban structure? The reasons are many; they include the broken topography of the county, and its location between the valleys of the Kansas and Missouri rivers. These two lowlands have always been development avenues for Kansas. The earliest cities were here, as were the first railroads and the biggest manufacturers. The road networks stringing out from the river cities of Lawrence, Topeka, Leavenworth, and Atchison tapped not only the rural parts of their own counties but also sections of Jefferson as well. Local towns never really had a chance to develop. The only place that could prosper to a degree was Valley Falls in the northwestern part of the county, most remote from the two major rivers.[29]

77.1 (0.05) Note the prefabricated steel building on the right, which houses the Meyer Lumber Company. Such buildings are changing the look of urban as well as rural America.

77.4 (0.3) *Old Jefferson Town.* The Jefferson County Historical Society, with the aid of a 0.1-mill tax levy, started Old Jefferson

Town in 1970. All the buildings are original, having been moved here from sites throughout the area. The church, for example, is old Edmonds Church, whose original foundation was viewed at mile 66.8. This project was conceived primarily for local pride, but it is also taking advantage of the increased traffic flow along the highway as people come to Perry Reservoir (note the various billboards for lakeshore developments). The "General Store" is leased to local craftsmen who ply the tourist trade.

» *Mile 77.5 (0.1) Turn left onto Jefferson Street, staying on Kansas Route 92.*

Pat's Thrift Way, on the corner, is also related to Lake Perry. The market opened fourteen years ago, just after the reservoir; it does a considerable business with the weekend visitors. Its Sunday-morning hours are an explicit response to this trade.

77.6 (0.1) On the right, note the low yellow building with the brick façade. The left part is a welding and body shop, and the right section is a unique place called the Book Barn. This is a nonprofit venture by the public libraries of northeast Kansas to recycle the old and duplicate books from their collections. The libraries receive a little money from the project, but they do it mainly to avoid the waste of throwing old books away. Prices are very reasonable, mostly under a dollar, and the shop is well worth a visit. Its hours are 9 A.M. to 5 P.M. on Saturdays only.

The Book Barn's name came from the barnlike building that housed the operation here prior to a fire in 1973. In light of previous discussion (mile 67.1), it is interesting to observe the vertical boards and the red paint used to establish a barn "atmosphere" in the new building.

77.65 (0.05) The masthead of the *Oskaloosa Independent* bears the slogan "Six Months Older Than the State." This age, however, has brought prosperity neither for the newspaper nor for the town. Perry Reservoir has helped some, but as the people say: "Sure cars go through town bumper to bumper on their way to Perry on weekends, but they don't stop." Most supplies are purchased in Kansas City or Topeka, and Oskaloosa gets only a few crumbs. The *Independent* is still published, but it is now owned by the *Valley*

Old bank building on the Oskaloosa courthouse square

Falls Vindicator and is printed in Valley Falls. Only an editor and a circulation clerk remain in Oskaloosa.

The Oskaloosa Square. The central courthouse square of Jefferson County is one of hundreds in the Midwest, but whereas many county seats now complain about poor traffic movement around the squares and resultant congestion, Oskaloosa finds the square well suited to its needs.[30] It seems as if city planners of the nineteenth century envisioned most county-seat towns as having a population of around two thousand. This would mean just enough businesses to fill the square and produce a nicely arranged city. Rapid urbanization soon spoiled this plan in many counties, but in Oskaloosa, one can still see how nicely it could work. Oskaloosa is actually not quite big enough for its square, as the empty buildings on the north side attest.

The new courthouse and the Leavenworth Mutual Savings office stand in marked contrast to the rest of the downtown architecture. The low horizontal lines and bright colors clash with the deep rusts and the verticality of the older buildings. This conflict bothers local residents somewhat, and they still speak lovingly of their old courthouse, a towering Victorian structure that was destroyed by a tornado more than two decades ago.

Along the south side of the square, note the old bank building (1892), which is listed in the National Historic Register. Note also that one house remains on the square. It is on the east side and has long been used as the sheriff's office.

77.8 (0.15) *The Origin of the Prairie.* For the next mile and a half, Kansas Route 92 follows the valley of Burr Oak Branch. A striking feature is the densely wooded rocky scarp land on either side of the stream. Wooded scarps like this have long interested people who are concerned with the natural vegetation of the Great Plains. The traditional theory held that grasses were the predominant vegetation on the plains because the climate was too arid to support trees other than along streams. The scarps challenge this thesis. If the deep soils of the upland could not support trees, how could the rocky, thin soils of the broken lands do so? An explanation of this phenomenon in terms of fire is growing in popularity. It says that the climate of the plains is conducive to tree growth, but periodic fires have favored grasses in most situations. Trees survived only along streams and on abrupt escarpments, which served as natural fire breaks.[31] Further evidence for this position is the success of trees on the plains upland in recent decades as prairie fires have been curtailed.

78.4 (0.6) A meat-processing plant, run by the Kansas Department of Corrections, is 0.2 mile to the left on a gravel road. After the original owners had abandoned the facility in 1984, the city of Oskaloosa interested prison officials in it. Thirty-five honor prisoners, who are bused to work here daily from Lansing, produce about fifty thousand pounds of meat per month. Prisons and other governmental institutions get the meat, the inmates learn a trade, and local farmers have an outlet for their livestock.

79.3 (0.9) *Slough Creek.* The bottom land here was originally wooded, like the scarps, but it has long been cleared for agriculture.

80.9 (1.6) The pasture on the left is being invaded by trees. This is a fairly common sight in the area and is support for the fire hypothesis of the prairie discussed above.

81.15 (0.25) Old Buck Point School, which has been converted into a house, is on the right. The ubiquitous schoolhouse well is in the yard.

81.5 (0.35) Begin the descent to the valley of Little Slough Creek

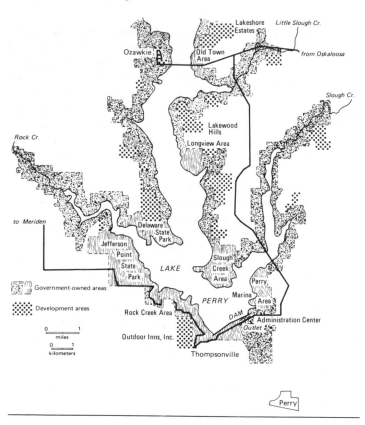

Perry Reservoir reference map

and Perry Reservoir. The next mile provides another good example of thickly wooded rocky escarpments.

82.4 (0.9) Cross Little Slough Creek. Even though the water is about three miles away, this is the official beginning of Perry Reservoir, because the federal government (U.S. Army Corps of Engineers) owns the flood plain from here downstream (see map). Public ownership of this area is necessary because of the large fluctuation in water level that occurs at Perry. The reservoir is one of about a dozen built in the Kansas River basin since a large flood in 1951 brought disaster to Kansas City, Topeka, and other cities in the lower valley. By storing floodwaters in the reservoirs and by temporarily inundating areas such as Little Slough Creek Valley, it is hoped that major downstream flooding can be prevented. This flood-control rationale and the whole phenomenon of reservoirs in Kansas has sparked much local interest and controversy. Several of the major arguments will be discussed in the ensuing miles.

82.8 (0.4) The dirt road on the right leads to the Midwest Regular Baptist Youth Camp, the first of many developments tied to the reservoir.

82.9 (0.1) Kansas Route 92 formerly followed the creek bottom, but for the next four miles the corps has relocated it on the upland. The old roadway is clearly visible, angling off to the left. Note the land use on the flood plain as the road climbs to the bluff. What was once intensively cultivated cropland is now in grass. The corps puts out haying contracts for the valley, but the return is only a small fraction of what it used to be. Acreages like this are one of the key elements in the reservoir dialogue. Does it make sense to forgo intensive agriculture on the bottoms, the best lands in this part of the state, when they will be flooded only very infrequently? The area involved is huge: many small valleys, such as Little Slough, and an extremely large tract on the main Delaware River at the head of the impoundment (see map).

» *Mile 84.4 (1.5) Intersection of two corps-improved roads; continue straight ahead on Kansas Route 92.*

The upland area around the lake is privately owned. This produced a flurry of land-speculation activity, most of it on a small scale. Signs advertising building lots and other land for sale are still common, but the homemade quality of most of them is obvious; only a few big-time operators have been attracted to Perry. The scarcity of major entrepreneurs was surprising to many area people because of the accessibility of the lake to both Kansas City and Topeka; it can be explained by the corp's absolute control of waterfront property. None of it is allowed in private hands because of the pool fluctuations discussed above, and a lake housing development that has no waterfront property is operating without its main selling point; even naming a development Lakeshore

Estates or Lakeside Village, as two local entrepreneurs have done, cannot fully overcome this fact.

84.6 (0.2) The first glimpse of the lake.

85.5 (0.9) *Old Town.* The corps has developed several public-use areas around the reservoir, but none can compare in interest with Old Town. This area is the former town site of Ozawkie, a community of about a hundred and fifty people that was founded in 1855. With the coming of the reservoir in the mid 1960s, the town was moved to a new location west of the lake. The only houses left on the old site are the three on the right, just north of Kansas Route 92.

Explore the Old Town area. The old retaining walls, sidewalks, and evergreen plantings all look a bit eerie among the new charcoal grills. The strangest site is old highway 92, which has been converted into a boat ramp at the southwest corner of the park. The American Legion Post 225, at the entrance to Old Town, sits just off governmental property. The sale of soft drinks to users of the lake helps to finance the post's activities.

85.8 (0.3) Causeway across the reservoir. Half a mile ahead, at the old channel of the Delaware River, a water connection between the north and south halves of the lake has been left.

» *Mile 86.9 (1.1) Turn right onto Kansa Avenue (the second exit) in Ozawkie. Complete a short tour of the new town site by turning right onto Coyote Avenue (0.3 mile), then right onto Sioux Drive (0.1), then right onto Sunflower Boulevard (0.2), then left onto Kansa Drive (0.1) once again.*

New Ozawkie. The character of Ozawkie before its move was similar to that of many midwestern villages. The businesses were collected in a compact central area, the streets were laid out in a square grid, the conditions and styles of the houses varied widely, and the population was an aging one composed largely of widows and retired farmers. New Ozawkie has undergone a metamorphosis. The townspeople formed a nonprofit corporation, sold lots, and used the money from this sale to finance a sewer, street, and water system for the new location. They were also able to implement a variety of new landscape tastes, since they were starting from scratch, rather than modifying an existing town. Some of these are rather sharp breaks with tradition and tell us much about our modern culture.

Ozawkie makes one aware that two-story houses are not commonly built in America today. Its streets also carry a message. The roads follow natural topographical lines for the most part, instead of the traditional grid; this enables a maximum number of houses to have a view of the water. The names of the roads are revealing, too. "Drive," "Avenue," and "Boulevard" have replaced the traditional "Street" appellation; and names such as Coyote, Goldenrod, Meadowlark, and Kansa are a far cry from Oak, Washington, or Second. The most significant change in the landscape, however, is probably in the location of businesses. A centrally located downtown is completely absent here. A few operations are dispersed among the houses, but most of them are along Kansas Route 92, at one end of the town and rather inaccessible on foot. If we needed documentation that American cities are being designed primarily for the automobile, this would be ideal. Sidewalks are scarce, and even the schoolhouse is remotely situated in the southeast corner of the town site.

New Ozawkie is a pleasant place in which to live—if you have a car. Sales of lots were sufficient to provide relief from local taxes for several years. This and the obvious amenities of lake-side living have swelled the local population to 250, most of whom commute to work in Topeka. The town has made a concerted effort to regulate the "lake crowd." Deed restrictions prevent mobile homes, and the people have voted against a proposed local boat ramp. Most businesses need the lake trade, however. The Donna and Family Café reflects this by posting different summer and winter hours and by stocking a supply of souvenir tee shirts and hats.

» *Mile 87.7 (0.8) Turn left onto Kansas Route 92 and return across the causeway.*

» *Mile 90.2 (2.5) Turn right onto the paved road, following the sign for Apple Valley Farm.*

90.5 (0.3) Notice the riprap ahead on the east side of the earth bridge across Little Slough Creek. The causeway is primarily clay filled, so it needs the stonework for erosion protection in high water.

90.85 (0.35) The old path of Route 92 passes beneath the roadway. The pavement can be seen off to the left.

91.5 (0.65) *Old Military Trail Campsite.* The corps has reserved this area for Boy Scouts and for other groups that want to camp. The site takes its name from the army road that once connected Forts Leavenworth and Riley. The nineteenth-century route paralleled Kansas Route 92 in this area and crossed the Delaware River at Ozawkie.

92.0 (0.5) A railroad dining car of undetermined origin sits rotting on the left.

92.5 (0.5) *Kansas Lakes vs. Ozark Lakes.* Many Missourians almost sneer at the mention of Perry and the other Kansas reservoirs, implying that these bodies of water do not compare with their own Lake of the Ozarks, Table Rock, and similar impoundments. A drive down this main lake road provides support for this opinion. There are scattered signs, pointing to places such as Apple Valley Farm and Lakewood Hills, but nearly twenty years after the dam was completed, the scene is still dominated by farmhouses and undeveloped land. The Ozark hubbub of activity is definitely lacking.

The contrast between the areas has impressed many people. Some attribute it simply to the relative newness of Perry and the other Kansas lakes. Others note the important factor of the corps's complete control of the waterfront here, in comparison to the private ownership available at Lake of the Ozarks and elsewhere. There may be a third factor involved, however: a difference in the natural settings of the two lake areas. Kansas City users of Ozark lakes are conscious of entering a different world as they journey southward. The soil turns from brown to red, the agricultural land is replaced by scrub forest, and the roads abandon their strict compass orientations. In brief, long before these people reach their lake destination they have passed into a new environment and are thus aware that they have left home and are now on vacation.

Users of Kansas lakes experience none of this, for their reservoirs are surrounded by ordinary agricultural lands. There are no visual cues to help them savor and anticipate their vacation destination until the water itself comes into view.

93.9 (1.9) *Lakeside Village.* Lakeside Village has been one of the most elaborately promoted of the reservoir housing developments. Its three-flagpoled entrance and stone pillars depict the combination luxury-rustic image that was marketed, while street names such as Briarwood Trail and Valleymead Lane contribute to the vision. A quick tour of the property suggests that the vision has not been achieved. Most of the lots remain undeveloped after having been on the market for more than a decade, and existing construction runs more to mobile homes and A-frames than to luxury retreats. A clubhouse exists near the main entrance, but its grounds are poorly maintained. Note the glacial erratics used for landscaping.

95.0 (1.1) Another access road to the reservoir is on the right. The rather brushy, semiabandoned look that has characterized the landscape for the last several miles continues down these access roads until governmental property or a housing development is reached. This is the result of land speculation. The area is in a state of limbo: the land is too valuable for growing crops (note the abandoned farmhouses), yet it is too far from the shoreline for immediate development. There are "Keep out" signs everywhere.

95.7 (0.7) Begin the descent to Slough Creek Arm of Perry Reservoir.

96.45 (0.75) Cross Slough Creek Arm. To the left notice the trees left standing at the head of the inlet. This was done to create a favorable habitat for fish.

98.1 (1.65) Perry Dam is visible momentarily ahead and to the right.

98.4 (0.3) Lake Perry Marina, on the right, is operated privately under a permit from the Corps of Engineers, the federal agency that built the reservoir and now administers it.

» *Mile 98.9 (0.5) Turn right and follow the sign to the Administration Center and Outlet Area.*

Corps land begins just beyond Bitler's Hickory House Bar-B-Q. Note the sign warning motorcycles to keep on the roadway. Cycles have been a problem for lake officials, because they destroy vegetation on hillsides and cause subsequent erosion.

99.1 (0.2) The earth embankment on the right, behind the row of trees, serves as the emergency spillway for Perry. During extremely high water, overflow can be channeled over this spillway, across the road, and into the small stream on the left. The stream will then carry the water into the main channel of the Delaware River.

» *Mile 99.6 (0.5) Turn right into the administration area. Follow the circle past the weather station and the administration building, and park at the dam overlook.*

A brochure with a map of the reservoir is available on request at the administration building. Quartzite erratics have again been used in the landscaping.

The Nature of Big Dams. The view of Perry Reservoir and Dam from the overlook is impressive, and the site is a fitting place to ponder the significance of big dams. Why do we build them? Are they the best way to deal with the flood hazard? These and similar questions are being asked in Kansas today, with varied responses.

Many people are opposed to big dams. They point out that floods and flood plains are natural phenomena, phenomena that people should adjust to, rather than expensively and perhaps futilely try to strait-jacket. Disasters such as the 1951 flood in Kansas City could have been prevented, they say, if the flood plain there had simply been zoned against settlement and if a system of "set-back" levees had been established. Set-back levees are ones built, not at the water's edge, but a couple of river widths away from the banks. They create a flow way for flood waters to pass through densely populated areas, and their cost is miniscule compared with the big dams. Also, the amount of land required for flow ways is a small fraction of that drowned by the reservoirs.

There are other arguments against big dams. Because of the accumulation of silt they cannot be effective as flood controls for much more than fifty years. Moreover, even at peak efficiency, they are not able to prevent all flooding, yet they lure us into a false sense of security and encourage more and more industrial development in the flood plains. Therefore, when a flood does come, the damage is greater than ever. A cycle is thus developed: more dams lead to more development of the flood plain, which leads to a call for more dams, and so forth. The best agricultural land in the area is thus progressively gobbled up and drowned. How much of this can we afford?[32]

There are better and cheaper ways than big dams for dealing with floods. Small dams located near the headwaters of streams are an obvious alternative. Little valuable bottom land would be inundated, and the impoundments would double as farm ponds for local landowners. Nevertheless, the number of reservoirs has continued to grow until they have become one of the most prominent features on midwestern maps. The reasons are not difficult to discern. Obvious proponents of the dams are industries that have a vested interest in flood-plain locations and local landowners who hope to profit from speculation in lake-side land. Chambers of Commerce from small, stagnating towns such as Oskaloosa, Perry, and Valley Falls also favor reservoirs, hoping for a business boom of some sort. These factors, in conjunction with the entrenched, efficient Corps of Engineers mechanism for constructing dams, make a combination that is difficult to thwart.

The public as a whole sees the reservoirs primarily for their recreation potential. The public enjoys this even as it realizes that big dams are tremendously expensive and that it probably would not vote to construct them with state or local funds. Federal money is another matter, however. The general attitude is that the dollars will be spent on some less-than-necessary project anyhow and that it is better for Kansas to get the construction funds and lake recreational benefits than for someplace else to do so.[33]

» *Mile 99.8 (0.2) Continue around the circle and leave the administration area. (Do not take the road across the top of the dam.)*

» *Mile 100.0 (0.2) Turn right and proceed along the base of the dam.*

Perry dam is an imposing structure. It is made of local materials, the exact mixture being determined by what was available on the construction site. The fill is primarily clay, with limestone riprap used on the water side to curtail erosion. Note the slight bend in the dam. This is not for strength or esthetic reasons; it was the result of engineers' utilizing a hill in the flood plain as part of the dam. The bend resulted when the hill was connected to the nearest points on the two bluffs.

100.4 (0.4) A tree nursery of the corps.

100.8 (0.4) *Fisherman's Paradise.* The road to the lake outlet is on the left, where water is periodically discharged into the Delaware River through a huge pipe that is twenty-three feet in diameter. It provides a spectacular display when the gates are fully open. The outlet is also the most popular fishing spot at Perry, as the current sweeps large numbers of fish from the lake. There are so many fish, in fact, that "snagging" (hooking fish in their side or tail) is a popular, though illegal, method of angling. Northern and walleye pike are prize catches.

» *Mile 101.6 (0.8) Turn right at the Thompsonville corner.*

Thompsonville. Thompsonville was once the site of a grist mill on the Delaware. The mill is long gone, and even the river has been relocated from its old channel along this western bluff. The second house on the left is a converted schoolhouse; the impressive but rapidly decaying stucco building, next on the right, was once a Methodist church.

101.8 (0.2) The road follows the edge of the Kansas River flood plain for the next three-quarters of a mile. Note that the farmhouses and other buildings are on the right-hand, or bluff, side. This portion of the lowland has never flooded in historic time, and the placement of the buildings is therefore probably more to get a good view and to save the plain for cropping than to avoid high water.

» *Mile 102.5 (0.7) Turn right just before the "Pavement ends" sign.*

The Outdoor Inn of Perry, on the left, is in the boat-storage business. The company also owns more than three hundred acres of adjoining land, which is choicely located near the lake outlet, two public-use areas just to the north, and U.S. 24 a mile to the south, which connects directly with Topeka and Kansas City. The land has probably the best development potential of any at the reservoir.

102.6 (0.1) *Thompsonville "Reservoir."* The small impound-ment on the left provides a vivid contrast with Perry. It was built for flood control in 1960, several years before Perry, by the local watershed district, with assistance from the county and the U.S. Department of Agriculture. As I mentioned at mile 99.6, numerous small dams like this one constitute a sound alternative to big reservoirs. The flooded areas are narrow valleys of marginal agricultural potential, and the lakes thus created are of an ap-propriate size for watering stock and for other local uses.

» *Mile 103.0 (0.4) Turn left and follow the corps's signs to the boat ramp.*

Nice picnicking facilities that have a good view of the reser-voir are scattered along the road for the next two miles.

103.7 (0.7) *Landscape Taste.* For the next couple of miles the route passes through the Rock Creek Public Use Area of the corps; then it enters the Jefferson Point section of Perry State Park. Although both of these areas serve the same general purpose, their appearances differ considerably. The corps's landscape could be termed "controlled natural" and is a result of policy established by Lynn Myers, the long-time project manager at Perry. Myers was an environmentalist who did not cater purely to picnickers and campers. As a result, the grounds are well maintained but are not mowed except in heavy-use areas. This aids the propagation of wildlife, prevents erosion, and keeps an overall "natural" ap-pearance. Many trees have also been left. As in the state park, some of the larger open acreages are leased for haying, but cutting is not permitted until after July 15 so as to allow time for nesting birds to hatch their young.

Jefferson Point, in contrast, presents a well-manicured appearance in its public areas, practicing what Myers has called the "cemetery caretaker approach." The state is in the camping business, he says, with camping fees being the major source of revenue for the park. Consequently, the landscaping and the design of the public-use areas are executed with the needs of people predominantly in mind, not those of the environment as a whole. The grass is all closely cropped; trees have been removed, and camping areas have been leveled, in order to be more comfortable for campers and trailers; and hillsides and open areas are hayed throughout the summer to keep them "neat." The slippage of mowers on hillsides and the removal of vegetation have initiated serious erosion in several places, especially along the roadways.

104.7 (1.0) As the road turns sharply to the left, the Rock Creek Arm of Perry comes clearly into view. The white bridge across the head of the arm is on the lake's main perimeter road.

106.2 (1.5) Leave the corps's area and enter Perry State Park.

106.3 (0.1) A typical manicured camping area is on the right across the small inlet.

106.6 (0.3) A steep, barren road cut such as this one would not be permitted on the corps's land.

107.1 (0.5) This is not an intensively used part of the park. The main access road, which you will join shortly, comes directly north from U.S. 24. The land here has pretty much been abandoned. What was once pastureland before the park has now been thickly invaded by sumac and fifteen-foot trees of various species.

» *Mile 107.5 (0.4) Stop sign. Turn right onto Route 237, the main perimeter road of Perry Reservoir.*

For most visitors this corner marks the entrance to Perry State Park, and it is here that the contrast in landscape with the Rock Creek Corps area noted at mile 103.7 is most vivid. Nature is forcibly subdued in catering to visitors' demands and expectations. Note the official entry sign, erected by the corps, and the various advertising billboards.

» *Mile 108.05 (0.55) Turn left onto a gravel road.*

Bordering the corps's property once again is a cluster of small, lake-oriented businesses. Goods and services available here include gasoline, bait, boat storage, boat sales, and food staples.

According to local people, one of the major needs of Perry is improved access roads. The corps has built a good perimeter route, but connectors are missing between it and the existing network of highways. The five-mile stretch of gravel you are now on joins popular Perry State Park with Meriden and Kansas 4. The corps, the county, and the state all agree that a paved road is needed; but thus far, other projects have taken priority. Meriden residents feel that the county will eventually make the improvement, as soon as taxes from lake-side developments have grown enough to replace the public funds that were formerly provided by the inundated farms in Delaware Valley.

» *Mile 109.2 (1.15) Stop sign. Continue straight ahead.*

» *Mile 110.2 (1.0) Turn right.*

111.0 (0.8) It is most unusual to find clusters of new houses such as you see here along a gravel road, but their occupants feel that the pavement will come soon. By building now, they got their land cheaper and got their choice of lots. Notice how the homes on the right side of the road are oriented eastward, away from the road and toward the lake. There can be little doubt about the amenity that brought these people here.

» *Mile 111.8 (0.8) Turn left, still on a gravel road.*

113.0 (1.2) The presence of a nearby lake brings all sorts of incongruous elements into a rural landscape. Observe the simple mobile home on the right, with its little rundown shed, which contains—of all things—two airplanes!

» *Mile 113.9 (0.9) Turn right onto Kansas 4.*

Even though there was some development along the last five miles, it is clear that a paved road makes a tremendous difference

Entrance display at Meriden

in roadside appearances. An obvious display of wealth is the white board fence enclosing the forty acres on the left.

» *Mile 115.4 (1.5) Junction of Kansas Routes 4 and 245. Continue ahead on Kansas 4.*

Meriden. The ostentatious entrance display of Meriden plainly reveals the connection the town feels for Perry Reservoir and why its people are pushing for adequate connector roads (see drawing). Viewed from the south, the town appears to be decadent, with the lake display being a grasping at straws, a last hope for rejuvenation. Driving farther along Kansas 4, however, another Meriden comes into view. The east side of the city is all new, revealing that, in truth, Meriden is in the midst of a boom. Roadside businesses include that sure sign of suburban influence—a small-animal hospital.

» *Mile 116.3 (0.9) Turn sharply left and follow the sign to Jefferson West High School.*

Although the lake has undoubtedly helped Meriden, the prosperity of the town actually dates back to 1960, paradoxically to a tornado disaster. A twister raked the heart of the town on May

19 of that year, heavily damaging or destroying more than sixty homes and businesses; within a year, however, Meriden had not only largely rebuilt, but had improved itself in the process. Kansas 4 was relocated away from the downtown area, businesses were modernized, a sewer system was installed to replace the old septic tanks, and the little community soon began to attract Topeka commuters in growing numbers.

Meriden is now totally Topeka dominated and oriented. Newcomers never hear about Oskaloosa, their county seat, until it is time to renew their car licenses, and they somewhat resent having to go "way up there" even once a year. There was even a local movement about ten years ago, when Perry Reservoir was being planned, to join this section of Jefferson County to Shawnee. The plan eventually failed, but a lingering sentiment remains.

116.5 (0.2) Another plus for Meriden is the new Jefferson West High School, one block to the right, which serves a consolidated district of Rock Creek and Ozawkie in addition to Meriden. Many of the new commuter residents say they came here to avoid the drug problems they perceive in the Topeka school system.

116.7 (0.2) City limit. Westward from here the houses still are quite new looking, even though they are in the older part of town. These homes are mostly reconstructions following the 1960 tornado. Note the frequency of silver maples. These fast-growing trees were promoted after the disaster, even to the extent of billing Meriden as the "silver maple city."[34] The fad did not last long, fortunately, for the shallow-rooted maple is not an ideal tree for a windy country.

116.9 (0.2) Two blocks north is another product of the tornado, a mobile-home park.

117.0 (0.1) Downtown Meriden features a new post office, a municipal building, a barber shop, a Methodist church, and the telephone company's office building as additional legacies of the 1960 storm.

A new bank was built too, ahead at the corner of Main and Palmberg. This has not survived. Banks that have a high percentage of agricultural loans have faced extreme financial difficulties

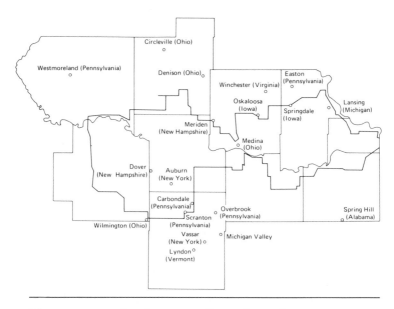

Place names transferred to eastern Kansas from other states

during the 1980s. Many farmers who borrowed for expansion during the prosperous 1970s have not been able to make payments. Thirteen Kansas banks failed in 1985, fourteen in 1986, and eight in 1987, the largest numbers since the 1930s. The Meriden bank is now the Hole in the Wall Video Vault, a wordplay on the sealed hole that was once used for night deposits.

» *Mile 117.05 (0.05) Turn right onto Palmberg Street, cross the railroad tracks, and leave Meriden.*

Names of Cities and the Origin of Settlers. When Meriden had its tornado, the town received aid from the citizens of Meriden, Connecticut. This friendly exchange between namesakes brings up the question of the origin of city names and what they can tell us about the migration of settlers. Meriden, Kansas, as it turns out, is actually the "grandchild" of Meriden, Connecticut, through the intermediary of Meriden, New Hampshire, as people moved across the country, giving new places the name of their old hometown.

A survey of the ten counties traversed in this tour reveals 119 city names whose origins are known.[35] The names come from a wide variety of sources: Indian words, such as Olathe and Ozawkie; physical traits, such as Maple Hill and Valley Falls; and surnames of local leaders; but many, such as Meriden, are simple repetitions of the names of old hometowns. The twenty towns in this category are indicated on the map.[36] Five Pennsylvania names; four Ohio ones; two each from Michigan, New York, Iowa, and New Hampshire; and single representations from Vermont, Alabama, and Virginia constitute the roster. The near absence of southern names, including the complete absence of Missouri names, is symbolic evidence of the triumph of the Free Staters in the "Bleeding Kansas" of the 1850s.

» *Mile 117.2 (0.15) Turn left, staying on the paved road.*

118.3 (1.1) Shawnee County line. Note the street sign at the intersection. This is N.E. Eighty-second Street, a designation out from Topeka, an indicator of the important role that the city plays even in the rural areas of the county.

118.5 (0.2) Kansas 4 used to follow this road, connecting Meriden with U.S. 75 four miles to the west, but now both highways have been relocated for more efficient flow of traffic. The old routes are thus less traveled, but they are still well maintained and have become favorite sites for ruralites, the urban commuters who live on small acreages in the country. Three examples appear on the left, although the land for the next two miles is bottom land and does not provide the scenic vistas preferred by these people. Two of these houses have post-and-rail fences, and two of them have elaborately decorated mailboxes—both characteristic of typical ruralite dwellings.

Notice the lack of fences in this bottom land. Fences are necessary only in areas that have both livestock and crops; and this rich level area is too valuable for stock raising.

119.5 (1.0) Muddy Creek. Here the road used to deviate slightly from its east-west course in order to avoid bridging the creek three different times (see sketch). A large infusion of money recently allowed order to triumph over practicality: the creek has been relocated and a new bridge constructed.

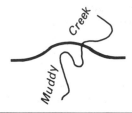

Muddy Creek

119.6 (0.1) The old roadway is visible on the right just after you cross Muddy Creek.

120.4 (0.8) Begin ascent back to the upland. Fences appear on both sides of the road just as the climb begins.

121.1 (0.7) The countryside now possesses all the attributes a ruralite could desire. Downtown Topeka is only eleven miles away on excellent roads, the traffic is not heavy, and the land has been dissected into a pleasing blend of hill and dale. The nice Cape Cod Revival home on the left is typical of the area, and several others are visible ahead. Note the predominance of hilltop sites, especially for the more luxurious dwellings.

122.3 (1.2) The old Capitol View School, on the left, benefited temporarily from the large ruralite population in this area. The school weathered the rural depopulation that killed so many of its kind, but it was recently declared too small to be cost efficient. Capitol View is true to its name, for from the hilltop the dome of the state capitol is visible away to the south.

"I" Houses. The traveler is constantly being made aware of the contrast between old and new on the Kansas landscape. The pace of technological advance has been so rapid during the last century that landscape elements belonging to a bygone era do not have time to disintegrate before later developments place new ideas and styles down beside them. By examining the variety of landscape features now existing, a sharp-eyed observer can practically read the history of changing tastes and technology since Kansas was settled. Houses provide an excellent illustration of this thesis.

"I" houses

The house that is most characteristic of nineteenth-century rural Kansas is called the "I" house, a modified example of which is the Humbert residence on the right. The designation "I" is used because this house style was first studied in Iowa, Illinois, and Indiana; the name also nicely describes the basic shape of the structure. In its purest form, it is a building two rooms wide, one room deep, and two stories high, with a simple gabled roof and no porches (see sketch). The windows on the front façade are regularly spaced and vary in number from two to five across the second story. Research done in the eastern states indicates that five was the number most favored in the northern states, whereas three was most popular in the South. No work has yet been done on the Kansas situation.

Gradually the "I" house underwent evolution. Porches were tacked on, and as more space was needed, additions were built onto the back of the dwelling, converting the "I" form into either an "L" or, more popularly, a "T" as you see here. At first the additions were usually one-story high, but later two stories became common, and occasionally houses were even planned initially in the full "L" or "T" form.

Changing fashion also affected the "I." Architects in the mid nineteenth century began to popularize the Gothic style in America, a style that stressed the vertical dimension and featured steeply pitched roofs and tall narrow windows. Slowly, in the latter part of the century, these notions filtered down to the local craftsmen who built Kansas farmhouses. The result can be seen on this house. A cross gable has been inserted in the front façade; this adds little to the interior space of the structure, but it provides the valued vertical lines with the roof angle and the tall central window. Occasionally one sees "I" houses with a cross gable for each of the second-story windows.[37]

» *Mile 122.5 (0.2) Turn right onto North Topeka Avenue (old U.S. 75).*

The small monument at the corner pays tribute to the United States veterans of the Spanish-American War, 1898–1902.

122.6 (0.1) Ruralites abound for the next several miles. Especially impressive is the seventy-acre Spring Valley Ranch, ahead at mile 123.8, where the road turns left. There, horses are raised on lush pasturage, with numerous trees, a corral, and a new lake adding classic touches. The highway, which curves around two sides, shows off the acreage nicely.

» *Mile 125.9 (3.3) Road turns to right.*

Enter Jackson County. The quality of the road changes markedly at this point, an indication of the relative wealth of Shawnee and Jackson counties.

126.8 (0.9) *The Origin of the "I" House.* The Thornburg dwelling on the left does not have the regular window placement typical of the "I", but it does possess a feature that hints at the origin of the house form: two front doors. Two of the mysteries of the "I" are this door arrangement and the rationale behind building only one room deep. Neither fits in well with the no-nonsense, most-for-the-money thinking evident in the rest of the house's design; the second front door was unnecessary, and the limitation on depth meant that expensive wings had to be added to get adequate living space. The answer to both mysteries probably lies in the log-cabin ancestry of the house form.

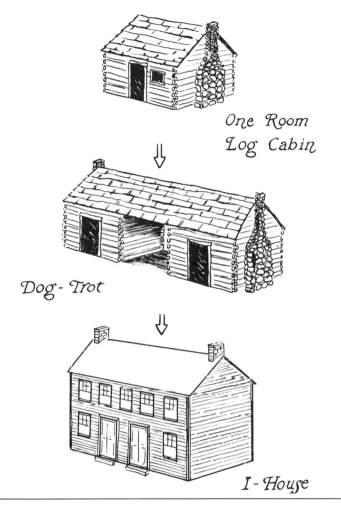

One Room Log Cabin

⇓

Dog - Trot

⇓

I - House

Hypothetical evolution of the "I" house

With logs it was difficult to build a large horizontal dwelling, since room width and length were limited by the length of available timbers. The common form was a single-room cabin, sometimes extended upward to a second story. If one needed more room, a second cabin was built near the original, and the two buildings were joined by a single roof. This is the famous "dog-trot" house, still found occasionally in the hill country of the southern United States, which contains, of course, two front doors.

One hypothesis is that the dog-trot is the direct ancestor of the "I" house, with the log form of the dog-trot being recreated in the balloon framing and clapboards of the "I" (see sketch).[38] The two-room width of the "I" corresponds to the original cabins; the two doors, of course, to their separate entries. The rationale for the two doors was apparently not questioned by the builders of "I" houses for many years. They simply perpetuated a form that was familiar to them.

127.8 (1.0) The increase in house frequency marks the entrance to *Hoyt.*

128.0 (0.2) A small but well-maintained three-window "I" house is on the right. Just beyond, on the corner, is a larger old home, which is also typical of many rural Kansas dwellings of the last century. If one looks beyond the porches and the bric-a-brac trim, the presence of the "I" form is easily detected. The house is essentially two "I" dwellings intersecting at right angles, which represents a further stage in the evolutionary process sketched at mile 126.8.

» *Mile 128.1 (0.1) Turn left, staying on paved road.*

Hoyt. Hoyt is about sixteen miles from Topeka; like Meriden, Hoyt is a commuter town. Unlike Meriden, however, Hoyt has had no recent lake or tornado to instill new vitality into the community. There is only the merest shell of a downtown business block, and the people obtain virtually all goods and services in Topeka. About the only integrating force in Hoyt is the consolidated Royal Valley High School at the south end of town. Drawn together at school functions are local people who, because they work and shop at diverse locations, would have little other opportunity for social exchange.[39] Take away Royal Valley and Hoyt might well die.

» *Mile 128.7 (0.6) Turn right onto Kansas Route 214.*

Kansas Route 214 is a spur that connects Hoyt with new U.S. 75, half a mile to the west. Most of Hoyt's new housing is on this "highway" side of town as is one of the few active local businesses, Calderwood's Grocery.

129.3 (0.6) The Delbert Boling residence on the left is a beautiful "I" house. Its cross gable and two-story "T" addition to the rear suggest a very-late-nineteenth or early-twentieth-century construction, but close inspection shows that the anachronistic second front door was once present. It occupied the blank space to the left of the existing entrance.

» *Mile 129.4 (0.1) The road turns to the left.*

» *Mile 130.0 (0.6) Junction with U.S. 75. Turn right onto it.*

132.1 (2.1) The snow-fenced enclosure on the right, studded with orange RW (highway right of way) posts, protects weed mowers and others from an old uncovered well.

133.0 (0.9) An old Santa Fe boxcar, being used as a storage shed, sits off to the right.

134.0 (1.0) An abandoned windmill marks a second old well on the right shoulder. It and the one at mile 132.1 were victims of a road-widening operation that placed them on state property.

Red cedars have invaded the pasture on the left. This juniper is the only evergreen tree native to the area; it thrives on pastures because cattle avoid its sharp spikes. Although it can be controlled by cutting or burning, some farmers enjoy the greenery and allow it to persist. Were this property a bit closer to Topeka, the young cedars would soon increase the land's potential for suburban development.

134.8 (0.8) *Mayetta.* As the road bends left to parallel the old Rock Island Railroad line, Mayetta is visible on the right. Mayetta was built as a railroad town, but it has become better known as the gateway to and the service center for the Potawatomi Indian Reservation, half a mile to the west.[40] The shuttling of Indians between depot and reservation and, especially, the selling of illegal alcohol to them were formerly major industries. Until recently, the ruins of a stone jail for the "drunken Indian" stood a block south of the business district. Ethnic conflict still flares up occasionally at the Silver Dollar Lounge.

Today Mayetta has about been abandoned by Indians and whites alike in favor of Holton to the north and Topeka to the south. Northside Antiques, one of the more successful businesses, still owes much of its prosperity to the reservation, however. The modest shop attracts a national clientele almost entirely because visitors see the Potawatomi Reservation on a map and come to Mayetta to investigate.

» *Mile 135.7 (0.9) Turn left just before the billboard that advertises bingo games on the reservation.*

» *Mile 136.2 (0.5) Turn right, staying on paved road.*

» *Mile 136.3 (0.1) Turn sharply left onto a gravel road.*

Potawatomi Indian Reservation. This road marks the eastern border of the eleven-mile-square reservation of the Prairie Band of the Potawatomis. It is a relic from the mid nineteenth century when reserves for displaced Indians once blanketed eastern Kansas. As other Indian groups were coerced into moving once again to Oklahoma, the Potawatomis stood firm, steadfastly resisting the governmental procedures whereby tribal land ownership was exchanged for individual allotments. The Prairie Band believed strongly in communal land holding and had seen how the allotment system quickly led to white ownership as individual tribesmen sold their homesteads or defaulted on tax payments.

Pow Wow Park is on the right. Traditionally, some members of the tribe staged a show here annually for the benefit of white tourists. The event was a moneymaker and served as a homecoming for urban Indians, but it was frowned on by conservative, introspective tribesmen who viewed it as a mockery of their culture. Powwows fell out of favor and were discontinued during the early 1980s but were revived again in 1984. The main stone building here once housed the local Bureau of Indian Affairs office. It was built as a Public Works Administration project in the 1930s.

Bingo is a more recent economic venture for the Potawatomis. Games are held three times weekly, with prizes amounting to

$5,000 per session. It is gambling of a sort in a state that traditionally has severely limited such activities. Because the reservation is under federal jurisdiction, the Indians have been exempt from such law and have been able to offer bigger prizes than their competitors. The games net approximately $4,000 monthly for the tribe. This bingo money may be in jeopardy. A state lottery was established in 1987, and the Potawatomis realize that Topekans may no longer want to drive to the reservation to do their gambling. The tribe thus has purchased land along U.S. 75 south of Mayetta and plans to build a new bingo facility there.[41]

» *Mile 136.9 (0.6) Turn right.*

The visitor who sees the reservation prominently displayed on a highway map and comes looking for an exotic landscape is in for a disappointment. Teepees and herds of antelope are nowhere to be found. Even when the Hollywood images are chased from one's mind, however, the reservation is still disappointing initially. Nearly three-quarters of the land is no longer owned by Indians, and only a few tribesmen actively farm on the remnant. In fact, the 547 Potawatomis who currently live here are a minority on their own reservation. The cultural landscape that one sees is thus predominantly a familiar midwestern one.

The Potawatomis resisted land allotments until nearly the turn of the century; but finally, after threats of force, imprisonment, and offering double allotments to any Indian who would take one, the system was implemented. The reservation remained in name, but the majority of the land eventually passed into white hands. Still, because of the cohesive nature of the tribe, about a quarter of the reservation has been retained. Since the early 1970s, Indian land holdings have expanded slightly as the tribe has purchased 2940 acres (3.8 percent of the reservation) back from the whites. The present ownership status is shown on the map.[42]

» *Mile 138.9 (2.0) Turn left.*

139.15 (0.25) *Land Use.* So far, the reservation land that you have traversed has all been owned by whites. The first Indian holding is on the left. Given that the Potawatomi considered it "a scandalous violation of tradition for a man to till the soil," it is in-

Land ownership on the Potawatomi Reservation

teresting to examine land usage on the reservation.[43] A survey that
compared land use on white-owned and on Indian-allotment land
showed that each group had a similar division between pasture
and cropland. This result is not surprising, given the paucity of
Indian farmers; almost all of the allotment land is rented to nearby white operators. A different pattern is found on the newly acquired tribal acreage, where only a small percentage is used for
growing crops. This may reflect traditional Potawatomi land-use
preference, but it might simply be a product of the quality of the
land on the market.

139.65 (0.5) The tribe recently purchased the land on the
left.

140.7 (1.05) *Indian Religion.* The Pottawatomi Methodist Church on the right, formerly the Mission Church, is one of two European faiths represented on the reservation. The Prairie Band has accepted Christian beliefs to a degree, but three Indian religious doctrines coexist as well, and many Indians belong to more than one group. It has been estimated, for example, that the principal native faith, the Drum Cult, includes many Catholics and about two-thirds of the local peyote ritualists (Native North American Church). It is interesting that both the Drum Cult and the Native North American Church are not parts of the original Potawatomi culture, having diffused to the reservation in the 1880s and in 1910, respectively, from other Indian groups. Anthropologists view the acceptance of these faiths as a "cultural revitalization movement," something Indian to cling to when traditional life styles were being rapidly eroded by white interference. The Drum Cult, especially, has prospered; it promises "the maintenance of some kind of a distinctive, identifiably Potawatomi, or more generally Indian way of life."[44]

» *Mile 140.9 (0.2) Turn right.*

141.9 (1.0) The large brush piles ahead and to the right are remnants of a large shelter belt that formerly ran parallel to the road for the next mile. Many of these distinctive long bands, several trees wide, were established on the reservation by the Public Works Administration during the 1930s. By planting parallel rows of deciduous and evergreen species, an effective wind screen was created. Shelter belts never caught on in this part of Kansas, but farther west and in the sand flats south of Great Bend, where blowing dirt and snow are more frequent, they are common along roads and around farmsteads. This landowner apparently felt that the shelter-belt gains were not enough to justify the acreage it occupied, so he had it bulldozed out.

143.6 (1.7) The first Indian residence on the route, the Wahwassucks, is on the right. Its small size suggests poverty, and indeed, this is characteristic of the reservation dwellers. Unemployment has ranged from 20 to nearly 25 percent during the 1980s, and about 11 percent of the homes lack plumbing facilities. There may be more than poverty accounting for the small size of Indian homes, however, as many who could afford larger houses do not seek them. According to a prominent anthropologist: "On the reservation, a house was (and is) primarily a refuge from the elements and a place to sleep. At other times, most people are busy out of doors, particularly in the summer. In cold weather, a small abode is easier to keep heated. This pattern probably descended 'from nomadic tent life where the shelter was portable and small; closeness and body heat were important in winter, and most life was spent in the out-of doors.' This is in contrast to the Anglo-Saxon tradition—at least in recent times. Here 'life takes place within the shelter and privacy of the walls of the house; hence the larger the house the more expansive the life.' "[45]

143.9 (0.3) *Shipshee Cemetery.* At first glance, Shipshee looks like many other rural Catholic cemeteries.[46] A large cross dominates the scene, and there are small madonnas on individual grave sites. Closer inspection reveals its Indian heritage. Wabaunsee and Wamego are common names here, for example, suggesting the large influence that Potawatomis have had on Kansas place names. An abundance of rough limestone tombstones and temporary grave markers which have become permanent ones denote poverty, as do the many small military stones (supplied free to any veteran). A large number of the military stones are from World War I, when influenza competed with bullets in striking down the Potawatomi men. The surnames in the cemetery are also revealing. Many are Indian (e.g., Mko-Quah-Wah and Nozachum), but others are French (e.g., Vieux and Cadue) or English (e.g., Thompson and Aitkens). The European names come from intermarriage, of course, first with the French, in their original lands near the Great Lakes, and later with the English in Kansas.

A few of the markers contain both a tribal and an Anglicized name, but the Potawatomi language is apparently dying out. In 1920 between a third and a half of the tribe knew only Potawatomi, but today all can speak English, and bilingualism is even on the decline. Researchers in 1955 reported that few people who were born after 1918 are able to speak Potawatomi, though many still understand it.[47] With native language essentially gone, the retention of Indian religions, as discussed at mile 140.7, looms crucial if the culture is to survive.

145.5 (1.6) The shelter belt on the right for the next quarter-mile has fallen into disrepair, but the basic form, including the alternate use of pine and deciduous trees, is clearly visible. Shelter belts serve a variety of purposes. With a typical belt, wind speeds are reduced by more than 10 percent for a distance of twenty times the tree height to the leeward.[48] Less wind results not only in less blowing debris but also in less evaporation of soil moisture, an important consideration farther west. The belts also catch snow and control drifting, thus helping to retain snow moisture for the fields.

146.0 (0.5) The pines of another shelter belt are visible a quarter-mile to the right.

» *Mile 146.5 (0.5) Turn right.*

146.95 (0.45) *Danceground Cemetery.* This cemetery occupies one of the most scenic spots on the reservation, a hill overlooking Soldier Creek Valley. Although it is only three miles from Shipshee, it is nearly a cultural world apart. The grounds are covered with ragged prairie grasses and a persimmon grove, not the manicured bluegrass and pine trees of other American cemeteries. A few of the graves are marked by ordinary tombstones, but the large majority are bounded on all four sides by a short stone or a concrete wall. On the markers, Indian names are more common than Anglicized ones. This is clearly the traditional Potawatomi burial ground.

Among the "walled" graves a time sequence can be discerned. The oldest are three made of limestone covered with large, flat "roof" stones. These "houses" belong to the first chiefs of the Prairie Band in Kansas. The next-oldest graves have walls of poured concrete, a practice that began about 1917 and lasted into the 1940s. They have no roofs. A third form, executed in cement block and also roofless, dates from the 1930s to the present. Recent graves indicate a further stylization of the original stone-house form. Plastic picket fencing has been used as "walls" on two graves, and others have only a rock at the head and at the foot.

The rationale for the walled graves is somewhat obscure, but they apparently began as grave houses, or residences for the spirit of the vacated body.[49] Early ones were always roofed and were con-

Scenes at Danceground Cemetery

structed of stone or wood. Over the years, the wooden structures have all burned, and the stone forms have gradually degenerated into the highly stylized version represented by the plastic fence.

» *Mile 146.95 (0.0) Turn around and return to the Shipshee Cemetery intersection by the route just taken.*

» *Mile 150.0 (3.05) Turn left at the Shipshee intersection.*

150.6 (0.6) *New Tribal Facilities.* Although the Danceground Cemetery has always provided a cultural focus for the reservation, no comparable economic or political center existed until nine years ago. The two clusters of buildings that are visible ahead from this hilltop now serve this need. Both were financed by federal grants. The first cluster includes two large steel buildings and a mobile home. Offices for the tribal council are here, together with a storage building for agricultural equipment and a commodities warehouse that belongs to the U.S. Department of Agriculture. The second and more impressive cluster includes a fire station, a day-care facility, and a $450,000 multipurpose center. This center has the size and look of a high school; it has a large gymnasium, a library, offices for the Four Tribes Social Services, and a cafeteria and center for senior citizens. The building's name, O Ketche-Show-O-Now, is that of the original allotee of this piece of land.

The gymnasium in the O Ketche-Show-O-Now Center houses the weekend bingo games discussed at mile 136.3, but the other offices are of more direct relevance to residents of the reservation. The senior center provides the closest thing to a restaurant available, and it is frequented by people of all ages. Penotte Wigwam, the day-care facility, is heavily used too; it enables mothers to work in Topeka with the assurance that their children are being cared for in a safe and culturally consistent environment. Advice on legal matters, child welfare, and general counseling are available at the social-services office.

A Private People. Traditional Potawatomi culture places high values on independence and privacy. These traits have been responsible for the survival of this reservation (see mile 136.9), and they continue today. The people deal with the federal bureaucracy no more than necessary, and they resist the probings of anthropologists and others. They deliberately have avoided the placement of signs at the reservation's borders in an effort to discourage visitors and similarly resist the idea of a museum and craft shop in O Ketche-Show-O-Now Center. Even the location of these tribal buildings suggests privacy. They are more than seven miles from a paved road and are not even on the main east-west route across the reservation (it is a half mile north of the center). The concept of privacy has been violated only by the bingo games, but if the proposed new site for this on U.S. 75 is adopted, serenity should return to the tribal heartland.

150.9 (0.3) The high fence on the right encloses a symbolic "herd" of three buffalo. The placement of these animals between clusters of federally financed buildings is interesting in that the Potawatomi speak of their grant applications as "hunting the federal buffalo." Clearly the modern hunt has been successful.

151.4 (0.5) The solar design of the Penotte Wigwam is a product of the federal program that sponsored it.

151.5 (0.1) The jumble of materials just north of the fire station may soon be a tribal-owned and -operated gasoline station. Plans for it have existed for five years, but construction has been delayed.

151.7 (0.2) *New Housing.* The concrete road on the right leads to one of three housing developments that have been built by the tribe since 1976. All the units are substantial single-family dwellings with three or four bedrooms, full basements, and carports. More than one hundred such homes now exist, and they are largely responsible for the population increase on the reservation, from 225 in the early 1970s to the current estimate of 575.

» *Mile 151.7 (0.0) Turn around and return to the Shipshee Cemetery intersection.*

» *Mile 153.4 (1.7) Continue straight ahead at the Shipshee intersection.*

Allotment Land. The land on the left, just beyond Shipshee, is Indian owned, as is, in fact, half of the land along the remaining three miles of the reservation tour. Nearly all of it is leased to white farmers, as discussed at mile 139.15, mostly through the intermediary of the Bureau of Indian Affairs (BIA) office at Horton. Although Indians complain that the leases are too generous, the BIA's role is necessary because of the multiple ownership of most allotment land. As a result of Potawatomi inheritance custom, aggravated by poverty conditions, some small plots have as many as sixty owners. Describing the 1930s, one observer noted that after the death of a landowner, "impossibly numerous claimants appeared, thirty being not uncommon. Among them would be the legal wife or wives, their children, brothers, sisters, parents, uncles, cousins, 'Indian-custom' (officially unrecognized 'shacking-up') wives, individuals declaring the deceased to be the illegitimate parent, and tradesmen presenting bills. The settlements portioned out fractions of tiny fractions of lands."[50] The annual lease money totaled about $120,000 in the 1970s, which is very little when it is divided among some twenty-one hundred Potawatomis on and off the reservation.

153.9 (0.5) Another Indian home, the Wahbnosahs.

154.7 (0.8) From the top of the rise, observe the landscape ahead. It is a definite departure from what has characterized the tour route thus far. Prairie grass, steep ridges, and a big sky are the key elements, with accents of scattered trees and cattle. Only a single house is in view, and there is no plowed ground. The silence is almost frightening at first. This collage is classic Flint Hills country. It is rare in Jackson County, but in Wabaunsee County, you will see it become the dominant landscape.

156.5 (1.8) The fence row marks the boundary of the Potawatomi Reservation. No billboard or change in road conditions announces this fact, but it is clearly defined by a change in the farmsteads. Houses and outbuildings seem immediately to become larger and better maintained off the reservation. The Max Bailey farm on the left, for example, exhibits an air of rural prosperity that we have not seen since the Mayetta vicinity. A general explanation is the relatively low quality of the land in the reservation area. The northern part of Jackson County is mantled by glacial till and generally has deep soils and a smooth surface. Good soils also characterize the far southern portion of the county, where streams cutting back from the Kaw have created numerous lowland areas. The reservation region, in contrast, is mostly an old upland surface, with thinner soils and steeper slopes than those to the north and less lowland area than to the south. A human element is also important in the observed contrast in farms, for the dividing line is too sharp for the physical factor alone to explain. It may be related to the type of whites who bought reservation land. An observer in 1936 called them "poor," and apparently little change has occurred since then, if one is to judge from the appearance of the farms.[51]

» *Mile 158.0 (1.5) Turn right.*

A good idea spreads easily within an isolated rural neighborhood. An example is on the right, where two "no hunting" signs have been fashioned on old tires mounted on fence posts. Similarly crafted signs are common on the Potawatomi Reservation; they continue along the tour route for several more miles but stop abruptly near the Delia community.

159.0 (1.0) An alternative means of expanding the standard "I" farmhouse from the "L" and "T" forms, which I discussed at mile 122.3, can be seen on the left. The side view shows a shedlike

A saltbox house

addition tacked onto the back of the "I" (see sketch). This simple method of enlargement was common in eighteenth-century
New England, where the completed structure was known as a saltbox house. The form had been largely discarded by the Yankees
before they settled in Kansas, however, and it is rare in the local
countryside. Who built this now abandoned home?

159.3 (0.3) Another saltbox!

The mile-wide lowland ahead is the Soldier Creek flood plain.
Its fertile acres were once scheduled to be put beneath another
Corps of Engineers impoundment. The project, called Grove Reservoir, was authorized in 1962, and the planning was all completed
before federal budget deficits prompted people to pay attention
to the arguments against big dams, which I noted previously (mile
99.6). The Grove project is now dead, but it is interesting to ponder
the effect it might have had on the Potawatomi Reservation to the
north. Undoubtedly it would have increased the value of adjacent
allotment lands and, with it, Indian incomes; but some Indians
saw Grove as just another scheme for the whites to get Indian land.
The mood and quality of Danceground Cemetery would surely
have been threatened.

159.8 (0.5) *Slavic Area.* The Charles Kovar farm on the right
marks the beginning of a rural ethnic community of Moravian
heritage. These Slavic peoples began to come to Kansas in 1869
and occupied land recently vacated by the Potawatomis. Some 145

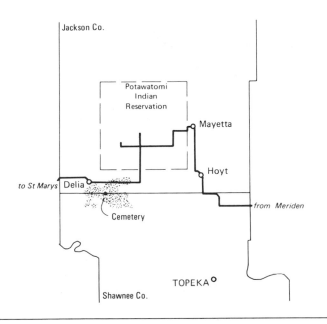

Concentrated Slavic settlement in the Delia area

had come by 1895, enough to constitute (along with their children) about 31 percent of the township population in 1930 (see map).[62]

160.05 (0.25) Soldier Creek. The land on the left is owned by Mary Simecka—another Moravian name.

163.1 (3.05) The cultural heart of the Moravian community —its cemetery—lies a mile and a half to the south and then a half-mile back east. It is one of the most beautiful places in the tour area. A hilltop location and rows of towering cedars create a cathedral illusion, and the grounds show the effects of loving care. Family names (all Slavic) include Badura, Cerny, Hejtmanek, Matyak, Olejnik, Zlatnik, and about fifteen others. Several stones contain non-English inscriptions, but the widespread use of the old tongue died out about 1942.[53] Today the cemetery and traditional recipes are the main physical links that the Moravians have with their past.[54]

163.6 (0.5) *Delia.* The town of Delia lies in the valley below. It is a relatively new Kansas town; it was founded in 1904 in anticipation of the Union Pacific Railroad track you see running through it. The town was not originally Moravian, but it became more so over time. All three stores that were present in 1977 bore Slavic names: Olejnik Welding and Blacksmith, Macha Hardware, and Matyak Garage. In 1987 the Matyak Garage was the only business in town.

Most of Delia's workers commute to Topeka, many to the large Goodyear plant about sixteen miles away. They follow the paved road that leads off to the left, the town's only hard-surfaced link with the outside world.

» *Mile 164.1 (0.5) Turn right.*

Two brick school buildings are on the left, but only the grade school is still operating. The high school has been deemed too small, and Delia students are now bussed south to Rossville.

» *Mile 164.3 (0.2) Turn left and enter Delia.*

Observe the housing. In spite of the railroad and the rich bottom land of Cross Creek, the town has never seen wealth. By the time Delia was founded, the growth pattern of the state had already been set. The houses are nearly all small frame structures, many with a square form and a hipped roof. Two churches survive, but residents must travel elsewhere for their groceries.

» *Mile 164.8 (0.5) The road bends to the right.*

» *Mile 165.0 (0.2) Turn left and leave Delia.*

165.4 (0.4) The Union Pacific Railroad.

166.0 (0.6) *Sullivan Creek.* The Moravians are not the only ethnic group in Cross Creek Valley. As the name Sullivan Creek suggests, Irish immigrants also came to the area, focusing on the village of Emmett, a few miles to the northwest. The two groups used to engage in friendly rivalry, including weekend sporting events and accompanying parties. Occasional pranks and fights enlivened the area, but since the Emmett vicinity produced heavyweight boxing champion Jess Willard, one wonders how the Moravian contingent fared. Today the rivalry has about ended, as the populations have mixed and contact with other cities has increased.

167.6 (1.6) *Reddy School and the Flint Hills Border.* Unlike the old country schoolhouses that you saw earlier, Reddy (on the left) has been deserted, not converted to another use. Abandonment is a characteristic feature of the margins of the Flint Hills (notice the grass-covered section-line road off to the left). The scarps and bench lands of this area seem to have repelled the small farmer with their often thin soils and, perhaps, with their broad, somewhat lonely vistas.

It is difficult to define a precise border for the Flint Hills because its nature is complex, involving a variety of physical and cultural factors. One common measure of the boundary lies directly ahead, however, the prominent scarp of the Foraker Limestone, rising about a hundred feet above Reddy School. The scarp is what students of land forms call a *cuesta*, an erosional feature that developed on slightly tilted rock beds which have alternating hard and soft layers (see sketch). In this area the harder layers are limestone, the softer ones are shale, and since the beds dip gently westward, the product is an east facing escarpment. Most of eastern Kansas south of the glaciated region contains cuesta topography, but east of the Flint Hills its form is more subdued.[55]

167.85 (0.25) The capstone layer of the Foraker Limestone is clearly visible on both sides of the road. At the top of the escarpment note the huge limestone blocks that were taken up during road construction. The exceptional hardness and convenient thickness of this layer make it a good building stone, although none of it is now being quarried locally.

» *Mile 168.5 (0.65) Turn left.*

168.85 (0.35) A road cut in the Foraker Limestone.

» *Mile 168.9 (0.05) Road turns right.*

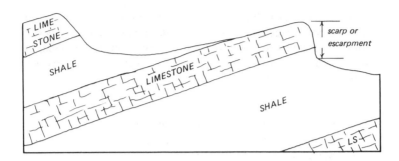

A cuesta landscape in profile

The Pottawatomie County line. The road surface changes from gravel to hardtop, and the road becomes County Route 108. A section-line road formerly continued straight ahead, but it has now been abandoned.

169.3 (0.4) Bourbonais Creek. This creek takes its name from François Bourbonais, one of the far-ranging explorers and traders who ventured into the plains ahead of the main European advance. Uncharacteristically, Americans have kept the original pronunciation of this word relatively intact, although they occasionally corrupt the spelling to Bourbonny.

169.4 (0.1) A stone house on the right is constructed of local limestone. The tour has passed very few of these since Leavenworth, as the route has lain mainly over glacial till and loess (see mile 71.1). Stone construction will become increasingly common south of the Kaw, where native limestones arc not mantled by glacial debris.

» *Mile 170.5 (1.1) Junction with Kansas Route 63. Turn left.*

St. Marys is only two and a half miles ahead on Kansas Route 63. One thus might expect the roadside to be strewn with the homes of ruralites, but only two old farmhouses and two newer dwellings are present. Is this a function of the bleak, windswept bench land, especially in contrast to the snug valley setting of St. Marys proper?

171.7 (1.2) Microwave towers, such as the example on the right, now encircle major urban centers like a loose picket fence. They are relay stations that receive, amplify, and retransmit signals for television and other communications media. Each tower has a range of about thirty miles, and this one, predictably, is just that distance northwest of Topeka.

172.2 (0.5) A nice three-window "I" house with a cross gable.

172.9 (0.7) Begin descent to St. Marys and the Kaw Valley.

St. Marys. St. Marys is a pretty community of about sixteen hundred people, the kind of a town many Americans still like to think characterizes the nation. Local businesses are healthy, the population is stable, and the homes are well maintained. This healthy situation is not all that typical of small towns today, however; St. Marys owes its vitality to several special circumstances. Foremost, perhaps, is the town's Kaw Valley location midway between Topeka and Manhattan. The river bottoms provide a solid agricultural base for the economy, and the accessible yet isolated position relative to larger cities keeps both businesses and townspeople happy. It is a delicate distance balance: the cities are close enough for St. Marys commuters yet remote enough so that local businesses do not face excessive competition. St. Marys people travel the twenty-five miles to Topeka to buy furniture and personal luxuries, but they usually purchase cars, jewelry, groceries, and similar items at home.

173.3 (0.4) Note the purple house at the Walnut Street intersection. Few college rivalries are as intense as that between the University of Kansas and Kansas State University, and one can often discern loyalties by displays of school colors. Usually these are restricted to banners or clothing, but the residents here leave no doubts about their Kansas State allegiance.

» *Mile 173.7 (0.4) Junction of U.S. 24. Turn left and proceed through downtown St. Marys.*

The Bayer Stone Company, on the right just before the turn, literally makes a business of the Flint Hills. From quarries here and in Chase and Riley counties, Max Bayer and his sons have supplied the stone for more than half of the buildings at Kansas State University, plus the new state historical museum in Topeka, the Eisenhower Chapel in Abilene, and the Hereford Building in Kansas City.[56] The Bayers are also responsible for the distinctive concrete-and-stone signs that welcome you to St. Marys.

» *Mile 174.35 (0.65) Pull off to the right at the historical marker opposite St. Marys College.*

St. Marys College. An additional factor in creating the pleasant atmosphere of St. Marys has undoubtedly been the presence of St. Marys College. This venerable institution, which began as a mission to the Potawatomi Indians in 1848, was the reason for the town's very existence. Then, as the mission evolved into a college in 1869 and then into a Jesuit seminary in 1931, other benefits accrued to the city. These ranged from a grass-green golf course to the more subtle work of the teachers and students in community affairs. Just the fact that about half of the townspeople are Catholic has probably meant a somewhat more united effort for community projects than is sometimes found elsewhere.

The college has been in turmoil for most of the last two decades. It was abandoned as a seminary in 1967, when the Jesuit theologate decided to move its training facilities to St. Louis, Missouri, citing the need for close access to university resources (St. Louis University is a Jesuit school) and the inconsistency of training students for predominantly urban work in rural St. Marys. A major controversy quickly arose over the future of the college facilities (some 1,380 acres and eleven major buildings). The grounds were originally part of the Potawatomi Indian Reservation, and the Jesuits hoped to turn them back to the Indians, but this apparently simple move became a legal snarl.

The problem involved both an intratribal dispute and a dispute between the Indians and the Bureau of Indian Affairs. Because of conservative-liberal feuding within the Potawatomi nation, the tribe did not have a self-governing constitution. According to the BIA, this meant the Indians could not accept and administer the St. Marys property. The federal agency wanted itself named as trustee, but neither the Indians nor the Jesuits liked that idea. A stalemate resulted, and the buildings stood practically empty for more than a decade. The Potawatomis had use of the library but could only dream about the St. Marys land and buildings becoming the basis for an Indian revitalization movement in Kansas.

The Jesuits finally sold the golf course to the city and the rest of the campus to local interests in 1976 and channeled the money into various Indian-aid programs. A planned housing development never materialized, and the property changed hands again in 1978. The buyer this time was the Society of St. Pius X, a conservative group within the Catholic Church. The society originally hoped to have a seminary here but decided instead to open an academy and college. Both began modestly but seem to be prospering. In 1987/88 the academy enrolled 310 children in its K–12 program, which draws from many states and countries. The college, which was established in 1981, has about twenty-five students in its two-year liberal-arts program.

Note the entrance sign for the college, which advertises the traditional Latin mass. The golf course, mentioned above, is just northeast of the campus proper; the Jesuit cemetery and most of the college's farmland lie to the northwest. The centerpiece of the St. Marys campus used to be Assumption Chapel, directly in front of you, which burned in December 1978. Most of its stone walls remain, including part of the frame for a large and beautiful rosette window. The Society of St. Pius X hopes to raise money to restore it.

» *Mile 174.35 (0.0) Turn around and proceed back through downtown St. Marys on U.S. 24.*

175.0 (0.65) Note the large Knights of Columbus hall at the intersection of Sixth Street, an indication of the town's significant Catholic population.

175.25 (0.25) A half-mile down the road on your left is a bridge over a small creek. Before 1903 the Kaw River occupied this channel, but the major flood of that year shifted the stream bed a mile and a half southward. This shifting of seventy years ago still profoundly affects about ten families who live between the old and the new channels, because the Pottawatomie-Wabaunsee County line continues to follow the old watercourse. These people live

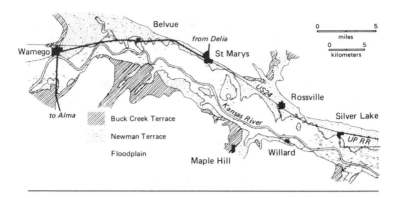

Kansas River terraces between Wamego and Silver Lake

in Wabaunsee County but cannot get to their county seat without a long detour through Pottawatomie. Imagine the problems if the Kaw had happened to be a state or a national boundary!

175.6 (0.35) *Kaw Valley Terraces.* The broad, flat, and fertile Kansas River Valley is a natural location for cities, farms, and transportation routes. The only significant hazard is flooding, and even this danger has been lessened by the utilization of two natural river terraces. Known locally as the Newman and the Buck Creek terraces, they are benches that stand about fifteen and forty feet, respectively, above the current flood plain. This section of U.S. 24 is on the Newman Terrace, which closely parallels the edge of the flood plain. The scarp, which lies just a few yards off to the left, produces cornfields that are fifteen feet below the roadway.

There is a general correlation between the Newman Terrace and both town sites and transportation routes (see map).[57] The terrace is level, nearly continuous, and high enough to be safe from all but the most severe flooding.[58] Buck Creek Terrace, although it is too discontinuous to be used as a transportation route, provides a convenient perch for Wamego and other towns.

The river terraces are another product of the glacial era, this time of an alternating advance and retreat of the ice that is thought to have occurred. The second of four advances is the only one that blanketed northeast Kansas, and its outwash left the Kaw Valley choked with sediment to a level some seventy feet above its current flood plain. The next advance of ice caused a temporary drop in sea level because its ice tied up such a large quantity of water; and this drop in sea level initiated a down-cutting cycle for the Kaw before it finally produced a new and lower flood plain. Buck Creek Terrace is a remnant of this plain. During the final advance of ice, the erosion cycle was repeated again, creating an even newer and lower plain and, in the process, erasing many of the Buck Creek deposits. The new plain, of course, was the Newman Terrace. Modern erosion has meant even more down-cutting for the Kaw, the creation of the current flood plain, and further erosion of the older terraces.

176.9 (1.3) Note the big cottonwood trees for the next 0.2 mile in the slough between the highway and the railroad tracks. The cottonwood, so-called because of the white and fluffy airborne seeds of the female plant, is the state tree of Kansas; it becomes an ever-more-dominant tree as one travels westward. Although it tolerates droughty uplands well, its natural habitat is valleys and other moist sites such as this.

178.8 (1.9) *Irrigation.* Irrigation is taken for granted in much of western Kansas, but the sprinkler equipment that is visible on both sides of the road for the next several miles seems to be out of place at first thought; rainfall is relatively abundant here, and the soil is deep and rich. The great agricultural potential of the Kaw Valley accounts for the anomaly. Farmers have found that a little irrigation water, applied at critical times during the growing season, can make the difference between a good crop and a great one. Because water is easily and cheaply accessible in the valley, irrigation makes sense if a farmer has enough capital to invest in the equipment.

Note the brand name "Valley" on the irrigation rigs. This refers to the Platte Valley of Nebraska, where sprinkler irrigation systems (as opposed to ditch systems) were pioneered during the 1950s. A line of sprinklers is mounted on a series of wheeled A-frames, and the whole assemblage pivots around a centrally located well. Some systems irrigate 160 acres at a time, and all create the circular field patterns that are familiar to anyone who has flown over the Great Plains.

179.0 (0.2) Just ahead the road descends from Newman Terrace to the flood plain. The buildings on the left and the short hedgerow on the right are just on the tip of the terrace.

179.1 (0.1) Descend the scarp. The drop is about fifteen feet, but highway engineering has rendered it nearly imperceptible in an automobile. It is quite visible when one looks back, however, and in the fields on either side.

179.8 (0.7) The farmhouse on the left is on a small spur of the Newman Terrace, but the land form is difficult to see from the road.

180.1 (0.3) The stream you are now crossing has been extensively modified by people. In order to utilize more of the fertile Kaw bottom land, the naturally meandering course of the creek has been replaced by a straight ditch. Artificial levees line it on both sides to keep its waters in place. Just beyond the creek observe how the roadbed has been built up above the surrounding farmland. This procedure is not necessary where the highway is on Newman Terrace; thus it serves as a good indicator for the terrace hunter.

180.4 (0.3) Pass under a series of high-tension electric wires. The source is a huge blue-and-white generating plant, which is visible on the right, just north of the valley.

181.1 (0.7) *Belvue.* The hamlct of Belvue sits on another small spur of the Newman Terrace. In the past, the town's chief claim to fame was being the northernmost point on the Union Pacific's main line between Kansas City and Denver, but in 1970 Belvue became newsworthy as the focus of a power-plant controversy. The Kansas Power and Light Company proposed and then built the huge 13,500-acre 2.8-million-kilowatt coal generating station noted at mile 180.4. The site was accessible to the population cluster in the Kaw Valley, yet it was remote enough that not many residents had to be displaced. A railroad to bring in the coal was nearby, as was a place to build a large cooling reservoir. Only twelve homesteads were on the plant site, but the landowners nevertheless objected to being pushed off their farms. A suit was filed which delayed the construction plans, but the new unit came on line in 1978. Its name, the Jeffrey Energy Center, honors a former president of Kansas Power and Light Company, Balfour Jeffrey.

Belvue is almost extinct as a business center. A grocery store and a motel survived into the 1970s but no longer exist. The motel was an interesting three-unit affair called Modern Cabins. The sign and the building remain at the east end of town. They provide a link to the 1940s, when rapidly growing automobile tourism led to a building fever on the part of small entrepreneurs. Shoestring operations flourished for about a decade before the inevitable takeover by big franchised operations such as Holiday Inn. Today, decaying remnants of tourist "cabins" can be found all across the land, particularly along routes that are now paralleled by interstate highways, such as this section of U.S. 24.

181.8 (0.7) Ascend to the Newman Terrace.

182.2 (0.4) Pass over the Union Pacific Railroad.

183.15 (0.95) Vermillion Creek. The road is again on the floodplain level.

183.7 (0.55) *The Pyramid House.* Observe the residence on the right, a two-story box with a hipped roof. This type of house is known as the pyramid or the cube, both of which are appropriately descriptive terms. Pyramid houses were the primary successors to "I" structures on the rural Kansas scene. They were most popular in the 1900 to 1920 period and probably developed as central heating replaced fireplaces in homes. The rangy form of the "I" house could not be adequately served by the new technology, but the compact shape of the pyramid was ideal.

The classic pyramid house was stark and uncompromising, but most versions had softening touches. A bay window might be added, as here, or some form of porch. The ultimate change was to imitate European design. Whereas the "I" house eventually received Gothic trimmings, the pyramid became overlaid with Italian Renaissance touches. "Italianate," as the Anglicized version was known, featured a flattening of the roof line and heavy brackets to support the overhanging eaves. A few went to the extreme of having cupolas placed at the apex of the roof. Pyramid houses

A pyramid house

were usually built of wood and were painted white, but brick versions are fairly common. Interestingly, the brick renditions are more often buff in color, instead of the familiar red, apparently an imitation of the light tones of the Mediterranean shore.

184.3 (0.6) *The Vermillion River.* The highway crosses the Vermillion almost at its junction with the Kaw. A bend of the larger river is plainly visible across the railroad tracks. As on most of the other major tributaries to the Kaw, the Corps of Engineers had planned a reservoir for the Vermillion before costs increased and public sentiment changed (see miles 99.6 and 159.3).

184.8 (0.5) The best view yet of Newman Terrace is on the right, where the road parallels the scarp for the next 0.2 mile before finally ascending it.

» *Mile 185.65 (0.85) Angle left, leaving U.S. 24 and turning onto the old highway pavement paralleling the railroad. The old road is now called County Route 72. A sign advertising the Stewart Funeral Home marks the intersection.*

Oscar Mayer Plant Site. A decade ago, Kansans were abuzz about a $20-million pork-processing plant proposed for this site. It would slaughter five thousand hogs per day (more than a million head annually) and would be part of a national trend toward moving meat-packing facilities from large cities to smaller places such as Wamego. Hogs are no longer raised in small bunches by general farmers; they are produced on large, specialized confinement operations. Packing plants have been relocating where conditions are favorable for these confinement facilities, such as the Kaw Valley. This area is a large producer of hog feed grains, it has a fairly dry climate to aid in disease control, and it has an excellent transportation system to reach consumer markets. Oscar Mayer bought this land, held it for two years, and then decided against construction. Some people attribute the change of heart to a decline in demand for pork; others attribute it to a switch in company policy from building new plants to buying out competitors (e.g., the Louis Rich Company).

Wamego townspeople enthusiastically courted Oscar Mayer and its five hundred new jobs in the 1970s, but some residents doubt that they would do so again. Possible environmental degradation concerns them, as well as the loss of their small-town atmosphere. If Wamego were in financial difficulty, the feelings might be different, but the town is thriving because of a combination of local businesses and commuters to Manhattan, Fort Riley, and Topeka.

186.2 (0.55) A second example of the pyramid house is on the left.

186.9 (0.7) The pyramid house in its pure form is a two- or a two-and-a-half story structure, but a one-story version also became popular in Kansas. Delia (mile 164.3) was characterized by this type of house; another example appears on the right.

187.4 (0.5) Two more pyramid houses. Note especially the Calvin Worden residence on the right, which possesses several of the Italianate features mentioned above. The heavy eaves brackets, the porch molding, and the low pitch of the roof are all distinctive.

187.6 (0.2) *Wamego and the Balderson Company.* Wamego, like St. Marys, is a pleasant small town, although our route is not the city's most scenic entrance. The tour route does reveal some of the bases for local prosperity, however: the good soil, the railroad, and now the Balderson Company, on the right. Balderson, a major manufacturer of blades for snowplows and bulldozers, has been an economic mainstay of Wamego since the company's founding in 1929.

It is somewhat unusual for a small Kansas community to have a thriving, locally owned manufacturing establishment such as Balderson's. Whereas a great many such plants are found in the smaller towns of New England and the eastern Midwest, by the time Kansas and the plains were settled, considerations in regard to locations for businesses had changed. Companies had become larger and wanted the better transportation and larger supportive services and labor pools that major cities offered. Small towns were left with only rural service and minor administrative functions. The Balderson Company, which was founded by a local man who wanted to stay in his hometown, is thus rather exceptional. The company began by repairing old snowplows for the State Highway Department and rapidly progressed to the manufacture of snowplow blades and then bulldozer blades after it became affiliated with the Caterpillar Tractor Company in 1935.

Alfalfa Dehydrator. The big revolving drum on the left, along with its associated storage tanks and equipment, is an alfalfa dehydrating operation, one of the growing forms of agribusiness in Kansas. By rapidly drying alfalfa under intense heat and converting it into small pellets, a dehydrating facility provides a high-protein product that is rich in vitamins A, E, and K. The pellets are widely used as a livestock feed supplement; they are of special importance to poultrymen because they give good color to egg yolks.

187.9 (0.3) Coming up on the right is Wamego's city park, a real showplace for a town of thirty-eight hundred. Directly ahead is the main attraction, a forty-foot European-style windmill, which was built as a commercial grinding mill in 1879 by a Dutch immigrant. It was moved to the park in 1925.

188.0 (0.1) The entrance to the park is on the right. In addition to the windmill, the park features a rose garden, a bandstand, a duck pond, statues representing Science and Art, and a small assemblage of pioneer buildings similar to those at Old Jefferson Town (mile 77.4). Tennis courts, a swimming pool, and swing sets are also present. Note the extensive use of red glacial erratics to outline roadways and in the construction of the picnic areas and the bandstand.

» *Mile 188.2 (0.2) Junction with Kansas Route 99. Turn left.*

Downtown Wamego stretches in both directions on Kansas Route 99. An interesting side trip is to go north four miles to Louisville, Wamego's old rival town. Louisville is on the main route of the old Oregon Trail and the old Fort Leavenworth–Fort Riley Road; it was also the county seat from 1861 until the early 1880s. Its death knell was sounded when the Union Pacific Railroad decided not to bend its tracks north to the town, and Wamego quickly changed from Louisville's port of entry to the major city in the county. Louisville now has only about two hundred people, but it still has a lot of interesting nineteenth-century houses. Its old jail now resides in Wamego's city park.

188.4 (0.2) The Kansas River. Enter Wabaunsee County.

189.0 (0.6) *Kaw Valley Agriculture.* The Kansas River Valley is the agricultural heartland of eastern Kansas, but its production is rather specialized. Because the topography is flat and the soils are deep and stone-free, bottom lands are so ideal for crop farming that extensive land uses are rarely found. Cattle, for example, are a rarity because fields are too valuable to keep in pasture. Corn, which has a very high dollar-per-acre value, is normally the dominant crop. Of the hay crops, only alfalfa, which yields several cuttings per season, is profitable enough to compete for space here.

Vegetables, of course, are among the most valuable crops per acre, and many truck-farming operations are found throughout the lowlands. On the right is the Bergsten Berry Patch, and on the left is Armendariz's Farm Market. A third intensive agricultural operation is the Leisure Acres Fish Farm, down the side road to the right (see discussion at mile 253.05).

189.9 (0.9) A well-maintained one-story pyramid house.

190.0 (0.1) Another old rural schoolhouse is on the right. It has been converted into the Cottonwood Community Club, a place for neighborhood social gatherings. This seems an appropriate use for the old building as it is an attempt to bind a rural society together as the school once did.

190.3 (0.3) At the bridge the road crosses a small slough, similar to the one near the Cottonwood Community Club. These small bodies of water are scattered across the plain. They are caused by an impermeable blue clay, which is laid down by floodwater, and they form small wooded oases on the otherwise intensively tilled lowland.

» *Mile 190.4 (0.1) Pull onto the shoulder just past the bridge.*

Ahead is a clear stair-step view of the Newman and Buck Creek terraces. Newman Terrace is about fifty yards away; its top is crowned by a sign for Key Work Clothes and by a farmstead on the left. Three-tenths of a mile beyond are the much-higher Buck Creek deposits.

190.5 (0.1) Ascend Newman Terrace.

191.0 (0.5) Begin to ascend Buck Creek Terrace. Notice the reddish soil in the barnlot on the right, a characteristic of Buck Creek deposits.

» *Mile 191.6 (0.6) Pull onto the shoulder and stop near the junction of Kansas Route 18 with Kansas Route 99. Then continue south on Kansas Route 99.*

Two miles to the west on Kansas Route 18 is the small community of Wabaunsee. Like Louisville, it was once the leading town in its county, but it was later by-passed by the principal railroads and highways and went into decline. The remaining residents commute to either Wamego or Manhattan. Wabaunsee is famous for the Beecher Bible and Rifle Church, established in 1862 as a Free-State rallying point. Construction funds were provided by Dr. Henry Ward Beecher, the abolitionist father of Harriet Beecher Stowe. Regular services are still held in the dignified little stone structure.

A quarter-mile east of the junction of Kansas Routes 99 and 18 is the old Mitchell farmstead, the home of one of the original

Landscape in the Flint Hills

Beecher colonists who came to Wabaunsee in 1856. The rambling house has been documented as having a log-cabin core (see discussion of the evolution of housing at mile 126.8).

Flint Hills Topography. A half-mile ahead the tour route enters a physical environment very different from the rolling uplands that we have generally been traversing; the new landscape is the Flint Hills, or, as they were formerly known, the Kansas Mountains. There are no real mountains, of course, as the elevations are rarely more than two hundred feet above the plains to the east, but the contrasts in physical characteristics and land use are so great between the two regions that perhaps the word *mountains* does convey the proper perceptual mood.

Ahead and to the left there is a good view of one of the characteristic features of the Flint Hills, a layered bench land that is formed by alternating strata of nearly flat limestones and shales. At least five distinct bands of resistant limestone influence the shape; they create a bold stair-step effect, like the parapets of a medieval fortress. Masculine comes to mind as a descriptive term for the harsh lines of this land form. It certainly stands in marked contrast to the subtler, rather feminine forms of the loess-and-till-mantled surface of Kansas north of the Kaw.

192.8 (1.2) Kansas Route 99 uses the small valley of Antelope Creek, on the right, as a means for ascending to the upland surface.

193.8 (1.0) Cross Antelope Creek and pass through some deep road cuts. Plainly visible are the alternating layers of limestone and

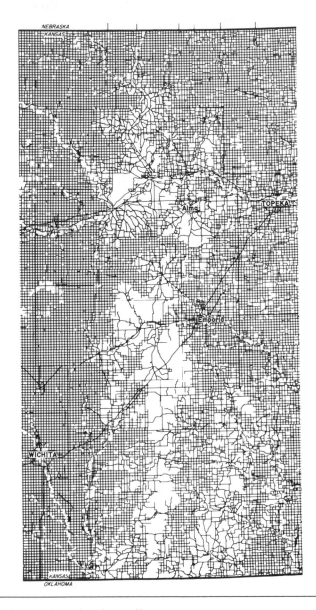

Road network in the Flint Hills

shale that form the bench lands just seen. Observe how little soil is present, as the uppermost layer of limestone outcrops at the land surface. Extremely shallow soils like this are characteristic of the Flint Hills; they are a principal reason why the land has been left in native prairie grasses. The land-use situation is considerably more complex than this, however, as many potentially plowable acres also retain their original grass covers.

195.1 (1.3) *Flint Hills Ranching.* The large sign for Fritz Clark's Flint Hills Charolais Ranch is a fitting welcome to the big-pasture country of Kansas. It is a very different world from the areas both east and west of it: one leaves crop agriculture, tractors, and gently rolling terrain behind and enters a ranching country that is characterized by cowboy boots, horses, and a coarser, seemingly less-human-scaled landscape. Although the Flint Hills have been defined in many ways, one of the best is by its road pattern (see map). Where ranching and big pastures are common, the density and regularity of the road grid falls off markedly. As the map shows, Wabaunsee County has a strong Flint Hills character.

The development of the Flint Hills as a grazing area is tied to the early cattle drives from Texas to the Kansas railheads during the 1870s. Drovers found that the grasses in this relatively humid area produced excellent weight gains on trail-worn cattle and thus significantly increased their market value. As most of the upland pasture was still unclaimed at this time because local farmers either preferred valley locations or could not afford to enter the cattle business, outside entrepreneurs rapidly acquired the Flint Hills pastureland during the early 1880s. The ranching economy that these people have developed is the primary reason for keeping potentially arable parts of the upland in grass.

The grazing of transient Texas cattle soon became the way of life in the Flint Hills, providing large amounts of grass-fattened beef. Since the late 1940s, however, American tastes have increasingly turned to grain-fattened beef, and this has affected the nature of Flint Hills ranching. Fewer transient cattle come in, and more attention is being given to cow-calf operations, the raising of young animals to send to feed lots for fattening.[59]

Several aspects of the changing ranch economy are apparent on the landscape. Cow-calf herds use the pastures for a longer period of the year than did transient cattle, and several areas now show the effects of overgrazing for this reason. Another visible change is an increase in the number of local hay sheds and barns, as more and more animals are wintering in the region.

195.6 (0.5) Nice vistas of the big-pasture country appear as the road descends briefly into the small Pretty Creek Valley.

196.7 (1.1) The cropped fields of the valley contrast sharply with the upland pasture. One might hypothesize that bottom-land and the upland areas would frequently be under one ownership, with the valleys providing shelter and feed for the cattle-grazing operations. Research suggests that this does not occur, however. Ranching and farming developed as distinctive enterprises early in the history of the area, and this distinction remains today.[60]

197.3 (0.6) Hinerville School, a nice 1898 stone structure, is now deserted.

197.8 (0.5) Pass under Interstate 70. The road cuts made for the underpass and access roads provide excellent cross-sectional views of the Flint Hills' physical structure. The rock beds dip slightly to the west, but so slightly that it is difficult for the eye to detect. Note again the thinness of the soil layer on the upland surface.

198.1 (0.3) *Wabaunsee County Germans.* For about the next ten miles the route passes through one of the most prominent of Kansas' ethnic communities: the Wabaunsee County–Alma Germans (see map). A combination of large numbers of immigrants (some 2,300) and a relatively isolated Flint Hills setting has aided the retention of Old World customs. Most of these are intangible things, difficult or impossible to see on the landscape, but the German preference for building with stone is clearly in evidence.

This entrance to the region was traditionally marked by the stone "I" house sketched here. It was recently razed, but stone buildings are still very common in this area. The hypothesis that they were built because quality stone was available here whereas wood was scarce is partially true but is not complete. Non-German areas in the Flint Hills where stone is just as common and wood is just as scarce do not have nearly the number of stone struc-

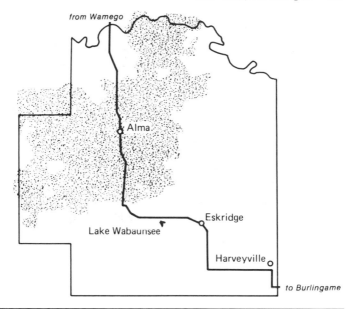

Concentrated German settlement in the Alma area

tures that one finds around Alma. The full explanation for this phenomenon is not as yet known. How much can be explained by the remembrance of Old World stone buildings? How much by a determination to use the building materials closest at hand? How much by a lack of familiarity with wood construction methods? What role did the availability of capital play in the choice of building material?

198.5 (0.4) An abandoned stone house is on the right, partially hidden by brush. Many of these deserted stone structures dot the area, and one wonders about their future. Some say they are in demand for restoration by urban people but that the local land-owners will not sell them. Others say that the abandonment is strictly a practical thing: the homes are small and mostly in poor repair, the thick walls are hard to remodel, and most need complete insulation jobs in order to be comfortable.

199.1 (0.6) *Stone Walls.* Stone walls are even-more-ubiquitous features on the Wabaunsee County landscape than are stone houses. A short example appears on the right. These, too, seem

Abandoned stone house north of Alma

to be tied to German settlement. Although one might think that a stony field would inevitably lead to a stone fence, the time and the skill that are evident in these carefully layered walls argue otherwise. It would have been much simpler just to have thrown the stones in a pile someplace and to have built a fence of something else. The unresolved questions that I raised about stone houses apply here as well.

The Kansas Legislature in 1867, in a move to encourage fences made of materials other than wood, voted to give a bounty for the construction of either stone or hedge fences. The bonus amounted to $128 per mile, payable over eight years—undoubtedly a large incentive for capital-short pioneers. Why the Germans should have taken special advantage of the law is still unknown, however.

199.2 (0.1) As the road curves, look at the fence to the right. A large limestone slab is leaning against a post where the fence bends. This phenomenon, which is common on the Flint Hills upland, is caused by shallow soils. Rock at or near the surface prevents fence posts from being sunk deeply, and without the use of stone slabs for reinforcement at corners and critical bends, stock could easily push the fences down.

Stone slab fence support

199.3 (0.1) A wall-less hay storage shed stands on the left. As discussed at mile 195.1, these structures have become increasingly common as the grazing economy has changed. The absence of sides makes the shed not only cheaper to construct but also easier to load and unload. Moisture problems are not severe if the bales of hay are tightly stacked.

200.0 (0.7) Just beyond the McFarland Road intersection, Kansas Route 99 begins to leave the upland. Ahead is Alma, almost idyllically nestled in beautiful Mill Creek Valley. Valleys assume a special meaning in the Flint Hills; they are something like oases, places of lushness and life on a scale quite different from the open spaces surrounding them.

There is another stone wall on the right, paralleling the road.

200.5 (0.5) Two more wall-less hay sheds are on the left.

200.7 (0.2) On the right, partially hidden by trees, is the stone house of G. W. Diehl, built in 1942. The Wabaunsee Germans apparently did not use Old World house styles, only Old World building materials. Most of the local stone farmhouses are "I" types, and the Diehl home is a classic pyramid form. It was built by the father of the present owner, who died before he could complete a stone roof over the front door. Later a more contemporary material was chosen for the job—redwood.

» *Mile 201.4 (0.7) Turn right, following Kansas Route 99, and enter Alma. Turn left in one block, just before the roadside table, onto Railroad Street.*

» *Mile 201.6 (0.2) Turn right onto Fourth Street.*

Alma. Alma, like Oskaloosa (mile 77.05), is one of the smallest county seats in eastern Kansas, with a population of about eleven hundred. It is located not only near the center of the county but also in the midst of a mass of extremely rough land. Both were factors in its selection as county seat, for rival towns were generally located at the edges of the rough topography, near the outer boundaries of the county. Their votes canceled each other out, and Alma was the compromise choice. Today, county business constitutes a significant portion of the local economy.

201.7 (0.1) Fourth Street, one of the nice old residential streets in town, contains several well-maintained stone homes. On the left, just beyond Illinois Street, is the largest of them, the Schroeder house. It is a three-story structure with an elaborate mansard roof, arched wine cellar, and stone carvings. The builder-owner was a stonemason.

On the northwest corner of Fourth and Grand is the old German Evangelical Church. This was one of five churches in nineteenth-century Alma. Significantly, the three German ones (Evangelical, Catholic, Lutheran) were built of stone, whereas both the Methodist and the Congregational were wooden structures.

» *Mile 201.85 (0.15) Intersect Missouri Street (Kansas Route 99). Turn left through downtown.*

Missouri Street is the main business street of Alma. Its name reflects the immediate St. Louis origins of many of the early town settlers. At the northeast corner of the intersection is the Alma Hotel, an 1888 stone structure. Another old hotel, the Royce, survived until recently on Missouri Street. That there were two hotels in a town the size of Alma is difficult for young people today to imagine. When Topeka was a full day, rather than thirty-five minutes, away, however, the prestige and business of the county seat were increased immeasurably. Salesmen and even people from the county periphery had to have places to stay while they completed their activities.[61]

201.95 (0.1) The Wabaunsee County Historical Museum, housed in still-another stone building at the corner of Third and Missouri, is well worth a visit. Betty Roberts, its curator, is a storehouse of local information. Hours are 10 A.M. to 4 P.M. Tuesday through Saturday and 1 P.M. to 4 P.M. on Sunday.

202.05 (0.1) A block to the right on Third Street are the Wabaunsee County Courthouse and the stone Lutheran and Catholic churches just mentioned. The choice of building material for the courthouse is ironic: in a region known for quality native stone, the people decided to import limestone from Indiana for their principal county building!

Flint Hills Foods, a block to the left on First Street, is the largest business in Alma. Appropriately for its name and location, its workers are billed as "Specialists in Kansas Meats." In 1986 the company bought out another local institution, Alma Cheese, which continues to produce good-quality cheddars and colbys.

» *Mile 202.15 (0.1) Bear left, continuing to follow Kansas Route 99.*

202.2 (0.05) *The Rock Island Railroad Tracks.* This is currently the only rail line serving Alma since the Santa Fe decided to abandon its Manhattan to Burlingame section some fifteen years ago. A Lake Tahoe promoter, Donald Steinmeyer, purchased a ten-mile section of the old track in 1973, planning to turn it into a tourist railroad through the scenic Flint Hills countryside southeast of Alma. The project failed to materialize, however; and now even the tracks are gone.

202.4 (0.2) Pools from the local water-treatment plant are on the left as the road bends back south. Note the lushness of the Mill Creek Valley cropland. Bank cuts by the stream reveal many feet of alluvial soil, very much in contrast with the local uplands.

203.0 (0.6) Cross the west branch of Mill Creek.

203.6 (0.6) The road that branches off to the left here is one of the few that exist for the next sixteen miles as the route reenters the big-pasture country of the Flint Hills (see map at mile 195.1). Follow the branch road for an interesting side trip along the Skyline–Mill Creek Scenic Drive. The skyline section is especially pretty, as the road snakes along a high, winding divide that separates various tributaries of Mill Creek.

Note also at this intersection the two rural directories, with metal plates showing mileages to area farms. This is a project of a local club; but it is one of doubtful utility. Friends and neighbors already know the addresses, and most farmers do not really want others informed.

204.5 (0.9) *The Walter Wilkerson Farm.* The Wilkerson farm is a showcase operation: it features an 1867 mansard-roofed house and a 1906 mammoth red barn, both beautifully restored and maintained. The farm is a retirement hobby for the Wilkersons, who finance it from money he made as a Wichita oilman. The farmland is leased out, and their efforts are all concentrated on the farmstead.

The barn is one of the most magnificent in the area. Its star and circle designs are reminiscent of Pennsylvania German structures, as is its large size, though the absence of that area's distinctive cantilevered upper floor throws doubt on a direct tie. Note how the barn is constructed to allow easy wagon access to both the lower stables level and the upper grain and hay areas. A cupola on top aids both style and ventilation.

204.7 (0.2) The Lester Martin residence on the left is a nice example of a one-story pyramid house executed in stone.

205.1 (0.4) The Flint Hills area is not entirely given over to the production of beef. The two silos on the left mark the former headquarters of a 500-acre dairy operation. The owners, J. R. and Sandra Maike, have now decided to abandon the difficult daily grind of milking in favor of raising pheasants and maintaining a kennel.

205.7 (0.6) More wall-less hay sheds.

206.15 (0.45) Something about the Flint Hills seems to draw former residents back for retirement. The Wilkerson farm just seen was in Mrs. Wilkerson's family; and the George Egerts, who lived on the left until their health failed recently, were also returnees. Mr. Egert was born in the old stone house standing to the left of the new ranch-style dwelling. He cites the "good air" in Kansas as a primary reason why he came back after living thirty years in southern California.

206.4 (0.25) Stone fences are extremely common for the next four miles. On the left is the beginning of one that stretches for nearly a mile.

» *Mile 206.8 (0.4) Pull off the road on the left just beyond the row of trees.*

Oil. Kansas is a fairly important oil-producing state, but most of the wells are south and west of the tour area. Wabaunsee County has a small amount of activity, some of which is visible here. Just behind the row of trees there is a complex of holding tanks which collect the oil that is pumped from the wells you see across the field. Tank trucks periodically empty the holding facilities.

Kansas oil fields have seen better days, and dwindling production has led most major companies to pull out. Small independent operations remain to pump out the rest of the oil. The energy crisis in the 1970s aroused the hopes of some, and many new wells were drilled; nevertheless, the long-term local outlook is not bright. The pools are all small, and because this oil is a lighter variety than refineries prefer, the prices are discounted.

207.1 (0.3) A stone fence on the right joins the continuing one on the left.

207.3 (0.2) *Burning the Rangeland.* Across the valley there is a nice panorama of the hills. Note that in spite of their steep and rocky nature, timber covers them nearly to the top in some places. Trees can invade with remarkable speed on these pastures, and controlling them is one of the reasons that cattlemen have traditionally practiced the annual burning of pastures. This controversial spring rite provides Kansans with a spectacle of grand proportions. Tourists drive to see the blackened landscape, just as they do to view New England's fall foliage, and nighttime fires add another eerie dimension to the pageantry.

Burning used to be a universal practice, and many leasing contracts still specify an annual burning; but in recent years, certain drawbacks have been noted. These include air pollution, increased erosion when the vegetation cover is removed, and a loss of soil moisture; the last two factors lead to a long-term decrease in grazing capacity. The case for burning is also strong, however: it controls insects and woody vegetation, it encourages earlier and more uniform growth of grass in the spring, and by eliminating the dry stubble of species that cattle do not eat, it prevents these undesirable plants from expanding at the expense of the palatable grasses. With no trees or weeds and with an early, uniform growth of grass, a burned pasture is a pleasing, easily leased piece of land.

Range-management specialists have been juggling these variables for years. Their current recommendation is for occasional, although not annual, burnings, preferably done around May 1. This compromise gives the benefits of burning while restricting its drawbacks. Late burning is a key, for if timed correctly, the soil is exposed to erosion and moisture loss for only a brief period before new growth restores the vegetation mantle.

207.45 (0.15) The small cattle lot on the right is fairly blanketed with stones. Some of these probably outcropped originally, but erosion of the bare soil has undoubtedly made the lot rockier than it was originally.

207.6 (0.15) Five of the popular wall-less hay sheds are clustered near the stone farmhouse of Edwin Stuewe.

» *Mile 207.9 (0.3) Pull off the road briefly next to the small cluster of oil storage tanks on the left.*

A nagging bother in stock country is remembering to close gates, but where traffic is heavy enough to justify the expense, a cattle guard, such as the one you see at the entrance to the pasture behind you, is an ingenious solution. Several pipes are laid parallel to one another over a shallow pit dug the width of the road. Vehicles can easily pass, but cattle shy away from the unsure footing.[62]

There is another reinforcing limestone fence slab on the right.

208.3 (0.4) The road has now angled slightly away from the valley, and the nature of the Flint Hills upland becomes more obvious.

209.6 (1.3) A mile length of stone fence begins on the left.

210.0 (0.4) *Loading Pens.* Loading pens are a hallmark of the landscape of the Flint Hills. They are found occasionally in farming country (see mile 67.95) but reach their peak in both scale and frequency here. The pens on the right are extremely well constructed, using a combination of boards and heavy wire mesh, and their size gives some feeling for the large cattle trucks that use the facility. Generally, the cargo consists of Herefords. This red-and-white English breed is acknowledged to be the best forager of the major beef animals, and although its local dominance is not what it once was, the Flint Hills are still referred to sometimes as the "Kingdom of the White-Faced Steer."

210.5 (0.5) Observe the rock-choked stream bed below. Such streams are common here and constitute one of the reasons why other Kansans who are accustomed to murky, silt-laden waters flock to the Flint Hills for spiritual restoration.

210.6 (0.1) A beautiful illustration of the necessity for reinforcing limestone fence slabs is on the left. The corner post is on the top of a road cut, and the extremely shallow soil is clearly evident.

210.8 (0.2) One last stone fence is on the left, as the route now leaves the German area of Wabaunsee County. The correlation between these two things is amazingly high. A lot of Flint Hills country remains ahead, but almost no more stone walls.

» *Mile 211.05 (0.25) Turn left, staying on Kansas Route 99.*

211.45 (0.4) Cross the middle branch of Mill Creek. The gravel-barred, clear-water nature of Flint Hills streams is even more apparent here than at mile 210.5.

212.7 (1.25) The road now leaves the stream valley and its cropped land and begins to cut across the grain of the hills. The density of farmhouses declines markedly, and the vistas become more spectacular.

212.9 (0.2) The red layers in the road cut on the left are caused by iron oxides.

» *Mile 214.2 (1.3) Stop at the large, rocky road cut on the right.*

Flint. This exposure shows not only the alternating limestone and shale layers that have been visible elsewhere but also some nice examples of flint, the area's namesake mineral. Three thin lenses of flint run through the top limestone bed, and many small pieces have fallen to the shale slopes below.

Flint is an unusually hard and insoluble form of quartz. It is not nearly as common as limestone or shale in this area, but it accumulates in considerable quantities at the land surface. The reason for this is its insoluble nature. As water slowly eats away at a surface layer of limestone and dissolves it, the flint particles remain behind. More and more erosion thus produces a higher concentration of flint.

» *Mile 214.7 (0.5) Stop at the cattle pens on the left.*

Prairie National Park. The cattle pens sit on a stream divide that affords an excellent overview of the Flint Hills. No houses are in sight, and even fences are few. The vistas are immense and almost overwhelming in their simplicity. Green rolling terrain and blue sky together constitute the world as far as one can see. To the harassed city dweller the natural beauty is mentally refreshing.

Most Kansans love Flint Hills settings like this, and many are now proposing that a national park be established. There is virtually a united front behind the idea of preserving the tall-grass prairie, but the park proposal has sharply divided people over how this goal can best be achieved. Proponents of a park point to increased state tourism and the desirability of a place where the original species of prairie plants and animals can exist as a reminder of our national heritage. The opposition sees another side: loss of land from tax rolls and beef from the American table, the displacement of long-term landowners, and overall deterioration of the environment. The cattlemen have preserved the grasslands for more than a century, they argue, and a park would only bring neon, litter, and other trappings of "civilization" into a beautiful, wild place. Moreover, they doubt if tourists really would flock to the park. At midsummer, the time of greatest tourist travel, unshaded and overheated Kansas prairies are indeed no paradise.

Several solutions to the dilemma exist. Many people would like to see the park located adjacent to a reservoir or perhaps to the historic Cherokee Strip in order to provide an additional tourist attraction. Opponents of a park have suggested a compromise prairie-parkway idea, whereby small, especially scenic areas would be purchased throughout the hills and linked together by a road system with overlooks and rest facilities. The beauty would be there to see, but without the neon signs or the displacement of ranchers.

215.4 (0.7) Ahead in the distance are the waters of Lake Wabaunsee.

215.7 (0.3) The house on the right is the first one to be seen in more than four miles.

216.25 (0.55) Note the small log cabin in the yard of the farmhouse on the left.

216.45 (0.2) Lake Wabaunsee was made in the 1930s by damming the headwaters of the south branch of Mill Creek. Native stone forms the face of the dam. Notice on the right, between the dam and the roadway, how care was taken not to disturb a tiny cemetery, one of the numerous family plots that were characteristic of rural America in the past.

216.8 (0.35) *Lake Wabaunsee.* The main entrance to the lake ("Gem of the Flint Hills") is on the right. It has an interesting history. The lake was originally a project of the National Youth Administration (NYA) during the depression, with the town of Eskridge helping and eventually completing the construction work. Because of its remoteness the area was little used before World War II, when it was taken over first as a training camp for a tank outfit and then as a prisoner-of-war camp. After the war the lake was again abandoned briefly before William Lacey leased the old NYA camp buildings and started a resort business.

Lake Wabaunsee today is a thriving oasis in the midst of the Flint Hills. It is not as large as the newer Corps of Engineers reservoirs, but because it is private and not subject to abrupt changes in water level, people can purchase lakeshore lots and cottages. This practice, of course, is forbidden at the federal facilities (see mile 84.4). The city of Eskridge, four miles to the east, owns and maintains the lake proper. Most users and property owners are from Eskridge, Alma, and Topeka, although some live in Kansas City or even farther away.

217.5 (0.7) More cattle-loading pens are on the left. If you have not done so already, stop to examine the prairie grasses in detail. The major species include big bluestem, little bluestem, Indian grass, switch grass, and sideoats grama; they are most easily identified in the late summer and autumn, when their seed heads are visible (see sketches).[63]

220.1 (2.6) A section-line road leads off to the left, the first one you have encountered since Lake Wabaunsee and only the second one since Alma. From this point on, however, these roads occur regularly, signifying the end of the big-pasture country.

220.3 (0.2) The microwave tower on the left is owned by sister stations KSNT of Topeka and KSNW of Wichita; it is on a direct line between the two cities. Given the thirty-mile range of these towers (see discussion at mile 171.7), a second one in this string should exist near Strong City, and a third one near Burns, Kansas.

221.0 (0.7) The boundary of the Flint Hills is often indistinct, but along this section of Kansas Route 99 it is as sharp as a knife blade. Looking ahead to the east as the road begins to descend to Eskridge, a familiar midwestern pattern of rectangular fields and frequent farmsteads appears on a gently undulating terrain. Looking back, the scene is filled with the totally different physical, cultural, and economic landscapes that form the bluestem pastures.

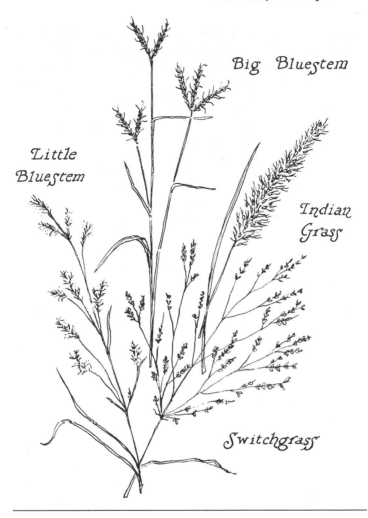

Big Bluestem

Little Bluestem

Indian Grass

Switchgrass

Grasses of the Flint Hills

221.2 (0.2) City limits of Eskridge. Eskridge, population about seven hundred, sits astraddle the ranching-farming border and serves people from both areas. Its self-identification, however, is decidedly toward ranching, as is evidenced by the Flint Hills Bank and other local names, as well as the town's annual Labor Day

Rodeo. The Flint Hills alignment of a border town probably should not be surprising. Americans have always romanticized ranching, and in this part of the Midwest the scarcity of ranching areas undoubtedly adds to their appeal.

An unusual feature of Eskridge is its street pattern. The familiar rectangular grid is present, but not in its typical cardinal-direction orientation. To anyone who is familiar with midwestern towns, this marks Eskridge as a child of the railroads, a settlement built after and aligned with the train tracks. The railroad here was the now-abandoned Santa Fe branch line that I mentioned at Alma (mile 202.2). The tracks have been pulled up, but their route is still visible at the northern end of the business district. The Eskridge Lumber Company, which formerly got its supplies by rail, marks the spot.[64]

» *Mile 221.5 (0.3) Junction of Kansas Routes 99 and 4. Continue straight ahead on Kansas Route 99.*

» *Mile 222.1 (0.6) Angle right, following Kansas Route 99.*

222.6 (0.5) *Sale Barns.* The large steel building on the right was built as the Flint Hills Livestock Auction and Café, a place where stock that local people brought in could be auctioned off weekly to slaughterhouse representatives and others. It has fallen victim not only to a series of bad years for cattle prices but also to the longer-term consolidation of farms and ranches. The economic role of small sales barns has been replaced, but a cultural void remains. Perhaps the majority of the people who attend a typical sale do not come with any serious intention of buying; the attraction is rather curiosity, the exchange of local news, and perhaps just an opportunity to get away from home occasionally.

224.3 (1.7) *Pipelines.* Kansas lies on a direct line between the major American oil fields of Texas and Oklahoma and the major consuming areas in the Northeast, and the state is crisscrossed by pipelines that carry oil, natural gas, and other petroleum products. Because the pipelines are buried, this oil activity generally escapes the traveler's eye. The only indicators are small marker poles (to warn construction workers where the pipes pass beneath roadways) and occasional pumping stations. Some of the markers can be seen on the left.

On the right is a station of the Mid-America Pipeline Company. Its two turbine and two electrical engines keep propane moving through an eight-to-ten-inch pipe from Skellyville, Texas, to Janesville, Wisconsin. Stations like this one occur at approximately fifty-mile intervals.

225.0 (0.7) Notice the barn on the right. A hay trolley projects outward on the roof's ridgepole, but it has no protecting hay hood (see discussion at mile 57.6). This characteristic of barns is rare in eastern Kansas, but its frequency increases throughout the intermontane west; it is the dominant form in Utah.[65] Its distribution seems to be a simple reflection of climate; in drier areas, less protection is needed for the trolley mechanism.

225.4 (0.4) A single oil pump and a holding tank are visible a quarter-mile off to the right.

226.7 (1.3) *Abused and Invaded Pasture.* Two interesting pastures appear along the left side of the road for the next three-quarters of a mile. First is a heavily overgrazed example. If you stop to examine the species present, you will find a complete absence not only of the native bluestem prairie grasses but also of bluegrass and other European forage species. These are replaced by a host of plants that are unpalatable to cattle: ironweed, daisy fleabane, prickly pear, and many others. The next pasture has suffered from an invasion of trees in addition to moderate overgrazing. Wood killer was sprayed on the trees in the mid 1970s in an attempt at reclamation. No other improvements followed, however, and therefore the trees have resprouted.

» *Mile 227.4 (0.7) Turn left onto Kansas Route 31.*

227.6 (0.2) *Fences, Fence Posts, and Good Roads.* The wire fences that parallel most Kansas highways are so common that they rarely attract our attention, yet contemplating them is both interesting and informative. In the early days of Kansas, livestock was accorded free range, but gradually during the last quarter of the nineteenth century, "herd laws" were passed, requiring stock fences. An important, but little appreciated, outgrowth of this decision was the encouragement of the first good roads in the state. When the range was open, individuals typically struck out overland from their homes, each one following a unique route. This diffuse pattern was not conducive to building and maintaining a small set of bridges and all-weather roads. Massive fencing changed all this. Travelers were now restricted to certain channels, and with this channelization came the volume of flow necessary to justify the construction of good roads and bridges.

A basic variation among modern fences is the type of wire used. Because barbed wire is relatively inexpensive, it is employed wherever possible. In contrast, the more expensive wire meshes are usually reliable indicators of an operation involving hogs or some other small animals. A second fence variation is in posts. On the left you see the old Kansas stand-bys; hedge posts; and on the right there are some orange steel ones. Historically, hedge has been more common. It is strong, and it was often available for the cutting on a farm's premises. More recently, steel has made inroads. These posts must be purchased, and they are not as strong as wooden ones, but they can be erected much more easily. Sometimes a compromise is made, by alternating hedge and steel, but always using the strong wooden ones at the corners, where stress is the greatest.

228.6 (1.0) In midsummer, day lilies bloom along the roadside on the right. This domesticated plant reverts easily to the wild and can sometimes survive other indications of man's presence for a long time. Perhaps an old farmhouse once occupied this site.

228.85 (0.25) More lilies are on the right.

229.0 (0.15) The price of fence posts has increased dramatically in recent years. Six-foot steel ones, for example, now cost several dollars apiece. Chain spacers offer one adjustment to this situation; examples of them can be seen in the fence on the left. They keep barbed wire strands apart and allow posts to be widely spaced.

230.0 (1.0) Pass under high-tension electrical wires that go to Topeka.

232.4 (2.4) Part of a Christmas-tree farm appears on the hill off to the right; it is owned by C. C. Converse. Because the public's taste has switched from a northern species, balsam fir, to the more adaptable Scotch pine, many midwestern farmers have gotten into the tree business. It is a fairly intensive land use compared with grain or stock farming, so it has been a salvation to farmers with limited acreages. Shearing by hand twice each year is no fun, but Americans were willing to pay $3 to $5 per foot for 33.3 million trees in 1987.[66] The most profitable enterprises are usually ones that are close enough to urban areas so that the city family (somewhat symbolically) can pick its own tree from the "forest."

234.1 (1.7) To the left is the back entrance to Harveyville; a mile to the right is the birthplace of the area's most famous son, the Viet Nam Marine leader Gen. Lewis Walt.

234.35 (0.25) *Harveyville.* Harveyville has only a few hundred people, but it is isolated enough to have retained a fair range of businesses: a bank, a law office, a library, a grade school, and an insurance office, in addition to the basic stores one would expect. Ten years ago it also had a hardware store, a newspaper, and a dry-goods store. Like Eskridge and Alma, Harveyville is on the abandoned Santa Fe spur, but the loss of the railroad does not seem to have had much effect on the local economy. A grain elevator was the railroad's only user.

》 *Mile 234.6 (0.25) Turn right, staying on Kansas Route 31.*

235.1 (0.5) A small, ill-maintained cattle-loading pen is situated on the left. In eastern Kansas, one can nicely correlate distance from the Flint Hills with the frequency and size of loading pens.

235.8 (0.7) Another tree-invaded pasture is on the right.

》 *Mile 236.65 (0.85) Turn left, staying on Kansas Route 31.*

Wilmington. Three-quarters of a mile south of this intersection and another quarter-mile west is the old settlement of Wilmington. Nothing remains today but a couple of houses, a church, an old schoolhouse, and a cemetery; but the place still has a certain fascination. It is located on the old Santa Fe Trail; it was a principal stop before the jumping-off place at Council Grove, thirty miles to the west. To me at least, the aura of the trail still permeates Wilmington, inducing mixed emotions of the fears and excitements of westering. One in a series of red-stone trail markers, placed by the Daughters of the American Revolution (DAR), is located in front of the old school.

Wilmington was the progenitor of Harveyville. The lifetime of the trail was from 1822 until about 1872, when the railroads rendered it obsolete. When the Santa Fe Railroad laid a spur line three miles north of town in 1880, nearly everyone moved. Connections between the old and the new settlements are easy to see. The grange at Harveyville still carries the name Wilmington, for example, and the Wilmington cemetery contains several Harvey tombstones.

237.1 (0.45) Enter Osage County.

237.15 (0.05) A pipeline passes beneath the road; note the marker pole on the right.

237.3 (0.15) Observe the beautiful barn on the right; it features two cupolas and a traditional wood-shingle roof. The outward flare of the lower edge of the roof is known as a "Dutch kick." This architectural feature is now widely used by many people, but on a structure as old as this barn, it probably accurately reflects the ancestry of its builder.

237.5 (0.2) Pass over the Kansas Turnpike, about midway on its path between Topeka and Emporia. There are no nearby entrances.

238.6 (1.1) *The Santa Fe Trail and the Transit Nature of the Plains.* In the fence row on the left there is another DAR monument marking the Santa Fe Trail. For the next fourteen miles, our tour generally parallels the old route.[67]

Kansas and the plains are famous for their trails, which took people across the so-called Great American Desert to the West Coast. To these travelers the region was seen primarily, not as a destination in its own right, but as a place to be crossed—a transit area. In more recent years, railroads and interstate highways have replaced the trails, but the transit nature of the region continues. This condition has affected the residents of the area.

Nomadic tendencies are strong. People nonchalantly drive long distances to football games and movies and do not get excited in the least by out-of-state license plates.

The movements may have even had deeper impacts. A great many people visit the plains, but most of them have destinations elsewhere and travel along a few major east-west highways. Because these roads do not intersect the physical variety of the plains and because they are deliberately located on flat terrain wherever this is possible, visitors receive an impression of incredible dullness in the landscape. This image is heightened by the concentration of most travel in midsummer, which is not one of the region's better seasons. A sign that used to stand along Interstate 70 in Wabaunsee County said more than it intended to say: "Salina Tonight, Rockies Tomorrow."

It is not a difficult transition to connect a dull landscape to dull people. Who else would live in such a bleak, hot place? There is some evidence to suggest that even area residents feel this way. They hear visitors talk, they notice how everyone passes through but nobody stays, and they feel a little bit ashamed of their origins. Whereas one easily detects regional pride among the residents of such diverse places as New York, Alabama, and Oregon, the young citizen of the plains is apt to say, "I'm only from Kansas (or Oklahoma or Nebraska or the Dakotas)." This slight inferiority complex is probably declining as Americans are becoming more disillusioned with urban life, and it certainly applies more to young plains people than to older ones. Although much is not yet known about this phenomenon, the probable explanation is that the more disillusioned young people migrate from the area, and those who stay behind gradually see more and more of the virtues of the region.[68]

238.85 (0.25) One of the few remaining stage stations from the Santa Fe Trail era stands in ruins among the farm buildings on the right. Its limestone walls are visible just to the right of the red barn and in front of the gray barn.

239.15 (0.3) The rapidly decaying school building on the left, together with the stage station, are about the only remnants of the old Havanna community. Settlement began in 1858, and this school was constructed in 1882. The building functioned until recently as a community center.

240.2 (1.05) As you cross Dragoon Creek, mentally contrast the murky, silt-laden waters here with the sparkling middle branch of Mill Creek (mile 211.45). The Flint Hills are indeed far behind.

A dragoon is a mounted infantryman armed with a short musket; the name goes back to the days of the Santa Fe Trail. The word ultimately derives from *dragon*, a reference to the shape of a particular pistol hammer. It was subsequently applied to a firearm and then to the troops who carried it.

240.75 (0.55) The Santa Fe spur line that I previously discussed used to intersect the highway at this point, just as the road begins to leave the flood plain. The route is clearly visible off to the right, along the east edge of the field. The fate of old rights of way poses an interesting problem. Should the grades be converted into roadways? Should they become bicycle trails (their gentle slopes and natural beauty make them ideal)? Or should they simply revert back to farmland?

242.0 (1.25) On the left there is a nice example of a five-window "I" house. Notice especially the shuttered arched openings in both the end and the cross gables. These carry the Gothic vertical motif a step further than was seen in earlier examples (mile 122.3).

242.85 (0.85) City limits of *Burlingame.*

People who are accustomed to visiting small towns can quickly differentiate two types: ones that were always small and ones that once enjoyed prosperity or at least had visions of such enjoyment. Eskridge and Harveyville fall into the former category, but Burlingame, population about 1,250, is definitely in the latter. The signs are everywhere. An extremely broad main street and a large contingent of once-elegant Victorian houses are two obvious manifestations; another is the quality of workmanship in the old downtown buildings. One wonders what happened: Why does one prairie town prosper and another fade?

In the case of Burlingame the answer lies partly with transportation but more with politics and mining. The town was a principal station on the Santa Fe Trail, as one can tell not only by the DAR marker at the corner of Dacatoh Street (mile 243.3) but also by the place names, such as Santa Fe Trail Antiques, Santa Fe Trail

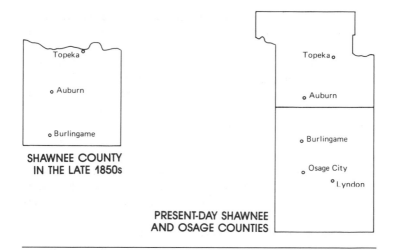

Shawnee County in the late 1850s and present-day Shawnee and Osage counties

Garage, and Santa Fe Avenue (Kansas Route 31). Burlingame boomed with the trail and declined a bit with it; but given the town's head start over competitors and the position that it secured on the main line of the Santa Fe Railroad, there was plenty of reason to expect growth.

Town leaders felt that acquisition of the county seat would ensure the future. The problem was that Burlingame was in Shawnee County; the old boundary passed two miles south of the city. Burlingame and Topeka were pitted against each other; and tiny, centrally located Auburn was threatening to secure the prize (see sketch map). A political deal was made, and the boundary was moved ten miles north, thus depriving Auburn of its central position and leaving both of the larger cities nicely located to become county seats.

The move was immensely successful for Topeka and seemed so originally for Burlingame, as it had the county government between 1861 and 1870. It eventually lost out, however, as big coalmining developments at Osage City created a powerful county rival. Lyndon emerged as a compromise choice for the seat of Osage County, and the county's power became dispersed among the three towns. All have therefore had to settle for second-class status.

» *Mile 243.4 (0.55) Junction of Kansas Route 31 and U.S. 56. Continue straight ahead on U.S. 56.*

Verticality and Horizontality. Note the predominance of two-story buildings along the main street of Burlingame. This verticality, which is characteristic of nineteenth-century American architecture, has already been sampled with "I" houses, two-story pyramids, and big general-purpose barns. Now, curiously, all are in decline. The old types of houses have yielded to one-story ranchers; big barns, to low steel structures; and the old store buildings, to new horizontal operations such as the local post office. Most of the second stories of Burlingame's buildings, which used to contain the offices of doctors and lawyers, are now vacant. America seems to be substituting the horizontal for the vertical dimension. Explanations for this are not fully available; modern technology favors horizontal flows of information and goods to some extent, but it has also been suggested that increasing American familiarity with mobility and speed has contributed to our preference for horizontal space.[69]

243.7 (0.3) Pass under the main line of the Atchison, Topeka and Santa Fe Railroad.

244.3 (0.6) Note the newly relocated Burlingame railroad depot on the right.

245.3 (1.0) This intersection was the site of Fostoria, a settlement that sprang up during the coal-boom days. It was much too close to Burlingame to survive as a rural service center after mining collapsed, and so it died. The only remnant on the landscape is a cement well cover near the southwest corner of the intersection. The well once supplied the Fostoria school.

245.5 (0.2) *Coal Mining in Osage County.* Adjacent to the road on the right is a large reddish-gray pile of material called gob. This is a mine dump, a refuse heap created by coal-mining shafts. Some twenty dumps are within sight of the road between Burlingame and Scranton, and many more dot the countryside from Carbondale south and west to Arvonia (see map). Coal mining was once a big business in Osage County, and although mining has now

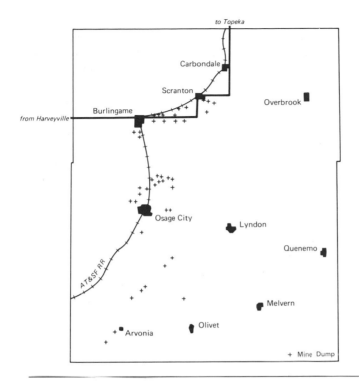

Osage County mine dumps

virtually ceased, the coal legacy is still clearly visible on the landscape that the tour will pass through for the next eleven miles.

One of the most important legacies is the Santa Fe Railroad itself, which closely parallels the highway between Burlingame and Topeka. Original plans called for it to go straight southwest from Topeka, along the base of the Flint Hills near Eskridge, and hence to Council Grove and Great Bend; but the present course was adopted when coal was discovered near Carbondale in 1869. The railroad needed coal for fuel, of course, and it saw that the mineral would also be valuable as cargo. The decision was made, and Osage County enjoyed a tremendous mining boom between 1869 and 1890.

The prosperous era ended when the Santa Fe's demand for coal had grown to such proportions that it exceeded the local supply.

The railroad was forced to build a branch line to tap the larger coal deposits of southeast Kansas, and this decision effectively caused the collapse of the Osage County boom. Southeast Kansas coal occurred in thicker, easier-to-mine seams than the Osage County product, its quality was higher, and the total reserves were greater. Furthermore, since the Santa Fe itself went into the mining business there, it established favorable haulage rates for southeast Kansas. Osage County retained only the domestic heating market for the immediate area. Local towns lost population rapidly, and a look of partial abandonment descended, a look that still characterizes the region.[70]

246.1 (0.6) Mining in Osage County was dominated by small entrepreneurs. In 1890, for example, the ninety operating mines were controlled by sixty-seven companies. The coal seams here were too thin for early mechanized equipment to be used, and this kept big operators out. One result is the virtual absence of mansions and other displays of wealth by a mining elite; such an elite did not exist in the area. The rather extravagant mansard-roofed and stained-glass-windowed house on the left is thus quite exceptional and is not related to mining money. Note the gazebo in the west yard.

246.35 (0.25) Mine dumps are especially numerous for the next mile. Most of them are at least forty years old, yet they are virtually bare of vegetation. The reason is their high acidity and sulfur content. Occasionally, when the dumps were not drained properly, leaching and erosion from the gob surface has led to the destruction of plant life over a considerable area.

247.7 (1.35) *Earth Berm Houses.* A new type of house has made a significant impact on the Kansas rural landscape in the past decade. It is a superinsulated passive-solar structure, such as the example on the right; it takes its name from the earth embankment that nearly surrounds it. The house's low profile contrasts with the verticality of the older one-story pyramid house just ahead. Its orientation is an even-more-radical departure from tradition because by opening to the south in order to capture solar energy, it turns its back on roadside society.

When Sun Day was celebrated in 1978, people predicted the

widespread construction of angular houses designed to incorporate solar panels. Only one such house exists along the tour route (near the Lake Wabaunsee entrance, mile 216.8), in contrast with dozens of the earth-berm structures. Some ascribe this contrast to a poor understanding of active solar technology and to inferior product quality during the early period of solar enthusiasm. Others would attribute the difference to the common-sense advantages of berm structures. The designs are simple and inexpensive and can be constructed with materials that are readily available.[71]

» *Mile 248.0 (0.3) Turn left, staying on U.S. 56.*

On the left, just after the turn, there is a remnant of a bygone era—an old barn with the sign "Six-O-Coffee" painted on its roof.

249.1 (1.1) *City limits of Scranton.* The town of Scranton is about a mile beyond its city-limits sign. This is not the result of a vigorously growing community's annexing new land. Rather, it is the opposite: a town that is declining to a shell of its former self. Scranton was a coal boom town, as its name suggests. It had more than seventeen hundred inhabitants in 1890, but it claims only about seven hundred today. Streets that run off to the left for the next half-mile are remnants from the prosperous era. Until recently they bore strictly functional names— for example, F, E, D—which bespoke a hurried platting. The streets are now named for plants, but they retain their former initial letters. For example, F has become Fern, E is Evergreen, and D is Dogwood.

There are no mining dumps in the immediate vicinity of Scranton today, although they once were very common. The county has hauled them away, having discovered that gob makes a cheap and adequate road fill.

» *Mile 249.7 (0.6) Angle right and follow U.S. 56 through town.*

249.85 (0.15) An Evangelical Covenant church is on the right. This is a small Swedish-American denomination which has only 545 congregations nationwide, 22 of which are in Kansas. The Swedish settlers southwest of Scranton came before the mining activity began, and they remained primarily farmers throughout the coal cycle.

249.9 (0.05) Note the sculptured catalpa trees in two yards on the right as the highway bends back north (412 Brownie Street and the corner of Brownie and Kenton). Catalpas, like ginkgoes (mile 39.8), have been faddishly popular in mid-America. The catalpa era was early in the present century, and fashion required owners to keep the trees trimmed carefully into ball shapes. Most catalpas that remain today have not received a trimming for several decades, but these in Scranton were well maintained until recently. A thorough study of landscaping taste in America has not yet been done, but the results would be interesting to compare with known patterns of fashion in interior decorating, clothing, and the like.

Another DAR Santa Fe Trail marker is located one block to the right on Boone Street, in a corner of Jones Park. Scranton and the trail did not coincide historically. The town, which was strictly a coal center, was not founded until 1872, about the time when the trail was finally abandoned.

250.0 (0.1) Downtown Scranton is not prospering. More buildings are vacant than are filled. Of the seven remaining businesses, three—a tire dealer, a gas station, and a car wash—are directly tied to the automobile. Scranton's residents have become commuters to Topeka.

Scranton was about the closest thing Kansas ever had to a company town. It was laid out by the Burlingame and Scranton Coal Company and later was controlled by the Santa Fe Railroad's Osage Carbon Company. Mining executives did not live here, but they carefully extracted the region's wealth. According to a local historian: "Scranton miners went through all the troubles and problems associated with any mining area. Many worked for the company, rented a house from the company and bought food and all supplies from a general store owned by the company."[72] Today all the "company" houses and stores are gone, but the town is still poor. Virtually no large homes can be found, either old or new.

Casey's General Store. Competition from Topeka merchants has continuously eroded the economic base of Scranton since commuting became a way of life in the 1950s. This erosion may now have reached its limit, for there are signs of a modest local resurgence. The most striking evidence of this in Scranton and about 150 similar-sized towns in the Midwest is Casey's General Store. Casey's occupies the garish red, white, and yellow building at the north end of the business cluster. It is part of a Des Moines–based chain that deliberately aims at the small-town market. The stores appeal to local needs by stocking dog food in 25-lb. bags, work gloves, video cassettes, and boxes of ammunition. Gasoline is the primary lure; food provides most of the profits. Casey's, like other convenience stores, takes advantage of the trend for busy Americans to buy their food where they buy their gasoline. They are unique in realizing that cheaper land prices and a monopoly of the local market can mean profits as high in Scranton as in the Topeka suburbs.[73]

250.5 (0.5) The old Scranton high school is on the right. Since 1970, students have attended the new consolidated Santa Fe Trail School, four miles to the east. Across the street is J. K. Hettinger's new earth-berm house, which is oriented toward the southeast to capture heat from the morning sun.

251.1 (0.6) *Satellite Dishes.* According to at least one authority, "the two most important possessions a farmer owns today are his diesel tractor and his satellite dish."[74] This may be an exaggeration, but certainly dishes have modified the look of American rural landscapes. The house on the right has one, and the density is especially high along this section of U.S. 56. Dishes concentrate, focus, and amplify microwave signals from communications satellites; they were first used by cable-television businesses in the mid 1970s. Individuals soon realized that they could bypass the cable companies by erecting their own "earth stations." Prices have always been the limiting factor. Dishes used to cost tens of thousand of dollars before the cable boom around 1980; they still retail for $2,000 or more. Most urban folk opt for the small monthly charges of the cable companies; but rural people, who do not have the cable option, have purchased dishes with a passion.

Kansas has some of the best satellite reception in the world. Each communications satellite hovers in a belt 22,279 miles above the equator so as to orbit at the same speed as the earth's rotation. Individual ones thus appear to be in fixed positions in the southern sky. Kansas' advantage lies in being midway across the country; satellites above the state can be received across most of the nation, and Kansas dishes receive stronger signals from more satellites than do dishes elsewhere.

251.45 (0.35) Cross 110 Mile Creek. This historic stream acquired its name, not from its length, but because it was 110 miles from Fort Osage, on the Missouri River near the beginning of the Santa Fe Trail. The old trail crossing was about one and a half miles southeast of here. The stone-and-frame McGee-Harris stage station at the old crossing is still standing. To view it (as well as some ruts at the creek crossing itself) take a short side trip south on *old* U.S. 75, 1.6 miles ahead. Go south one-half mile to where the old road rejoins new U.S. 75. On the left there will be another DAR marker; on the right there is a dirt trail that leads 0.2 mile to the station. The building can be seen from new U.S. 75 if one drives just beyond the DAR marker.

251.8 (0.35) The barn lot on the left is enclosed by a cyclone fence, an expensive and very unusual procedure.

» *Mile 253.05 (1.25) Turn left at the Four Corners intersection onto old U.S. 75. Do not take new 75, the divided highway that lies just ahead.*

Four Corners Fish Hatchery. At the extreme southwestern corner of the building complex at this intersection, thirteen small ponds cover a total of six or seven acres. They constitute Del Weidner's fish hatchery and farm, a wide-ranging operation that raises minnows for local bait shops, sells fingerlings to other fish raisers, and markets mature catfish direct to area restaurants and grocery stores.

Fish farms are still unusual in Kansas, but the business is booming in the South and is rapidly coming into the Midwest. Its popularity is primarily attributable to economics. It takes only about 1.3 pounds of feed to produce a pound of catfish. This compares extremely favorably with other common meats: poultry has a feed to meat ratio of 2.5 to 1; for hogs it is 5 to 1; and for beef cattle it is 8 to 1. Catfish, thus, are six times more efficient to produce than beef cattle, a factor of increasing importance in a time of rising food prices.

The technology of fish farming today lags behind that of other methods of producing meat. Not enough is known about feed rations, water temperature and filtration, disease control, and the like; and marketing systems are still primitive. These things so far have kept catfish prices higher than the feed conversion ratio would predict, but work is progressing rapidly at various university experiment stations and elsewhere. Catfish may soon be regular fare on American tables.[75]

254.05 (1.0) Note the sign for the Carbondale Cemetery, one mile to the east. The cemetery is two miles from town, a strange fact that is attributable to coal mining. The original strike was near the cemetery's site, and the first settlement was there. When the railroad came through, the town moved northwest a bit but left the cemetery behind.

254.8 (0.75) *Strip Mining and the Final Decline of the Osage County Coal Fields.* A quarter-mile to the left, extensive dirt and rubble piles mark the presence of strip-mined land. This is the same coal that was mined by shafts between Burlingame and Scranton, but here it is close enough to the surface to make it cheaper to scrape off the overlying material and expose the coal layer directly.

The coal in Osage County is contained primarily in a geologic formation called the Wabaunsee Group, which outcrops across the state along a north-south line from Brown County to Chautauqua County. A little mining has been done all along its length, but because the coal vein is thickest (about eighteen inches) in Osage County, most activity has been concentrated here. The coal bed, like the other strata of eastern Kansas, dips to the west, and mining has only been attempted within four miles of the outcrop line, which runs from Carbondale through Scranton and Osage City to Arvonia. On the eastern fringe, as here, strip mining was done; farther west, shafts had to be sunk, because the coal's depth drops off from thirty feet near Carbondale to some one hundred and twenty feet at Burlingame.

As was discussed earlier, a major decline in the Osage coal fields occurred in the 1890s with the opening of the large Pittsburg min-

Coal tipple at Bell Mine No. 4

ing district (mile 245.5). Small production continued locally for many years, in order to supply nearby towns with heating fuel, but the collapse of even this market came soon after World War II. Young miners went off to fight, saw the outside world, and decided against returning to the coal fields. Coincidentally, natural gas began to make massive inroads into the home-heating market, and the mines closed one by one. Osage City and Burlingame proudly resisted the natural gas takeover by refusing to allow local pipelines until 1953 and 1964, respectively; but this was all in vain. The last shaft mine closed in 1964, and stripping operations, too, have ceased. Plenty of coal remains in the ground, however, waiting for the gas wells to run dry or for other coal fields to falter. The last shaft mine was Bell #4, located 1.3 miles south of Burlingame on U.S. 56. Its tipple stood into the 1970s, the sole survivor of the scores that once punctuated the Osage County landscape (see sketch).

255.6 (0.8) *Carbondale.* Downtown is two blocks to the left, but many businesses have relocated along the highway. Just like Scranton, Carbondale was a company town, a creation of the Carbon Coal and Mining Company. It claimed a population of some fifteen hundred in the 1880s and featured nineteen saloons. The town declined rapidly after 1890 to a 1940 low of four hundred people. Since then there has been a revival because of the proximity of Topeka. Currently the population is about seventeen hundred.

The character of Carbondale still reflects its working-class origin. Wealthy Topekans who want to build in the country have shied away from the old mining towns, with their unreclaimed strip land and ingrained pessimism, born of decades of poor wages and slowly declining business. New residents are low- to middle-income families who fit in better with the existing populace.

255.7 (0.1) The development on the left for the next quarter-mile is typical of newer housing in Carbondale. Most of the houses have single-car garages and are built on slabs. Many driveways are graveled, and there are lots of swing sets, cyclone fences, and dogs.

257.1 (1.4) *Mineral Springs.* A tenth of a mile to the right down the gravel road there is a small, permanent marsh, covered by cat-tails and arrowhead plants. It is unimpressive today, but from 1887 until 1915 it was the site of the Merrill Springs Hotel, a fashionable resort spa that served a large part of eastern Kansas. According to local accounts, M. D. Merrill heard Indian stories about the spring's medicinal properties, so he sent samples to a chemist for analysis. When the report showed a high concentration of min-erals, Merrill gave the waters to some friends for treatment and received "enthusiastic" responses. Consequently he built a three-story, thirty-eight-room hotel and bath house, and there was a rash of customers in the spring of 1887:

> An estimated one hundred persons visit the spring daily on an average. At a low calculation over four hundred were there last Sunday. A continual stream of vehicles of every description, from the open barouche and road wagon to the typical Mex-ican burro, loaded with kegs, cans, big jugs, and little jugs to be filled with these marvelous waters, was maintained each day.[76]

The spa operated until its owner died in 1915, and the hotel building was razed in 1957. A trailer court occupies what once were the picnic grounds, and the spring now provides water for livestock. About the only visible remnant of the old era is the line of walnut trees along two sides of the hotel grounds.

The Merrill Springs Hotel is not an isolated example. Spas were popular all across the country at its time. A few have survived to the present, including nearby Excelsior Springs, Missouri, and Hot Springs, Arkansas. The spa era deserves to be studied. To what extent were the springs frequented for health reasons? To what extent were the waters just an excuse to get away for a sophisticated rural vacation?

257.8 (0.7) Downtown Topeka is less than fifteen miles from here, so one would expect to see large numbers of expensive ruralite homes lining the roadway and on adjacent hills. The handful of modest ranchers on the left stand virtually alone, however. For some reason U.S. 75 south is not perceived to be a highly desirable homesite. Two factors seem to be responsible: the depressed coal-country image at Carbondale and the presence, until 1973, of Forbes Air Force Base a few miles ahead. Both have been viewed as diseconomies by prospective builders of luxury homes, the coal area for reasons already discussed and Forbes because of its air of transience and the generating of heavy traffic and noise pollution. Interestingly, the closing of Forbes has not greatly affected the suburban growth pattern of Topeka. Some reasons for this will be examined later.

259.2 (1.4) Enter Shawnee County.

259.3 (0.1) Roadside businesses provide more insight into the nature of this area. Cut-rate gas stations are common, as are bait shops and camper dealers. On the left is an outlet for plaster deer, plastic flamingos, wagon wheels, and other lawn ornaments.

260.7 (1.4) Cross the *Wakarusa River.* Like many Indian place names, Wakarusa has had several spellings and interpretations. Some say the word means "river of weeds," but a more popular (though not necessarily more accurate) statement was told to an early traveler in 1857:

Many moons ago before white men ever saw these prairies, there was a great freshet. While the waters were rising, an Indian girl on horseback came to the stream and began fording it. Her steed went in deeper and deeper, until as she sat upon him she was half-immersed. Surprised and affrighted she ejaculated "Wau-ka-ru-sa!" which meant hip-deep. She finally crossed in safety, but after the invariable custom of savages; they commemorated her adventure by renaming both her and the stream "Waukarusa."[77]

The Wakarusa has been dammed some twenty miles downstream to form Clinton Reservoir. Lake waters do not back up this far, however.

260.8 (0.1) *Mobile Homes.* The hamlet of Wakarusa is to the left half a mile. Here and elsewhere along this section of U.S. 75, mobile homes largely take the place of ruralite ranch houses. Two small trailer parks have lined the road since Carbondale, and they increase rapidly in number and size ahead. Mobile homes are becoming amazingly popular all across the United States. About half a million of them are manufactured each year; they constitute more than a *quarter* of all new housing construction. One sees them nearly everywhere, but U.S. 75 seems to be a preferred setting.

Cost explains much of the mobile-home boom. The median price for a conventional new house in the late 1980s is nearly $100,000, or $40 per square foot, exclusive of furnishings, appliances, and land costs. This compares extremely unfavorably with the figures for mobile homes: a range from $15,000 to $40,000 overall, or, more importantly, $21 per square foot. A buyer's money thus goes nearly twice as far if he or she selects a mobile home.

Beyond simple costs, a mixed body of mythology and half-truths has always accompanied the mobile home and has influenced its distribution pattern. Many people still envision them as cramped, ill-heated cubicles, suitable only for vagabonding and inhabited permanently only by the extremely poor. This view is almost entirely wrong. Modern mobile homes commonly contain more than 900 square feet of living space and are equipped with the latest appliances, heating, and cooling equipment.

In fact, the term "mobile home" itself is almost a misnomer today, because few of the increasingly large "trailers" are ever moved after their initial placement. A preferred term is "manufactured home," which stresses the principal difference between this form and conventional housing, constructed at the site itself.

Although mobile homes are not totally luxurious, in quality and appearance they are the equivalent of many conventionally built houses. Because the public image has tended to lag behind reality, however, industry representatives feel that owners of mobile homes are discriminated against in terms of taxing procedures, interest rates, and zoning restrictions. According to one Kansas authority: "Zoning is our major obstacle. We still fight regulations set up years ago when the relatively flimsy house trailer was the primary image."[78]

260.9 (0.1) Another abandoned sale barn, "The Farmers Livestock Exchange," is on the right. Auctions used to be held here every Thursday, so as not to compete with the Wednesday sales in Eskridge (mile 222.6).

» *Mile 261.6 (0.7) Stop sign. Old and new highways U.S. 75 merge over the next quarter-mile. Continue straight ahead.*

262.2 (0.6) A sign announces that Topeka is five miles away. This refers to the official city limits, but in many senses, Topeka extends to this point and beyond. The beautiful Gothic-roofed dairy barn on the right is a case in point. It cannot last long here, for urban land speculation has forced property values and taxes so high that traditional farmers are being forced to sell out.

262.4 (0.2) Three large auto-salvage yards line the road for the next half-mile. They enjoy an excellent location: along a major highway for easy access to their product, and close to the Topeka market, yet just outside the city limits, to avoid municipal ordinances and taxes.

262.85 (0.45) Just beyond the last salvage yard there is a pumping station of the Williams Brothers pipeline. This moves refinery products to Kansas City from the El Dorado oil field east of Wichita.

262.9 (0.05) Another trailer court.

263.8 (0.9) *Forbes Air Force Base in Transition.* Until September 1973 the land on both sides of the road for the next two miles was occupied by more than four thousand military personnel at Forbes Air Force Base. Then the government announced the closing of Forbes as an economy measure, and since that time, the area has been in turmoil. What would happen to the base's hospital, golf course, and other facilities? Who would live in the base's housing? What businesses would survive without the military customers? Even after fifteen years these questions have not been completely answered, but it is interesting to see how a military landscape has been transformed into a civilian one.

264.4 (0.6) Topekans were at first shocked at the demise of Forbes and its large payroll, then they were elated over the possibility of acquiring the $80-million facility for their own use, and finally they became frustrated by dilemmas of how best to do this. Some things have been resolved: Cullen Village, a thousand-unit housing complex, located behind the warehouses on the left, is now privately owned by a Wichita firm and is called Montara Estates; the county operates the base's golf course; and the old forty-bed brick hospital on the right has become offices for the Kansas Department of Health and Environment.

264.6 (0.2) The old main entrance to the base is on the right. The road leads through the 3,100-acre Air Industrial Park (the old cantonment area) to the airport terminal. Both the airport and the industrial park face an uncertain future. City officials debated three years before deciding to operate Forbes Field. The facilities were magnificent, including one of the longest runways in the world (12,800 feet), but no one was certain that sufficient demand existed for a jet airport with annual maintenance costs estimated at $1.5 million. The gamble was to convince business travelers and others that quicker turnaround times for private planes and a general absence of congestion would outweigh problems of limited numbers of commercial flights. Topeka has invested $5 million in a beautiful new terminal building, but the level of use remains low. First Frontier and then United Airlines abandoned the city, and currently no passenger jet flights exist. The desks are not even staffed on Saturday afternoons and evenings.

The Air Industrial Park is also having problems. Its transportation facilities are excellent, but the cantonment buildings are small, and the park has not been able to compete for the limited number of users in Topeka. One superior rival, in fact, is immediately on your left: Forbes Industrial Park. The Forbes park occupies the site of the former General Services Administration warehousing facility. It couples access to transportation with quality buildings; thus it is fully occupied by major businesses, such as Frito-Lay, Del Monte, and Fleming Foods. The company list at Air Industrial, in contrast, changes frequently. Many buildings are in disrepair, and county/city agencies are occupying an increasing percentage of the sites. Some Topekans brand the complex as an eyesore and want to convert part of it into a race track (see discussion at mile 20.5).

265.0 (0.4) *Montara Estates.* The thousand units of the old Forbes housing complex are one-half mile to the left on University Boulevard. The military origin of this complex provides an interesting perspective for viewing civilian tract housing. Both types have only a few house styles, but the military has avoided the sham of adding minor, nonfunctional trim in an attempt to make each dwelling seem unique. The low ranch-type houses at Montara, with their wide roof overhangs, are the result of an honest, straightforward architecture. The simple, unadorned lines are in keeping with the classic folk designs of the "I" and pyramid houses.

The Montara people have modified the system of naming streets. The main access road (University Boulevard) formerly led to a warren of streets named after colleges (Drake, Tulane, Lehigh, etc.). These streets now bear rather syrupy names, such as Arborglade, Sunnyvale, and Timberway.

265.5 (0.5) *Pauline Businesses.* Before the establishment of Forbes in 1942, Pauline was a small agricultural community, but it rapidly became devoted to serving personnel from the base. As a result, the businesses in Pauline were not those typical of other small towns; they catered to the special needs of young single men and young couples and were calculated to take into account the goods and services available to these people at the base itself. A survey taken in 1973, before the closing, revealed some standard enterprises, such as a post office and a barber shop, but also a pawnshop, two bars, a large dealer in cheap furniture, and many vehicle-oriented places—a cycle center, a sports-car lot, car washes, and an auto-supply store. Of these things, only bars were available on the base, and the civilian bars offered their clients a different

Fifty-seventh Street Bargain Barn

atmosphere. In October 1987, all of the above-mentioned businesses except the sports-car lot and the cycle center were still operating, somewhat surprisingly. The survival of the others is probably because of the continued occupancy of large local trailer courts, originally established for military personnel. The present residents of the trailers apparently share many of the demands that were characteristic of the airmen.

265.7 (0.2) The large trailer courts mentioned above are just to the left on Fifty-seventh Street.

266.2 (0.5) No less than five mobile-home dealers and trailer parks line the highway for the next half-mile.

» *Mile 267.2 (1.0) Turn right onto Forty-fifth Street (the turn is just before the railroad underpass).*

Forty-fifth Street Development. Forty-fifth Street marks the edge of Topeka's growth. For about the next mile, one sees a startling variety and juxtaposition of human activity; a nineteenth-century barn is adjacent to a new skating rink, a luxurious golf course adjoins a rural shack. The current landscape is caused by extremely uneven suburban development, a characteristic of the fringes of American cities, yet a very inefficient and expensive operation. People who live in the dispersed housing developments demand city services, for example; yet the city is hard-pressed to provide them. Farmers face the pinch of rising taxes as speculation forces land values up. Moreover, they find that suburban neighbors are not always tolerant of barnyard smells or insecticides and that their properties often fall victim to youthful vandalism. Farmers may flee the area, leaving prime agricultural land unworked.

Zoning boards find it almost impossible to deal effectively with such areas. It is difficult to anticipate future development of an urban fringe, and because a wide variety of enterprises often exists before the city even annexes the land, there is a tendency to have either no zoning or far-too-restrictive ordinances. Either way, the future welfare of the city is in jeopardy.

267.4 (0.2) The South Village mobile home park is the last of the great trailer cluster around Forbes.

268.6 (1.2) Sheep and cattle are still being raised on the farm on the left, but for the most part, livestock have been removed from Forty-fifth Street. Stock require a bigger investment in barns and other permanent farm facilities than do cornfields; they are also more subject to vandalism and objectionable smells.

269.0 (0.4) A white board fence on the right marks the presence of the "country estate" that one would expect on the urban fringe. The fence is only a two-board affair, however, instead of the classic four-board design, thereby casting doubt on its owner's true country-gentleman status.

269.3 (0.3) This intersection marked the city limits of Topeka until recently, a change that is clearly reflected in the development on either side of the line. Ahead, in the county, suburban sprawl is much less visible. Apparently developers feel that city services are worth the higher taxes and zoning restrictions that accompany them. A fireworks stand used to occupy the northeast corner of the intersection every year, just managing to escape city regulations.

269.9 (0.6) One of the benefits of urban growth is the occasional salvage and restoration of an old farm house. A good example is on the left, where an 1885 two-story pyramid house has been beautifully restored. The brown-and-red trim sets off the native limestone well.

270.3 (0.4) The cyclone fence on the left marks the beginning of the Lake Shawnee property, a well-conceived public golf, camping, and boating facility. It is a fine place for a rest stop.

270.8 (0.5) Another excellent stone-house restoration is on the left, a three-window "I" with center chimney and a wood shingle roof.

272.0 (1.2) Small-animal hospitals, such as the Hoof and Paw Clinic on the left, are another characteristic of urban fringes.

272.9 (0.9) Look carefully at the fence row on the left for a two-foot-high concrete pillar. It is a bench mark, a spot whose elevation has been carefully determined by the U.S. Geological Survey. Bench marks are used as control points for local mapping and other surveying operations. The local elevation, by the way, is 1,051 feet above sea level.

273.4 (0.5) Bauer Cemetery, an old family burial ground.

274.5 (1.1) *Shawnee Heights and the Role of Rural Water Districts in Exurban Development.* Shawnee Heights is a sprawling agglomeration of houses that centers on the intersection of Forty-fifth Street and Shawnee Heights Road. It is easily accessible to Topeka but it is not the product of a single land-development company and is not within Topeka's city limits. One wonders why Shawnee Heights is located where it is.

Initial probing reveals several possibilities. A rural community once existed here, as the presence of the 1917 Watson Grange Hall on the corner testifies. Did Shawnee Heights simply evolve from Watson? Other possibilities are the high school and the Methodist church just north of the intersection. Did they initiate local development or did they come only as a response to it? Research indicates that there is little connection between old Watson and new Shawnee Heights and that the school, although it was a factor in the growth of the area, was not the real key. The prime mover is the mushroom-shaped tower off to the left that says R.W.D. No. 8. Houses in rural areas can easily acquire electricity, and if the building density is not too high, they do not need an integrated sewer system. The one essential element is a reliable water supply, made available here by Shawnee County's Rural Water District Number 8.

The importance of water to developers is not widely appreciated, yet it brings to mind some interesting questions. Rural water districts were originally conceived as aids to farmers. Loans and technology are supplied by the federal government when local landowners petition, and the district is run as a cooperative affair. But what is happening on the rural-urban fringe? Are city slickers duping the farmer out of his water, or are shrewd farmers perhaps voting for water in order to sell their land at an inflated price? Both forces undoubtedly operate, but at least in Shawnee Heights, enough water is available from the Kaw Valley to supply both farmers and urban developers.

274.95 (0.45) Another bench mark is on the left at the crest of the hill. It is about six inches tall and is located just behind the second fence post before the driveway. The local elevation is 1,121 feet.

275.0 (0.05) Zion Cemetery, on the left, is a remnant of the old Watson community.

275.25 (0.25) *The Watson Store.* Note the building close to the road on the left, whose roof projects forward to form a porch. This is the old Watson Store, which operated from 1927 until the late 1960s. Competition from Topeka killed it, of course, but it almost survived long enough to cater to the new Shawnee Heights residents. Surely a "7-11" type store, a breed not terribly dissimilar from an old general store, will be established there soon. We are seeing a full cycle of development: An isolated, diversified store succumbs to the competition of large, specialized businesses in the city; this is followed by a revival of the general-store idea as downtown crowding increases. If the Watson store could only have held on another ten years . . .

276.7 (1.45) A nice earth-berm house is on the left.

277.6 (0.9) Enter Douglas County. Forty-fifth Street now becomes Douglas County Route 442.

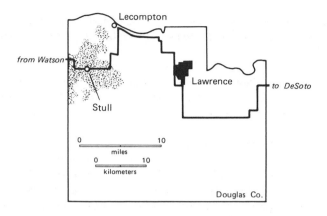

Concentrated German settlement in the Stull area

» *Mile 277.9 (0.3) The road bends to the right.*

Note the road sign on this corner: the north-south segment is labeled 050 E, and the east-west one is labeled 1700 N. The code refers to a classification system adopted by Douglas County to help emergency vehicles and others find their way. This intersection is one-half mile (050) east and 17 (1700) miles north of the county's southwestern corner.

278.2 (0.3) Three old cedar trees off to the right indicate the site of an old farmstead. This is confirmed by numerous stone walls just south of the trees, remnants of a barn lot.

278.5 (0.3) *Deer Creek Germans.* A long stone wall intersects the road on the right. It, along with the barn-lot stonework just seen, is a visual sign of another German ethnic community. Focused on the village of Stull two and a half miles ahead, this group is neither as numerous nor as isolated as the Alma Germans, but it still exhibits a striking dependence on stone construction (see map).

» *Mile 278.9 (0.4) Bend left, staying on Douglas County Route 442, and descend to the Deer Creek Valley. This intersection is 050E and 1600N.*

280.35 (1.45) The first local example of stone masonry is the outbuilding on the right. It was built in 1860 by the Buchheim family.

280.6 (0.25) More stonework on the right: the old Deister house (1870) and an outbuilding. Deer Creek flows just behind the farmstead; its course is marked by a wandering line of trees.

280.95 (0.35) *Stull.* Stull has had no economic functions since the brick garage at the southwest corner of the intersection closed in 1970, unless one counts the bait shop that recently opened in the same building to serve nearby Clinton Lake. The hamlet's general store once stood across from the garage. In spite of these losses, Stull continues to function as a community. The local families have been here for generations, they share a common ethnic heritage, and their ties are reinforced by the church that you see on the right. Culturally, in fact, Stull is as alive as it ever has been. This vitality, which is typical of many American hamlets, is often overlooked by those who think of towns strictly in economic terms.

The church now bears the United Methodist label as a result of a denominational merger, but it was originally a German Evangelical congregation, as one can see in the stained glass window over the main door. Services were given entirely in German as late as 1904, and monthly German meetings persisted until 1908. The Byzantine-like building, with its heavy buttresses and low hipped roof, was built during the prosperous 1920s; it is quite unusual for a rural midwestern area. The original 1867 church, a simple stone building more like what one would expect, is still standing a tenth of a mile ahead, just above the cemetery.

281.05 (0.1) German names heavily predominate in Stull Cemetery: Wulfkuhle, Koehler, Wittich, Buchheim, Kampschroeder, Stull, and Houk, to name only a few. The name Houk brings to mind the area's most famous son, the former major-league baseball player and manager Ralph Houk.

281.4 (0.35) The road now ascends abruptly from the Deer Creek Valley through a major road cut. Until about ten years ago, an easier gradient, which passed around the side of the hill on

Cemetery and old church building at Stull

the right, was used. Evidence of the old path can be seen three-tenths of a mile ahead, where the two routes rejoin.

281.7 (0.3) A stone fence intersects the road on the left.

282.1 (0.4) More stone structures: a barn on the right, a fence on the left. There is a much larger and better-maintained stone barn on the hill to the left, about a quarter-mile away from the road.

282.5 (0.4) The old Stull rural community is rapidly being eroded on its eastern margin. Beginning at the intersection with road 400E, Lawrence commuters become more and more common. The area meets all ruralite requirements: close to the city (ten miles); a paved, but not heavily traveled road; and hilly, scenic terrain.

283.25 (0.75) Another stone fence is on the left.

» *Mile 284.0 (0.75) Turn left onto Douglas County Route 1029, a gravel road.*

Stone fences parallel the road on the left side for most of the next mile. Then, they magically cease as the route leaves the German area, just as they did in Wabaunsee County. A tree-invaded native prairie appears on the right for the next half-mile. Bittersweet is common on the fence rows.

» *Mile 285.7 (1.7) Turn right, staying on Douglas County Route 1029 as it temporarily joins U.S. 40.*

U.S. 40 follows one of the oldest overland travelways in this area, the high divide between the watersheds of the Wakarusa and the Kansas rivers. The Oregon Trail, in particular, passed this way before it crossed the Kaw at Topeka. The divide is particularly narrow at this point, and there are nice valley vistas both to the north and to the south.[79]

» *Mile 286.2 (0.5) Turn left, back onto Douglas County Route 1029.*

The small roadside park on the right has good well water and pleasant shade trees, as well as historical information on Lecompton, the next destination.

286.75 (0.55) Pass under the Kansas Turnpike.

287.3 (0.55) Be sure to observe the nice stone wall on the right, lest you think these features belong exclusively to German communities.

287.9 (0.6) *Chicken Raising.* Notice the low sprawling steel barn on the left. Believe it or not, it is the focus of a large poultry farm, although you cannot see any hens or smell any smells. This is a modern confinement operation, and about the only similarity it has with an old-style chicken farm is the small amount of land and capital that each requires compared to other farming endeavors.

Thirty years ago, most of the American poultry industry was concentrated in the Midwest, where it was a side-line operation on nearly every farm. The rural wife usually managed the flock, and the "egg money" served as a familiar supplier of family treats and a hedge against minor disasters. Today the industry not only has become specialized but also has moved from the Midwest to the South. Poultry raising is not a glamorous business, but since it requires a minimum of land and money to enter, it offered an ideal situation for many southerners and others who wanted to stay on the farm but could not afford to compete in other forms of agriculture. Ralston-Purina and other major companies aided the process by supplying technology. The nearest major concentration of poultry production is in northwest Arkansas, centered on the city of Springdale.

288.4 (0.5) The same Mid-America pipeline that was encountered at Eskridge (mile 224.3) again crosses the tour route. The apparatus on the left is not another pumping station, however; it is a distribution terminal. Propane is taken from the pipeline here, is stored in a battery of large tanks, and is then sold for local distribution.

289.3 (0.9) *City Limits of Lecompton.* Lecompton was the capital of Kansas during the bitter and bloody 1850s, when the territorial government was controlled by proslavery forces. The legislature met here regularly between 1855 and 1858, but as Free-State influence grew, Lecompton declined quickly. The legislature maintained only a token presence from 1858 to 1861, meeting briefly before adjourning to Lawrence; and Topeka was named the permanent capital in 1861.

Sandwiched between the growing cities of Topeka and Lawrence, Lecompton has never again approached its 1856/57 peak, when it had not only the legislature but also a land office, a district court, a federal court, five hotels, and five thousand people. It is difficult to believe that this sleepy town of six hundred was once called the Wall Street of the West. Only two major buildings survive from the boom times: an undistinguished frame structure on Main Street, which was the old Constitution Hall, and the Lane University building, located just behind the old high school. Lane especially is worth a visit.

Lane is a stark but imposing two-story stone structure that has a simple hipped roof and tall, narrow windows. It sits on the site that the state capitol building was to have occupied, and in fact, it utilizes the foundation that was originally laid down for the capitol. Beyond this distinction, Lane is best known because the parents of Dwight D. Eisenhower met here while both of them were students. The university operated from 1882 until its merger with Campbell College of Holton in 1903. The building is now a museum, which is open on Sunday afternoons from 1:00 to 4:00.

Lecompton today is growing in population but is steadily losing economic functions. Not only Topeka and Lawrence but also Perry, just across the river, are capturing much of the local business. Perry is not on the river, and it cannot match Lecompton's history, but it is much better situated for modern growth, because it has a major highway (U.S. 24) and a new reservoir. A recent loss to Perry is the local high school.

» *Mile 289.35 (0.05) Turn right onto a gravel road (2057N) just past the city-limits sign and just before Kroeger's Country Store.*

The route now follows the river road between Lecompton and Lawrence. It is a little bumpy and dusty, but it offers some nice views of the Kaw and the river bluffs.

289.5 (0.15) There are ten or more Kentucky coffee trees in the fence row on the left. Their twice-compound leaves and heavy woody seed pods make them distinctive in the hardwood forest.

289.7 (0.2) The road jogs to the right for a tenth of a mile and then back left.

290.3 (0.6) The road descends to the flood plain and parallels the Kaw closely for the next two miles. The river is immediately adjacent to its bluffs over most of this distance and is actively engaged in cutting away at the upland surface, slowly enlarging its flood plain. The Santa Fe Railroad, which lies between the road and the river, fights a continuous battle to check the process; it is winning in the short run but will eventually lose to the relentless river.

290.7 (0.4) Cross Oakley Creek. The little cove carved by this stream pinches out just ahead and the bluffs come right up to the roadway. The Kaw is only about five hundred feet to the left at the line of gigantic cottonwoods. If you are touring during the winter months, you may be lucky enough to see bald eagles along the river. The birds like the numerous crags and the calm waters formed behind Bowersock Dam in Lawrence. Lecompton's original name—Bald Eagle—suggests that the birds may have wintered here for centuries.

291.35 (0.65) An access trail to the river goes off to the left. It is one of many that are maintained by local fishermen.

291.7 (0.35) *Bluffland Esthetics.* The driveway on the right leads to a private house on top of the bluff and to one of the best views in the state. It is strange how few Kansans know or appreciate the beauty of their large rivers and bluff lands. Highways tend to follow either the high stream divides or, if in the valley, the glacial terraces, and city river fronts are cluttered with old warehouses and railroad spurs. When one considers the vivid contrast between the deep woods, the long river vistas, and the varied terrain of the bluffs with the plainer topography of the upland prairies, the lack of use becomes rather appalling. A relatively inexpensive paving of this road and the cutting of a little brush would pay big esthetic dividends for Douglas County. With a little more money, the Kaw Valley cities could emulate Louisville, Kentucky, where urban-renewal projects have recently reclaimed part of the city's beautiful river front. Lawrence has taken tentative steps in this direction. City officials have created two parks that face the river, and there are plans to convert an old river-front factory complex into a shopping area.

292.3 (0.6) All at once, the flood plain reappears, and both the river and the bluffs diverge from the roadway.

292.4 (0.1) Two small seasonal dwellings perch on the bank of the Kaw. Note the absence of driveways; access is only from the river.

293.4 (1.0) A change in townships brings a change from gravel to paved road. Note the levee stretching from the road off to the left. It gives the valley a measure of protection, but because the levee is not high and because the land is flood plain rather than an old terrace, brief river inundations happen fairly regularly. Standing water also occurs after heavy rains, when the runoff cannot find a stream channel on this pancake topography.

» *Mile 293.65 (0.25) The road bends to the right.*

Soil textures vary considerably on flood plains, although they are usually deep, fertile, and good for agriculture. This area is extremely sandy, as you can see along the roadside and on the country lanes.

293.7 (0.05) In most years there is a small melon patch on the right. Although truck farming is not as developed here as in areas closer to Kansas City, a fair amount of produce is grown. Most of it is concentrated in fields away from the road, in order to prevent poaching.

» *Mile 294.1 (0.4) The road bends to the left, again paralleling the railroad tracks.*

294.3 (0.2) *Oxbow Lake.* If one looks to the left, a broad, cattail-covered swale can be seen, which breaks the monotonous flatness of the flood plain (see map). This shallow depression once marked the course of the Kaw. Just across the railroad tracks the swale is a little deeper and is filled with water to form a distinctive "U" shaped impoundment known as an oxbow lake.[80]

Oxbow lakes are characteristic features of mature-river flood plains; they are created when a stream abruptly shifts its channel during flood stage or at some other time. The old isolated channel persists on the landscape as a lake. Most of these are shallow; they usually do not last for more than a few decades before they silt up, but this one has endured for at least 135 and probably 145 years because of some special conditions that I will discuss below. It was in existence when Douglas County was founded in 1854 and was possibly created during a major flood that is thought to have occurred in 1844. Rumor has it that Daniel Boone hunted and trapped around the lake as an old man, a not unlikely story considering that his son had settled just across the valley in Jefferson County.[81]

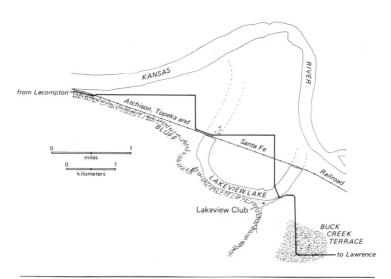

Lakeview area reference map

294.45 (0.15) The eastern edge of the old river depression, which is a bit deeper than the rest, forms a permanent marsh on the left.

294.7 (0.25) The curve of the river bluffs off to the right marks the shape and location of the lake. The road will turn shortly and intersect it.

» *Mile 295.15 (0.45) Road bends to the right.*

The levee that you saw at mile 293.4 is now an eighth of a mile to the left, running parallel to the river, which has turned south.

295.45 (0.3) Cross the Santa Fe Railroad. This little siding is called Lakeview, after the oxbow lake.

295.7 (0.25) An arm of the lake is visible on the left.

295.85 (0.15) Cross Lakeview Lake. The two factors that have maintained the oxbow lake beyond its expected lifetime are now in view: the Santa Fe grade, which dams it at either end (see map), and the Lakeview Club, whose cabins and clubhouse lie ahead and to the right. The Lakeview Club has owned the lake since 1892 and has periodically dredged the bottom to maintain the water depth.

>> *Mile 295.95 (0.1) Turn left, staying on the paved road.*

The *Lakeview Club.* Take a short side trip to drive past the cabins and to see the Lakeview Clubhouse, a large white stucco building that has eighteen bedrooms and a dining room with a hundred-person capacity. The Lakeview Club is something out of the past, a hunting-and-fishing resort for local enthusiasts that dates back to the last century. It currently has about sixty memberships, several of which have been handed down from fathers and grandfathers.

To appreciate the Lakeview Club, one must imagine Kansas before the rash of reservoir building during the last thirty years and before farm ponds and swimming pools were widespread. An oxbow lake was then a very valuable commodity. The club has weathered the passage of time remarkably well. Its small membership size lets each person have a prominent voice in management decisions, and the grounds are never overcrowded on summer weekends. Moreover, private waterfront cabins are possible here, unlike on the reservoirs. The only sector of the club that has been adversely affected by modern times is the clubhouse. As transportation has improved, members utilize its overnight and dining facilities less and less.

>> *Mile 296.15 (0.2) The road bends to the right.*

Just after turning south look ahead a quarter-mile. The sharp twenty-foot rise that you see is an escarpment of Buck Creek Terrace (see discussion at mile 175.6). There is no intermediate Newman Terrace between it and the flood plain here, as erosion has cut it all away. Even the Buck Creek deposit is quite small, about half a mile square (see map).

296.5 (0.35) Ascend Buck Creek Terrace.

296.65 (0.15) Buck Creek Terrace furnishes not only good soils and flood protection for a farm but also an impressive setting for a farmstead, which the Charles Taylor residence on the right occupies. The house is a noteworthy brick pyramid structure, but the pride of the area is the Baldwin barn, a magnificent 1879 stone building just to the left. Its numerous arched windows and rounded main entrances are unique in the region.

» *Mile 296.9 (0.25) Turn left and follow Douglas County Route 438.*

The traffic just to the south is on the Kansas Turnpike.

297.3 (0.4) Leave Buck Creek Terrace and ascend to the upland surface.

» *Mile 297.4 (0.1) Stop sign. Continue straight ahead on Lakeview Road.*

297.5 (0.1) Note the toolshed "barn" in the background of the McCurdys' on the right. It duplicates all the stereotypes that I discussed at mile 67.1: the red color, the gambrel roof, and even the hay hood. The old wooden barn is apparently near enough to extinction that it has become a nostalgic item.

297.9 (0.4) *KPL and Turnpike-Oriented Industry.* Industries flank the route for the next mile, but the agglomeration is of two distinct types and is located here for two different sets of reasons. On the immediate left is a generating plant of Kansas Power and Light Company, and a half-mile beyond is the old Callery Chemical Plant. These are here because of the railroad, which brings in coal and other materials, and the river, which furnishes water for cooling purposes. On the right is a plant of Aeroquip Corporation, makers of brakes and pipe fittings. The keys to its location are the large semitrailer trucks parked near the rear of the building. Shipments are by highway, and nearby Interstate 70 provides excellent east-west movement. Kansas' promotional phrase "Midway USA" is taken literally by Aeroquip and its neighboring companies, which use Lawrence as a distribution center for large sections of the country.

298.0 (0.1) Lawrence Paper Company, United States Building Products plant, and more trucks.

298.1 (0.1) Lawrence is a rapidly growing industrial city. Timberedge Industrial Park is under development on the left, and Packer Plastics, a major manufacturer of drinking cups and similar products, is a new tenant at the Santa Fe Park on the right. Ahead 0.3 of a mile is another new industrial area, the Anna Hope Park. Cultural amenities provided by the University of Kansas are cited by most observers as giving Lawrence an advantage over other sites that have equally good availability of transportation and water.

» *Mile 298.45 (0.35) The road bends to the right.*

The collection of steel buildings that you see ahead just before the turn is the dormant plant of Callery Chemical Company. It was a victim of rapidly changing technology. Built in 1958 at a cost of $4 million, it was supposed to make liquid rocket fuel from boron. Less than two years later the plant was empty, because the missile industry had switched to solid fuel.

Recent experiments by Atomic Energy Commission scientists have suggested that boron can be made to undergo nuclear fission without producing harmful amounts of radioactivity, thus providing a safe source of energy. If the process could be perfected, it might ease the nation's power crisis, and, incidently, lead to a reopening of the Lawrence plant.

298.8 (0.35) The houses on the left are not inside the city limits of Lawrence. They were annexed at one time but managed to get the decision reversed, thus preserving their privileged status of enjoying city amenities without paying city taxes. Two more major manufacturers are on the right: divisions of TRW Corporation, which makes oil-well cables, and Quaker Oats Company, which makes dog food here.

298.9 (0.1) Kresge Road, on the right, leads to the largest warehousing facility in the area, that of the Kresge (K-Mart) Company. The building is impressive from this side, but the façade faces south onto the busy turnpike.

A Schoolhouse History. Riverside School, at the corner of Kresge Road, has had a tumultuous existence. It once served a small country district and was nearly at the point of closing, before suburban growth led to increased enrollments and the decision to enlarge and modernize the building. Then, in the 1970s, enrollments in Lawrence grade schools fell as the baby-boom era passed. Crowded classrooms gave way to excess space, so the school board seriously considered closing Riverside. Growth began again in 1983, and Riverside now has 215 pupils, more than double its low point in 1977. A portable classroom has been added to handle the load.

299.2 (0.3) Pass over the Kansas Turnpike (Interstate 70).

299.6 (0.4) Another turnpike-oriented business is on the left, a Hallmark Cards plant. It faces east, toward the turnpike access road, but this rear view shows the trailer trucks that determined its location. Other factors that favor the Lawrence site are the large labor pool provided by the spouses of University of Kansas students and Lawrence's proximity to the headquarters of the Hallmark Company, which are in Kansas City.

» *Mile 299.9 (0.3) Stop sign. Turn left; then turn back to the right in half a block onto McDonald Road, which becomes U.S. 59 half a mile ahead.*

» *Mile 300.4 (0.5) Pass under U.S. 40 and merge onto U.S. 59 (Iowa Street).*

By-Pass Routes and Commercial Strips. The core of the city of Lawrence is enclosed by a rectangular highway grid (see map). Massachusetts Street, on the east, has always been a business and residential corridor, but the other three sides of the grid were conceived as by-passes, along which through traffic could flow quickly. The tour route passes along two of these streets, which vary markedly in their success at achieving the by-pass goal.

300.7 (0.3) Iowa Street is a fairly effective mover of traffic. Some congestion does exist in this section; it is created by franchise restaurants and gasoline stations, but in a quarter of a mile, residences begin to line the road, and cars travel without interruption. In another half-mile, even the houses stop, and open land borders the roadway. It is tempting to credit the city planners with

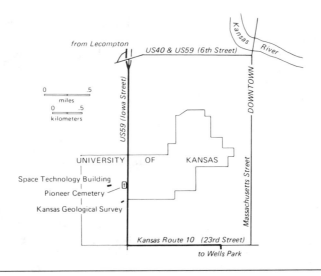

Lawrence highway grid

foresight and courage in keeping Iowa Street from becoming continuously fringed with hamburger stands and used-car lots, but
the situation was caused more by luck than by skill in planning.
This Iowa Street portion of the by-pass grid was completed only
about twenty years ago. Before this, residences lined the portions
of the road that existed, and the University of Kansas controlled
most of the land along the southern half of the route. When the
new road was opened, these two existing land uses remained, thus
severely limiting the frontage that was available for business
development.

301.55 (0.85) Fifteenth Street Intersection. University land
begins here on both sides of the highway. The large brick buildings
on the left are dormitories; the main campus starts two blocks
east on Fifteenth Street.

301.8 (0.25) On the right, just beyond the overpass, is Pioneer
Cemetery, an area landmark that contains graves of many people
who were killed in the famous sack of Lawrence by Missouri guer-
rilla leader William Quantrill. Residents of the nearby dormitories
sometimes use the site for sunbathing and studying.

302.05 (0.25) Nineteenth Street Intersection. Most of the land to the right is still undeveloped by the university because it is so remote from the center of the campus. Several research and quasi-university facilities are located here, however. The copper-roofed brick building adjacent to the road is the headquarters of the Kansas Geological Survey; the larger structure off to the north-west is the Space Technology Center. The buildings to the left of Iowa Street are fraternity and sorority houses.

» *Mile 302.6 (0.55) Turn left onto Twenty-third Street (Kansas 10).*

Twenty-third Street is a classic example of a commercial "strip" development, a solid mile of gaudily colored stores of wide variety, all striving to attract the attention of passing motorists. "Strips" are an original American phenomenon, a product of the automobile age which completely ignores the pedestrian. Sidewalks have been built as afterthoughts, and the advertising signs are almost impossible to read from a walker's perspective.

A serious study of the strip developments would tell us much about our present society, but the traffic congestion that they cause is a more pressing problem. Because Twenty-third Street no longer serves as a by-pass, Lawrence has been forced to plan another fringe highway far to the south.[82]

303.1 (0.5) The drainage ditch between the two lanes of Naismith Drive on the left carries runoff from much of Lawrence. This water occasionally floods the flat area south of Twenty-third Street, but city officials in 1986 foolishly allowed developers to extend Naismith Drive and to build a large apartment complex on the bottom land. Now, to protect this complex, the University of Kansas is being asked to donate land on which to construct holding ponds.

» *Mile 303.6 (0.5) At the stoplight turn right onto Louisiana Street.*

The retail complex at the corner is one of three small shopping malls that serve Lawrence. Developers say that the city is the largest in the country to be without a major mall. This fact angers some residents but is a source of pride to others. The anti-mall faction contrasts the homogeneity of malls with the unique character of Lawrence's downtown retail center.

304.2 (0.6) Ahead lies the Wakarusa River lowland, an effective barrier to Lawrence's residential expansion. The transition zone between urban and rural is occupied by two schools and a spacious park.

» *Mile 304.6 (0.4) Stop sign. Continue straight ahead on Louisiana Street.*

This flat surface is the Newman Terrace again, not the actual river flood plain. A remnant of the higher Buck Creek surface lies just off to the right. The old farmhouse at the intersection is on the easternmost edge of the deposits; the scarp can be seen retreating on either side.

304.7 (0.1) *Baker Wetlands.* The weedy-looking section of land on the left beyond the drainage ditch is an ecological treasure, one of the few remaining examples of wetland prairie in the Midwest. This type of biological community once dominated most of the major river valleys in the region and much of the total land surface in a broad arc from Detroit southwest around Lake Michigan and up into Minnesota. As settlement progressed, however, most of these marshes were drained.[83]

The wetlands here were preserved by chance. The federal government controlled them as a part of Haskell Institute, a local school for Indians, and planned to use them in agricultural instruction programs. This plan never developed, however, and in 1968 the property was deeded to Baker University of nearby Baldwin. The area is not yet a wilderness paradise, although that is the dream of Dr. Roger Boyd of Baker, who oversees the project. Only 50 of the 573 acres are in a virgin condition, and even these are threatened by drainage ditches that carry away needed water from the north and west sides of the tract. The proposed by-pass highway, noted at mile 302.6, poses another threat. Since 1968, Dr. Boyd and others have been reseeding the wasteland areas with prairie plants and have reintroduced native animals. If the water and highway problems can be solved, the wetlands may again become a home for prairie chickens and marsh wrens, as well as a place of natural inspiration for man.

305.8 (1.1) Cross the Wakarusa River. Immediately beyond is Dreher's Trailer Park, which is dominated by small trailers and old cars. Mature trees add greatly to the appearance of the area, even if they are the wind-damage-prone Siberian elms.

305.95 (0.15) A sign on the W. R. Meairs home on the right states that this is an 1854 family homestead. The house does not reveal the age of the place, but the yard does. Large cedar trees line the front, in the manner of the last century, and an old-fashioned trumpet vine winds around the front gate.

» *Mile 306.7 (0.75) Stop sign. Continue straight ahead onto a gravel road.*

306.75 (0.05) Note the large pile of red glacial erratics beside the driveway to the stone house on the right. Glaciation did reach beyond the Kaw in places. It has been suggested that this glacial extension is why the Wakarusa River has an unusually wide valley relative to the size of the stream. Ice that occupied the present site of Lawrence supposedly blocked the normal flow of water down the Kaw, and diversion occurred into the nearly parallel Wakarusa. This temporarily made a small stream into a major river and caused tremendous amounts of valley erosion. When the ice receded and the Kaw reclaimed its normal flow, the Wakarusa was pathetically undersized for its valley, an example of what geomorphologists call a misfit stream.

307.55 (0.8) Some nice prairie grasses grow along the road bank on the right.

» *Mile 307.7 (0.15) Stop sign. Turn right onto a paved road, Douglas County Route 458.*

» *Mile 308.0 (0.3) Turn left into Wells Overlook County Park, drive to the parking lot, and then walk to the observation tower.*

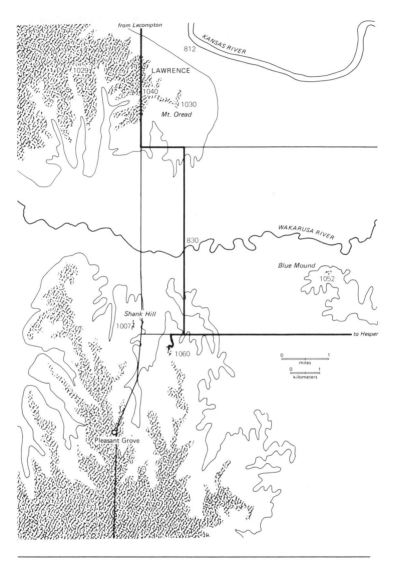

Topography of Lawrence and vicinity

Landscape Evolution in Eastern Kansas. The Wells Park observation tower, built atop a high ridge, affords a broad panorama of the region. As happens in a view from an airplane, ground detail is somewhat obscured, but a more generalized picture takes its place and reveals new insights into the landscape. The pervasive influence of the grid land-survey system is clear, for example, as arrow-straight roads persevere regardless of topography and as fields and pastures repeat the square pattern on a smaller scale. Even the farmhouses and the barns seldom deviate from rigid orientations that are either parallel or at right angles to the roads. Another highly visible feature of the land is its farm ponds. Although these are not found on the flood plains, they dot the upland surface liberally, a testimony not only to the area's livestock economy but also to the pond-building subsidization programs of the U.S. Department of Agriculture.

The evolution of local land forms can also be studied from the Wells Park vantage point. As one looks around from the tower, it becomes obvious that several features stand at about the same elevation as the park itself (see map). Most of the land to the south is at this level, as is the campus of the university to the north. Moreover, an isolated hill off to the northeast (Blue Mound) seems to be at a comparable height, and another hill to the west (Shank Hill) is only slightly lower. The reason for this similarity is that all of these surfaces except Shank Hill are composed of the same rock material; they were joined into a continuous surface at some time in the distant past.

The exposed rock on the high surfaces is called Oread Limestone, a term derived from the Mount Oread setting of the University of Kansas. Like all of the sedimentary rocks of eastern Kansas, the Oread Limestone was laid down flat and later became tilted slightly so that it dips gently to the west. Because of this development, the surface rocks are of different ages across the area. In Shawnee County, for example, they are newer than in Douglas County, because they overlie the Oread formation. To the east, in Johnson County, the Oread formation is not found, and underlying, older rock layers appear at the surface.

Where the Oread Limestone and other resistant rocks outcrop at the land surface, escarpments are formed (see discussion at mile 167.6). The major ones are shown on the map. To understand the present terrain forms in this area, the key to remember is that

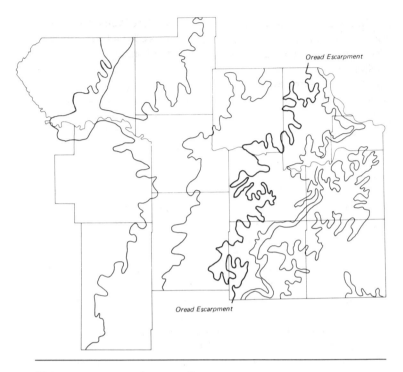

Major escarpments of eastern Kansas

the geologic system that I have just described is not static. Slowly, over the course of hundreds of thousands of years, streams have been eating away at the surface. The result is an irregular westward recession of the surface escarpments, the irregularities having been caused by minor variations in rock composition and especially by the location and size of the eroding streams. Stream cutting leaves peninsular ridges of the original surface on the divides. Occasionally, small sections of the rock will become completely separated from the main surface, forming islandlike hills known as monadnocks.

One can see the operation of this general pattern of evolution all over eastern Kansas south of the glaciated section. The accompanying diagrams show three stages in the development of the Douglas County topography as an example. The first two maps are hypothetical: one is just as the Oread formation is becoming

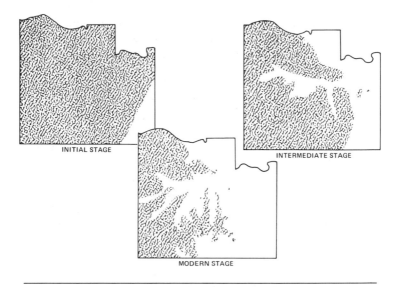

INITIAL STAGE

INTERMEDIATE STAGE

MODERN STAGE

Hypothetical recession of the Oread formation in Douglas County

exposed at the surface, before water has had a chance to begin erosion; the second is an intermediate stage. The back cutting of the Wakarusa early isolated the northern section of the surface, the portion that was to become the site of the university. One of its major south-bank tributaries, Coal Creek, can be seen on the intermediate stage map as it begins to isolate the eastern-most section of the southern block from the rest. As cutting continued, this became the monadnock known as Blue Mound. Earlier hypothesized monadnocks are shown on the intermediate stage farther to the east.

» *Mile 308.25 (0.25) Return to the park entrance and turn right, back onto Douglas County Route 458.*

» *Mile 308.55 (0.3) Louisiana Street junction. Continue straight ahead on Douglas County Route 458.*

309.8 (1.25) *Hedgerows.* Rows of Osage-orange trees form a partial enclosure around the three houses on the left. Hedgerows like these are found throughout Kansas, although they were once much more common than they are today. Natives of the area rarely comment on these familiar lines of trees, but a study of them can reveal much about Kansas history and culture. Hedge fences came into local prominence in 1867, when the legislature agreed to subsidize them to the amount of $128 per mile, a subsidy that was intended to keep Kansas' meager wood supplies from being devoured in making rail fences. This incentive disappeared in the mid 1870s, when barbed wire came on the scene and the subsidy expired; but hedgerows continued not only to persist but actually to increase. Why should this be?

Part of the explanation lies in an unfavorable initial response to barbed wire. Livestock, which were accustomed to solid fences, frequently rammed into the wire; this sometimes resulted in serious injuries. Also the wire was thought to attract lightning. One irate Atchison farmer in 1883 claimed that "the charges against barbed wire fences are so numerous that we cannot mention them. But it would be . . . a blessing to everything excepting the fish, if all barbed wire in Kansas were thrown into the Missouri River."[84]

Besides the charges against barbed wire, hedgerows had many positive factors in their favor. They gave farms a built-in supply of timber, for example; and they required much less initial cash outlay than did most other kinds of fences, because the seeds could be easily transported to prairie farms that were remote from roads or railroads. Moreover, trees physically transformed the appearance of the plains, and many persons found this the best point of all. Hedges sheltered the farmstead and cropland from incessant prairie winds and at the same time helped to change harsh Kansas into a sophisticated land like western Europe by providing the well-trimmed hedges that seemed to be the very essence of the French and English countryside.

A final important motive for planting, which intermixed with the above ideas, was the widespread contemporary view that the planting of trees would increase the local rainfall. The notion was based on the tremendous transpiration rates of trees and was encouraged by generally above average rainfall amounts during the main settlement years of eastern and central Kansas.[85] A typical local view in 1880 was this one:

Kansas was, 25 years ago, an almost treeless region, and severe drouths, followed by terrific storms, were much more frequent than they are now. The planting of trees all over our prairie has undoubtedly worked the beneficial changes in our seasons. The rain-falls are more frequent and timely, and extreme drouths are rare. . . . Tree planting is the best paying business in which farmers can engage. A forest of trees on a farm and rows of trees along the highway and about the farms houses add largely to the money value of a quarter section.[86]

Osage-orange hedgerows have existed in Kansas for more than a century now, but their days are probably numbered. Cattle long ago became accustomed to wire fencing, and other species of trees are now preferred for shade and for esthetic considerations. More importantly, modern farmers can less well afford the time necessary to maintain hedgerows as tight fences, and they increasingly begrudge the land near the fence that is taken out of production by the trees' shade and by their sapping of moisture. The U.S. Department of Agriculture has estimated that two acres of land are taken out of production for every mile of hedge.[87]

310.45 (0.65) Cedarwood Hills, an incipient rural housing development on the right, is taking advantage of a paved road that leads north to Lawrence. When this land was still in pasture a few years ago, small cedars had been allowed to spring up, giving the development its name. Most of the trees have now been cleared away, thus removing the distinctiveness of the tract.

» *Mile 310.55 (0.1) Intersection of Douglas County Routes 458 and 1055. Continue straight ahead on Douglas County Route 458.*

An interesting side trip is to follow the paved road south for a few miles. The hamlet of Vinland is 3.8 miles away; it features the oldest library in Kansas and several restored stone homes. Another 2.3 miles beyond Vinland the road ascends the thickly wooded scarp of the Oread Limestone, providing an excellent view of a cuesta.

310.65 (0.1) The bottom land for the next half-mile is the flood plain of Coal Creek, a major south-bank tributary of the Wakarusa River. Coal Creek long ago cut off Blue Mound from the main body of the Oread escarpment.

311.05 (0.4) Just beyond the bridge over Coal Creek, a trail branches off to the right. It follows the old right of way of an Atchison, Topeka and Santa Fe spur line that connected Lawrence and Baldwin. This intersection was known as Sibleyville, although there were never more than a half-dozen homes here. It is too bad that the Santa Fe abandoned this stretch of track before the bicycling renaissance came to America, for the colleges in Lawrence and Baldwin would now provide an abundant clientele for a riding trail along this route.

311.45 (0.4) Note the "Covered Bridge Ranch" sign above the entrance pylons to the property on the right. Sure enough, just down the driveway there is a genuine covered bridge, newly constructed on this 40-acre "ranch." The mailbox also repeats the covered-bridge theme.

311.55 (0.1) The road to the left leads to Blue Mound, 1.5 miles north.

311.85 (0.3) *Mont Bleu, nee Blue Mound.* Blue Mound is visible off to the left for the next quarter-mile, as is a smaller, lower hill just to the right and in front of it. The lower hill, which had the same origin as Blue Mound, has now lost its caprock of Oread Limestone and is thus eroding much more rapidly than its larger neighbor. Both hills were forested until recently, when the smaller one was cleared in order to erect a radio tower.

In the 1970s the north slope of Blue Mound was the site of Kansas' only ski resort. The operation depended heavily on artificial snow manufactured from Wakarusa River water; it existed primarily to prepare University of Kansas students for their winter excursions to Colorado. As the name Blue Mound did not have the proper alpine ring for a ski area, the local operators decided to rechristen it Mont Bleu. A recent plan to reopen the area is facing competition from a similar ski development on the Missouri River bluffs near Weston, Missouri.

312.85 (1.0) A prominent remnant of old rural America stands on the farmstead to the left, an Aeromotor Company windmill. This particular one, like most of its kin, is no longer operating. Although it turns in the wind, the drive is not connected to the pump. Windmills were marvelous inventions —water pumps that required no electricity or animal power; but they have almost disappeared in the Midwest because their pumping capacity is low and irregular compared to electrical motors.[88]

Somewhat surprisingly, there has been a recent revival of interest in windmills. Along with covered bridges, Cape Cod style houses, and eagles over front doors, windmills are being adopted by affluent Americans as symbols. People seem to be turning from Europe as their sole source of cultural inspiration and finding desirable traits and values in the American past.

313.05 (0.2) Six oil wells and some storage tanks appear on the left. Another cluster is 0.2 mile ahead. These wells are marginal ventures (see the discussion at mile 206.8). They are about 1,000 feet deep and yield only one to two barrels per day. Profits were adequate when they were drilled around 1980, but since then the price of oil has dropped from $32 to $16 per barrel; therefore, many pumps have been shut down.

» *Mile 313.55 (0.5) Intersect Douglas County Route 1057; then continue straight ahead.*

313.6 (0.05) A bench mark (935 ft.) is in the fence row on the left.

314.1 (0.5) A hedgerow that used to parallel the road for the next tenth of a mile has recently been cut down. It is now resprouting vigorously, and by so doing, it provides a hint of its original purpose. Then, slightly less intensive pruning was employed to keep the trees squat and broad, a growth so dense as to be "hog tight."

315.25 (1.15) Another hedgerow meets the road on the left. In this setting, as the surrounding land is quite flat, the importance that nineteenth-century Kansans attached to having the hedges produce small, intimate enclosures can be better understood. Those Kansans needed to "protect" their farms from a seemingly all-pervasive and sometimes cruel natural environment.

316.05 (0.8) The lath-and-wire snow fence that parallels the road on the left is needed in order to restrict drifting. Flat, open stretches of east-west roads, such as the one here, are especially prone to being closed by snow.

316.25 (0.2) Cross Little Wakarusa Creek.

» *Mile 316.55 (0.3) Turn left onto Douglas County Route 1061.*

316.75 (0.2) A very unusual barn is located on the left, expensively constructed of brick and gray stucco. Each of the huge windows features numerous small panes of glass. It is neither the product of an eccentric farmer nor the work of an obscure European folk culture; it is merely an old maintenance and storage facility of the Kansas Highway Department. The building design was once standard for the department.

317.5 (0.75) *Cattle and Hogs.* A small feed lot for cattle is on the right. Note that the animals rarely have the coloration of purebred animals—the jet black of the Angus or Shorthorn or the mottled red and white of the Hereford. Feeders have found that crossbred cattle tend to gain weight more rapidly than the traditional breeds; thus they have turned their lots into a medley of color. Here one can usually even see strains of Zebu cattle, an Indian breed that was brought into this country for purposes of crossbreeding. These animals are marked by a lanky, light-colored body, a prominent hump over the shoulders, and a pendulous fold of skin under the neck.

Across the road from the feed lot, Cliff Neis combines raising cattle with raising hogs. Hog raising, though not as glamorous as cattle ranching, is more lucrative. It requires only a modest investment in land, and fluctuations in market price are usually less severe and more manageable than those for cattle because the turnover time from baby animal to salable product is shorter. Farmers can therefore better adjust production to suit current market conditions.

» *Mile 317.55 (0.05) Turn right just beyond the feed lot and follow the sign to the Hesper Friends Church.*

318.55 (1.0) *Hesper.* The Quaker community of Hesper stretches along the road for the next half-mile. It is not quite as old as the

Springdale Quaker settlement, which you saw previously (mile 62.3), but it became a much more important center. The first settlers arrived here in 1858 to lend their votes to the Free-State cause in territorial Kansas, and by 1869 the congregation numbered 350. Hesper became the hub from which Quakers went to form new communities in Lawrence, Kansas City, Shawnee, and Wichita. Friends University in Wichita, for example, was not only founded by a Hesper native but also had Hesperites for two of its early presidents.

319.2 (0.65) Hesper reached its peak as a settlement in the 1880s. The meeting house on the right was constructed in 1881, and three years later the Hesper Academy was completed a quarter-mile to the west. This was one of the best and earliest of the area's secondary schools, and it attracted many non-Quaker students. Also operating at this time was the Hesper Lyceum, said to be the first literary society in Kansas (1859), and numerous businesses.

The community began to decline around 1910. Major transportation routes by-passed Hesper, preferring to parallel the Kansas River Valley four miles to the north, and competition developed for local businesses and educational facilities. The academy closed in 1912, followed by the businesses, and finally the grade school. Only the Quaker meeting house has remained active.[89]

» *Mile 319.2 (0.0) Turn around and return 0.65 mile to the road intersection.*

» *Mile 319.85 (0.65) Turn right.*

Most of the houses in Hesper date from the 1880s or before; the "I" style is the rule. The grade school that I referred to above stood on the northwest corner of the intersection until 1976.

320.05 (0.2) *Outwash Plain.* The countryside around Hesper is extremely flat for eastern Kansas, and because of this, the land is extensively cropped. Livestock are rare, and fences are scarce. This unique region is an outwash plain, another product of the glaciation era (see map).

A lobe of ice penetrated south of the Kansas River here, reworking the soft shale and sandstone rocks that occupied the site. Then,

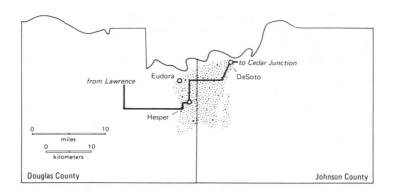

Hesper outwash plain

as the ice began to recede, meltwaters sorted the debris, shaping it into a nearly flat surface. The receding ice also temporarily acted as a dam to impound lakes on its southern side. Soil deposits on these old lake bottoms helped to create the present flat topography.

320.6 (0.55) The farmstead on the right is old, but a new mobile home has replaced the original house. This sight is becoming increasingly common in the Midwest; it is often cheaper to tear down sagging, poorly insulated structures than to renovate them.

321.85 (1.25) From this approach the Community Baptist Church appears to be a rare feature on the landscape: a new rural church. It is new, but it is not really rural, since the growing edge of Eudora is only a quarter-mile to the left.

321.95 (0.1) The deposits that form the Hesper Outwash Plain are about thirty to sixty feet deep, and various streams have cut through them near the edges. Just as you reach the series of four boxlike houses on the left, the road descends into an unnamed creek valley and reveals the older sediments that underlie the glacial ones.

» *Mile 322.85 (0.9) Stop sign. Continue straight ahead onto Douglas County Route 442. Do not jog left onto new Kansas 10.*

Douglas County Route 442, which is the old Kansas 10, continues to traverse the Hesper plain for the next 7 miles, but because this section is near the entrenched Kansas River and its rapidly down-cutting tributaries, it is much more dissected than the area around Hesper.

323.25 (0.4) One of the largest and prettiest wooden barns on the tour route sits just off to the right, a majestic structure with flanking shed extensions on three sides and six small dormer windows for light and ventilation. Everything about it seems to be perfectly proportioned, an example of folk architecture at its best. There used to be a farmhouse at this site, and the barn has suffered since the house's demise. Although the building is still solid, it badly needs a new coat of paint.

323.85 (0.6) Enter Johnson County. Note the final example of signs that mark Douglas County's rural roads (2400E). The county is 24 miles wide.

323.9 (0.05) The estate beyond the small lake on the right belongs to architect Kenneth von Achen. The main house is an old stone five-window "I," with wooden pillars added. To its right is von Achen's studio-office, a new stone building.

324.35 (0.45) The number of "I" houses along Kansas 10 makes it obvious that this is an old trafficway. The brick home on the right is one of the oldest and least altered of these. The highway has changed character radically over the last twenty years. With the spread of Johnson County suburbs south and west from Kansas City and with the growth of the University of Kansas, Kansas 10 has become one of the busiest and most dangerous routes in the state. A new four-lane limited-access version (just to the north) has made the 1980s a safer decade for commuters.

324.85 (0.5) *Sunflower Army Ammunition Plant.* Just beyond the intersection on the right, a sturdily constructed barbed-wire fence marks the northwest corner of a 16,000-acre governmental facility that produces explosive powders and rocket propellants. Because of the inherent danger of fire and explosion in the manufacturing process, operations are dispersed into some five thousand individual buildings, almost all of which are out of sight from the highway. The particularly hazardous buildings are further protected by encircling earthen barricades, and special construction methods are designed to divert explosions upward instead of into surrounding structures.[90]

325.0 (0.15) The entrance for powder trucks is on the right.

325.55 (0.55) The copse on the right is part of a University of Kansas experiment on the feasibility of growing its own fuel.

325.8 (0.25) The Sunflower plant let the city of DeSoto build this ball field on its property as a gesture of neighborliness. Johnson County's Sunflower Park, 0.5 mile ahead, has a similar origin.

326.5 (0.7) The main entrance to the plant. Sunflower is a product of World War II; it was constructed on a crash basis in 1942 at a cost of $100 million. It was located primarily with regard to Kansas City, to be far enough away not to scare anyone yet close enough for workers to commute. The wartime years were chaotic, as twenty thousand construction workers descended on the site, followed by twelve thousand permanent employees. A newspaper account in 1942 claimed that "traffic is so heavy on the Kansas City side of the plant at shift changing time that one could walk the entire distance stepping from one car to another."[91]

Since the 1940s the history of employment at Sunflower has been erratic, though it generally has shown a slow decline. The plant was placed on stand-by status in 1948, but it was partially reactivated in 1951 for the Korean War. Small-scale production has been maintained since, with Viet Nam causing a spurt in employment to 3,500 in 1968. Twenty-one buildings were added in 1980 to produce nitroguanidine, an artillery propellant. About 790 people are now employed, and a second entrance to the plant, 0.65 mile ahead, has been closed because of the decrease in activity.

326.6 (0.1) *Sunflower Village.* Stretching for the next mile on the left side of the road is Sunflower Village, one of the most unusual communities in Kansas. It was created in 1943 for powder-plant workers when the general problems of mass commuting from

Kansas City were aggravated by wartime shortages of automobile tires.[92] Some 850 stark concrete-block units were built originally—the ones you see on the left—and about 580 wooden prefabricated buildings were added to the east in 1945. Soon businesses came in, and Dynamite Junction (as it was dubbed) began to function.

Residents came from all over the Midwest, with an emphasis on the deprived Ozarks hill country. Kids were everywhere, and even two local grade schools were not enough; the surplus had to be bussed to DeSoto. Then, during the late 1940s, Sunflower Village changed character markedly. Units that had been vacated by workers at the plant were acquired by the University of Kansas as housing for its postwar explosion of students. At one time a thousand single students and another thousand student families lived here. Thus Dynamite Junction became Jayhawkville.

After a flurry of activity during the Korean War, Sunflower Village declined along with the powder plant. The wooden buildings on the east side of town were removed, and businesses gradually closed. Only 147 units were occupied in 1956, when title passed from the government to a private developer. In recent years, however, the community has undergone a modest renaissance. The name has been officially changed to Clearview City, and it now caters to retired people in the low- to medium-income brackets. The long white stucco building on the left was until recently the Clearview Market. Only a beauty shop and an "odds and ends" business remain active.

326.85 (0.25) The large abandoned pink building on the left housed a combination of a theater, bowling alley, and restaurant until it closed in 1957 at the nadir of Sunflower Village.[93]

326.95 (0.1) Several old roadways can be seen on the left, marking the former site of the wooden prefab houses mentioned above. The area is in the process of being turned into a trailer court.

327.2 (0.25) The newer of the two Sunflower schools (Countryside Elementary) is on the left; it was built in 1953.

327.7 (0.5) Two small service stations stand abandoned on the left, victims of the change in traffic flow from old to new Kansas 10.

328.55 (0.85) Pass under new Kansas 10.

» *Mile 329.15 (0.6) Angle right, following old Kansas 10, which is here called Lexington Avenue.*

DeSoto. The road that continues straight ahead is the original path of Kansas 10 and runs through downtown DeSoto. It was by-passed in 1943 to eliminate a major bottleneck for Sunflower commuters. Now the by-pass has been by-passed.

The Sunflower plant and village have had a tremendous, though mixed, impact on DeSoto. During the early boom days, the town suffered from severe traffic jams and housing shortages; it still endures the boom-and-bust economics created by erratic production contracts at the plant. Renting out everything from garages to chicken houses and tents in the 1940s, however, and selling supplies to the new workers brought undreamed of prosperity to the townspeople. They paid off mortgages, remodeled homes, and even had money enough to erect a somewhat pretentious civic-center building.[94] Population shot up from four hundred to one thousand and held there until the 1950s, when commuters to Kansas City began to raise the total to twenty-five hundred or so.

DeSoto High School, on the left, represents a microcosm of the above story. Its programs were aided substantially by federal money paid for the children of workers at Sunflower. On the other hand, it had problems stemming from the learning disabilities suffered by a number of the children from Sunflower Village. The background of the average DeSoto youngster differed substantially from that of the average Sunflower child, so the two cultures did not always mix easily at the high school.

329.4 (0.25) Pass under a railroad spur built by the government to supply Sunflower.

329.95 (0.55) Intersecting the highway on the left is Ottawa Street, and coming up at tenth-of-a-mile intervals are Peoria and Wea Streets. These are three of the original seven north-south streets in DeSoto, all named for eastern Indian tribes who were relocated in Kansas during the 1830s and 1840s.[95]

Liquor in Kansas. To the right, opposite the Ottawa Street junction, note the round neon sign Retail Liquor Store in one section of the Mini-Mart building. One can see this sign in unvaried format all across the state, a symbol of Kansas' rather puritanical liquor laws. The legal sale of liquor was banned from 1881 until 1948; even now, strict limitations are in effect. All package outlets, such as this example, must be licensed and must not be internally connected with any other building. The stores cannot advertise prices, cannot use promotional lures, cannot sell mixers or other nonliquor items, and most importantly, cannot sell by the drink.

Several interesting upshots have developed from these restrictions. The state is blanketed with so-called private clubs, where members bring their liquor bottles to be dispensed by a bartender. They are saloons in all ways except by letter of the law. Another result of the liquor situation is 3.2 beer. The state has declared that beer with an alcoholic percentage of 3.2 or less is nonintoxicating and therefore is not subject to the above liquor restrictions. Public bars that dispense it are quite legal (an example exists 0.1 mile to the west). Legislation passed in 1987 has created still-another type of outlet. In counties where voters approve, restaurants may now sell liquor by the drink. The average town in Johnson and other approving counties ironically now has four types of establishments for liquor because of the state's unique laws.

Another part of the 1987 liquor legislation raised the legal age for drinking to 21. This applies to all kinds of alcohol, even the previously exempt 3.2 beer. License applications for beer bars plummeted across the state in 1988, evidence that many of these bars depended heavily on the 18–20 age group. The effect was especially noticeable in the state's border counties, where bars served a youthful clientele from two states. Officials who count tax receipts in Johnson County hope that the increases from the new restaurant/bar combinations will be enough to counter the decline from sales of 3.2 beer.

330.45 (0.5) DeSoto Plaza, on the right, is one of the few prosperous business clusters visible along this mile of strip development. A decline in local population is not the problem, for DeSoto is on the margin of Kansas City's expansion and is growing rapidly. Heavy traffic flow does not come along Lexington Avenue anymore, however; and store owners know that a proposed shopping center at the exit for new Kansas 10 will take their business, just as they themselves had taken it from downtown merchants forty-five years ago. El Rancho Motel, across from the Plaza, is a case in point. It looks fancy when compared with Belvue's "Modern Cabins" (mile 181.1), but it pales when compared with the franchise establishments along the newer highways.

330.55 (0.1) Just beyond the DeSoto Plaza shopping area on the right note the large field devoted to the production of vegetables. It is part of the large truck-farming operation of Fred Morse and Sons, whose headquarters are just ahead.

330.75 (0.2) *DeSoto Truck Farming.* The green steel building on the left, just at the point where the old path of Kansas 10 rejoins the present highway, is the focus of Riverview Farms. The Morse family annually produces 2,000 acres of vegetables, an amazing figure, almost beyond the comprehension of the average gardener.

Truck farming is an old tradition in the rich soils of the Kansas River bottoms. Before the 1950s the big crop was potatoes, with an estimated 18,800 acres being planted in 1925 between Lecompton and DeSoto. Shipments went out by the railroad carload. Blights of various sorts, combined with depressed prices and erratic growing seasons, gradually reduced the potato acreage, and the crop was down to about 500 acres in 1951 before the disastrous flood in that year ended the season. For the ensuing twenty-five years, truck growers turned exclusively to other crops, but potatoes are now making a comeback. This time the growers are aiming for the potato-chip market.

The Morse operation at Riverview Farms is only one of several in the DeSoto area, but is by far the largest. Its crops, as well as its markets, are quite diversified. Some produce is raised on contract for supermarkets, but much of it is marketed independently all over the country. Some, of course, is sold over the counter locally. The major vegetable fields are to the northwest and northeast of DeSoto, where the river bends north, leaving large bottomland acreages on its south bank. Northwest of town, Morse maintains some housing facilities for Mexican laborers who help with the harvest. Working relations are good, and most of the migrants return year after year.

330.85 (0.1) Cross Kill Creek. The origin of this name is uncertain. If may refer to a frontier slaying or it might be the result of early Dutch settlers. The Dutch word for a small stream is *kill;* the term is widespread along the Hudson River area of colonial Dutch settlement. Non-Dutch peoples at DeSoto might have retained the word *kill*, but, not understanding its meaning, added the redundant term *creek* after it.[96]

330.95 (0.1) An excellent vegetable stand is on the left.

332.05 (1.1) *Cedar Junction and the Fate of Cities.* If you blink, you will miss it, but the old settlement of Cedar Junction is along and just off the road to the left for the next two-tenths of a mile. It has no church, business, or school today, but the town was a principal actor in a historical drama that tried to make Lawrence the major metropolis of the Missouri-Kansas frontier.

As discussed at mile 34.1, Kansas City and Leavenworth were major rivals for metropolitan supremacy, with the acquisition of crucial railroad connections holding the key to victory. The idea was to become the intersection of a railroad running west from St. Louis with one running southwest from Chicago. For a period of several years, from the late 1850s until the 1870s, Lawrence made a serious attempt to triumph over both Kansas City and Leavenworth. The Lawrence vision is diagrammed here; it should be compared with the maps at mile 34.1.

The prime mover in the Lawrence plan was Senator James Lane. He backed Leavenworth's attempt to get the rail connection from Chicago, as he hoped for an extension to Lawrence. The St. Louis link was to be achieved by laying track between Pleasant Hill, Missouri, where the Missouri Pacific was, and Cedar Junction. This would by-pass Kansas City and, with a simple extension from Cedar Junction westward, make Lawrence a regional rail center.

The dream might have come true had Senator Lane not become politically unpopular during the mid 1860s. The railroad link between Pleasant Hill and Cedar Junction was actually completed, but not until 1872, after Kansas City had already become established. The connector railroad failed in a few years, and Cedar Junction faded to its present obscurity.

332.25 (0.2) Descend into the valley of Cedar Creek.

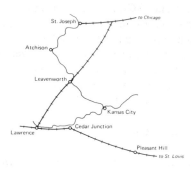

Railroad vision of Lawrence

332.55 (0.3) The road to the left leads to the Kaw flood plain and another vegetable farm. The Caldwells appeal to nearby urban residents with their pick-it-yourself pumpkin operation.

332.85 (0.3) Cedar Valley Forest, an estate nestled in this pretty setting, is another landscape sign that a large city is ahead. Downtown Kansas City is 25 miles away, close enough for serious land speculation to begin. Pressures for development at this distance depend on a combination of access and scenic quality. The winding nature of old Kansas 10 is not inviting to builders of tract housing and commercial property, but it has appeal to wealthy individuals who do not have to keep regular office hours. Note the contrast between the expensive, massive wooden entrance gates to Cedar Valley Forest and its simple graveled driveway. Attempts to "buy" a simple Arcadian existence lead to many such paradoxes.

333.05 (0.2) More typical of the urban influence along byways at this distance from the city are small matchbox homes that are occupied by lower-income urban commuters. Some examples appear on the left. These people may soon be forced farther out, given the active land speculation that is apparent ahead.

333.45 (0.4) A third type of urban-influenced housing now begins, the middle-income ruralite ranch houses that have been sampled elsewhere on the tour. They occupy the zone between the older matchbox homes on the far side and the organized tract developments on the near side of the city. Their development is sporadic, as it depends on finding farmers who are willing to part with small acreages, but in places, as for the next few miles, a nearly continuous strip is formed.

Evidence that these ruralite homes are oriented toward Kansas City, rather than toward DeSoto, can be noted in the numerous "for sale" signs on the highway property: all the realtors represented are from the city.

334.35 (0.9) *Highways and the Ravenswood and Cedar Creek Developments.* Two miles ahead the roadway recently has been widened to four lanes. The Ravenswood housing complex, nestled in the bluff lands to the left, is partly a response to this improved access. New highways on the urban fringe are one of the surest predictors of land development. The construction of Interstate 35 some twenty years ago has led to sustained booms for Overland Park, Lenexa, and most recently, Olathe. Now the Interstate 435 and Kansas 10 developments are switching the emphasis westward. Ravenswood's twenty or so lots are dwarfed by the scale of a whole new "city" under construction along Kansas 10 just 2 miles southeast of the DeSoto city limits. Cedar Creek, as it is called, will be for an elite market. Fourteen thousand homes are planned on 3,300 acres, with prices ranging upward from $120,000. The local professional Tom Watson is designing the golf course, and 315 acres have been reserved for a plush office complex, retail shops, and a hotel/convention center. Within twenty years, thirty thousand residents are expected; DeSoto's days as a small town are numbered.[97]

335.05 (0.7) *Amenity Agriculture.* Note Windcrest Farm on the left, which specializes in Arabian horses. This is an example of a rapidly growing new type of agriculture, oriented not toward food or industrial purposes but toward the aesthetic and recreational needs of urban America. Such pursuits have been termed amenity agriculture by geographer Cotton Mather.

Amenity agriculture has boomed on city peripheries since the 1950s, a direct product of increased leisure time and affluence. Its forms are varied: Christmas-tree farms, dog kennels, shooting preserves, sod farms, and plant nurseries, for example, in addition to the types of enterprises to be sampled along the remainder of the tour route. They could be owned by converted traditional farmers, but evidence suggests that urban businesspeople control most of them.

335.25 (0.2) *The Demise of Traditional Farms.* The decaying Clear Creek Grange Hall on the left ironically emphasizes the tremendous changes in land use and occupance that have occurred along this section of highway. Grange halls were meeting places for farmers, places where isolated people could go occasionally not only to exchange farming ideas but simply to see people socially. Today not only is the isolation gone, but the farmers themselves are getting scarce.

From the farmers' point of view there are both push and pull factors urging them to sell. The positive lure is the large profit that they can make as a result of tremendous increases in land value. Unimproved acreages that sold for a hundred dollars per acre twenty-five years ago now bring several thousand dollars per acre, and by selling out, a farmer can make enough to retire.

If one decides to forsake selling, other factors conspire to almost "force" the farmer out as the city begins to encroach. Increased land values become a double-edged sword, as soaring taxes, based on this value, begin to erode incomes. Finally come other plagues. Suburban children innocently and otherwise begin to leave gates open and to vandalize machinery. Their mothers complain about animal odors and the dangers of herbicides, and their fathers object to farm machinery being on the roads. Restrictions and objections build, and soon the farmer either must go or must consent to some form of amenity agriculture geared expressly to the new urban surroundings.

335.7 (0.45) The first of the tract developments along the route begins on the left and is joined just ahead by one on the right. Both are located on unattractive flat uplands and are aimed at lower-middle-income commuters. The upper middle class can afford locations both more scenic and closer in than this, as will be sampled ahead.

335.85 (0.15) The Lenexa city-limit sign officially announces the presence of suburbia. A city fire station is 0.4 mile ahead. Note also that the tour route is now called Eighty-third Street, part of an urban numbering system emanating from downtown Kansas City, Missouri.

336.55 (0.7) The Rural Water District tower on the left supplies not only the housing tracts but also the small roadside Cole Industrial Park. Manufacturing began here when the spot was rather isolated, having originally been attracted by low taxes and good access for workers via Kansas highways 10 and 7.[98] There is a parking area for commuters next to the water tower.

» *Mile 336.7 (0.15) Intersect Kansas 7. Continue straight ahead on the newly widened Eighty-third Street.*

Before 1984 and the completion of the new interstate-quality Kansas 10, 2 miles to the south, this section of Eighty-third Street carried extremely heavy traffic. Consequently, it was a prime site for business and housing developments. Competition has slowed the frenetic action momentarily and has forced several under-financed entrepreneurs out of business, but Eighty-third Street is still a place in rapid transition. Interstate 435 is only 4.5 miles ahead, and Interstate 35 is another 3 miles beyond that. As a yardstick on which to measure future change, a land-use map of this area, as it existed in mid 1974, is presented here.

336.85 (0.15) Two ends of the spectrum for suburban fringe businesses are represented on opposite sides of the road. Ruf Construction Company, in the large new steel building on the right, does finish carpentry work for the building boom; occupants of the small older house on the left sell firewood, bales of hay, and bird baths from their front yard.

337.55 (0.7) *Horses and Urban America.* Look carefully at the building and grounds now housing the NCS Precision Manufacturing Company. The weathered gray boards on the front façade and the western-style porch suggest a different past, as do remnants of expensive board fencing. This site used to be Whispering Downs Arena and Turf Club, one of the plushest members of the local amenity-agriculture establishment. It was originally conceived as a private club for an exclusive housing development,

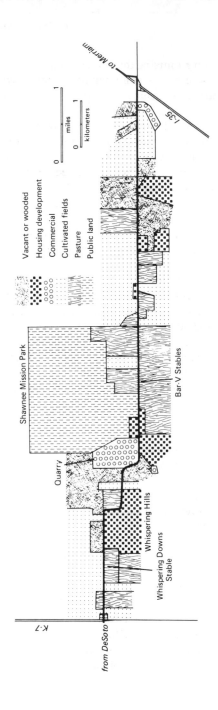

Land use along a portion of 83rd and 87th streets in Johnson County

but it seemed so promising that it was opened to a wider clientele. By the 1970s, there were stalls for 200 horses, with plans for an additional 750 before financial difficulties led to changes in ownership and then closure.

The Whispering Downs idea was a good one, for Americans' obsession with horses has grown steadily over the past several decades. Ever since you left DeSoto, in fact, horse pastures have been increasing in numbers, which suggests that ownership is now more an urban than a rural phenomenon. Certainly no farmers would pay Whispering Downs a thousand dollars a year (feed not included) to stable their work horse. Why are urbanites infatuated with horses? A Minneapolis–St. Paul survey revealed the following reasons: (1) they provide a wholesome, family type of recreation, (2) their care teaches children responsibility, and (3) the person-versus-animal challenge is a relaxing change of pace from normal person-against-person or person-against-machine activities. Status was rarely mentioned in the survey, but it seems to be an additional underlying factor. The growing popularity of "English" riding attire, for example, suggests an attempt to imitate the activities of a cultured European elite.[99]

» *Mile 338.25 (0.7) The road bends gently to the right. Make a sharp turn to the right onto Woodland Drive.*

On the left, just after the turn, there is a panorama of the beautiful Mill Creek Valley. A hardwood forest blankets the bluffs on either side, and through the lowland flows a remarkably clear stream, veritably sparkling as it passes over rock shoals. Given this setting and downtown Kansas City's location less than 20 miles ahead, it is easy to predict the existence of luxury homes here. Just as the beauty of Cedar Valley is now attracting development into a rural area, Mill Creek has created a landscape "island" of the wealthy in the midst of an otherwise middle-income area. The first part of this island, Whispering Hills, is visible in the woods on the right.

338.35 (0.1) The entrance to Whispering Hills. Take a short drive into the development to observe its expensive rustic trappings. A wide variety of floor plans is present, but the homes still all look similar, because of their woodsy character. Rock is used

House in Whispering Hills

extensively, roofs are all wood-shingled, half-timbering is common, and paint has been eschewed in favor of wood stain.[100] The image is further imprinted by the purposeful placing of huge slabs of limestone, the design of street signs, the selection of street names, and, most ostentatiously, by the erection of a large covered bridge over the main entrance road.[101] Most of the homes were built in the mid 1970s and sold then for $70,000 to $300,000.

» *Mile 338.35 (0.0) Turn around and return to Eighty-third Street. Then turn right and descend into the valley.*

338.5 (0.15) This section of gently curving road, including the graceful bridge over Mill Creek, is new. It replaced an angular route, part of which is now Woodland Drive. An almost perfect setting for an ostentatious hobby farm was created inside the elevated curve of the new roadway, and someone has capitalized on it. Not a trick seems to have been missed: a columned, plantation-style house, lots of white board fencing, a pond, and even a new wooden barn.

The bluff land to the south, just before the bridge, is a newer section of Whispering Hills, developed during the early 1980s.

338.85 (0.35) Pass over Mill Creek and the Atchison, Topeka and Santa Fe tracks that connect Kansas City with the main line of the railroad at Emporia. The old roadway is visible below on the right, before the overpass, and on the left afterwards.

339.3 (0.45) A large abandoned quarry is on the left, cut into the Mill Creek bluffs. It was developed prior to the suburbanization of this area but then came under great pressure to cease its noisy, dusty business. Trucks continued to haul out stockpiled material until the late 1970s.

339.65 (0.35) The road on the right leads to Hidden Valley, another collection of luxurious homes overlooking Mill Creek.

339.85 (0.2) *Run-Down Farms and Prosperity.* Examine the beautiful "farmstead" on the left—numerous outbuildings, all in good repair and tastefully painted to match the prosperous-appearing house. It fits the image of what farms in the Midwest, the richest agricultural region in the world, "ought" to look like. The paradox is that large and well-maintained farmsteads are not all that common on the tour route and in most of the area. This example, of course, is no longer a farm; the buildings are being used and maintained by a construction company.

Books about the Midwest that need pictures of prosperous farms almost always resort to shots from the dairy belt in the upper part of the region. Why is this? Are dairy farms in Wisconsin more prosperous than the agricultural operations in Illinois, Missouri, or Kansas? The problem lies in confusing the appearance of prosperity with the real thing. Local farmsteads often appear rundown because farming here, to a greater degree than in the dairy belt, has changed character drastically in the last generation. The general farm that produces a little bit of a lot of things has disappeared in favor of specialization. With this change have come many surplus, anachronistic buildings. Grain specialists do not need livestock barns, and so barns begin to fall into disrepair. Farm wives no longer keep chickens, and so tens of thousands of chicken houses are left to decay.

339.95 (0.1) Shawnee Mission Park, on the left, is an excellent place either to stretch your legs or to picnic. An observation tower which affords a nice view of the Mill Creek area, is just inside the park.

340.55 (0.6) Bar V Riding Stables, an older, much-less-luxurious version of Whispering Downs, used to occupy the land on the right. Its abandoned buildings still stand for the moment, but with the I-435 junction less than a mile away, this land is about to be converted to a more intensive use.

» *Mile 341.1 (0.55) Stop sign. Continue straight ahead on Eighty-seventh Street.*

This intersection with Renner Road provides the last glimpse of rural Kansas on the tour. For the moment a milo field occupies the southwest corner, with pastures elsewhere. A metal-sheathed old barn stands just ahead on the right. Given the frequency of "Will Develop" and "Zoned Commercial" signs in this vicinity, this bucolic scene cannot remain much longer.

341.25 (0.15) Pass under Interstate 435.

Lenexa. I-435 currently represents the limit of continuous development for the city of Lenexa. A sign just past the underpass announces the construction of a new K-Mart store, and beside it are the pristine Point West apartments. Across the road (now called a parkway instead of merely a street) 77 acres are devoted to a combination business park and "French Village" called the Loiret.

New developments such as these are a regular occurrence in Lenexa, once a sleepy town that had only 2,487 people as recently as 1960. Interstate 35 initiated the boom and, when I-435 was completed in 1985, the pace accelerated. Population rose to 5,242 in 1970 and to 18,639 in 1980, and was estimated at more than 31,000 in 1987. When the first edition of this guide was written in 1976, continuous development along Eighty-seventh Street did not begin for another mile to the east. Truly one has to be in almost daily contact with Lenexa to keep up with the expansion.

342.15 (0.9) One last farm house appears on the left, a two-window "I" structure.

342.25 (0.1) The Legler Farm Museum on the right symbolizes the difference in cultural worlds between Lenexa and DeSoto. Over a span of fifteen miles, barns have changed from being an everyday, unnoticed feature of the landscape, through a stage where they were undesirable objects standing in the way of commercial property development, to a rare and valued symbol of a nearly forgotten way of life. The Legler barn, a small stone building, was built in 1864; the museum opened in 1982.

342.45 (0.2) Note the horses on the hillside estate to the right.

343.05 (0.6) Pflumm Road leads to downtown Lenexa, half a mile south. The downtown area is worth a visit because of its contrast with the rest of Lenexa. Its store façades are those of small-town Kansas, not suburbia; they recall the not-so-remote days when Lenexa's only claim to fame was as a station on the interurban railroad that connected Olathe and Kansas City. The old district lends character to the city's otherwise rather bland appearance, but a major renovation project, now under way, threatens to make everything homogeneous.

343.6 (0.55) The property on the left, which is now occupied by the Central Church of the Nazarene and Greystone Estates South, was a beautiful tree-studded pasture in the late 1970s. The trees were mature sugar maples, and they enabled the land to command an incredibly high price. They also add elegance to the grounds of both complexes.

» *Mile 343.7 (0.1) Stop light (Monrovia Drive). Continue straight ahead on Eighty-seventh Street Parkway.*

» *Mile 343.95 (0.25) Stop light (Quivira Road). Continue straight ahead on Eighty-seventh Street Parkway.*

On the left side is one of fourteen new industrial parks that flank Interstates 35 and 435 in Lenexa. Similar parks are scattered along major highways near all major cities in the United States, but the concentration is heavier than normal in Lenexa. The Saint Louis and San Francisco (Frisco) Railroad tracks that parallel I-35 are one reason; they provide firms with rail access to supplement the interstate. In addition, Lenexa actively solicited industries by passing several large revenue bonds; it now draws new firms because of its reputation for supportive government, good schools, and the like. The local business directory currently lists several hundred firms, including a massive J. C. Penney warehouse and many high-tech industries. The city's assessed valuation has skyrocketed—from $1.9 million in 1960 to $220.5 million in 1987.

» *Mile 344.3 (0.35) Turn left onto Interstate 35 and follow the sign to Kansas City.*

345.05 (0.75) *Interstate "Cities."* The development of the interstate-highway network in the United States since the 1950s has engendered a transformation of urban structure. Places such as Lenexa, which were long assumed to be only bedroom communities dependent upon activity in the central city, are rapidly becoming self-sufficient. Some people would now call Lenexa an "outer city" and interpret it as a serious competitor for downtown Kansas City. The transformation began during the 1960s with the rise of suburban shopping malls and warehousing facilities. Then, in the 1970s, populations became large enough to attract regional headquarters of corporations, plus hotels, legal services, and the like. Finally, business offices began to move, often into high-rise buildings that rivaled downtowns in appearance as well as economic activity. The Pine Ridge Business Park on the right is an example of this trend. Its tenants include Xerox, Southwestern Bell, and the Southland Corporation.

Admirers of this roadside landscape stress how the clean lines and the smoke-free environment reflect the new service (as opposed to manufacturing) orientation of the U.S. economy. Critics note a certain blandness caused by similarities of architecture, culture, and wealth. In an ironic twist, labor shortages have begun to develop in these outer cities, while the old downtown areas have surplus workers. Reverse commuting is now underway.[102]

345.25 (0.2) There are several advantages of locations on interstate highways. The Lee Distribution Center on the right obviously needs excellent truck transportation (note the eight loading docks on the south side), but one should not overlook the advertising value in having thousands of motorists pass a plant daily. The careful architecture and landscaping of the Lee facility and its neighbors attest to their awareness of this potential. Additional advantages of such sites are the clean air of a suburban location and its accessibility for customers and employees alike.

345.55 (0.3) The Heritage Yachting Center on the right uses its interstate location to "work on the minds" of passing motorists. A person may not think he or she wants a yacht, but seeing the sign twice a day sometimes is enough to plant a seed of desire. A "BMW Gallery," 0.3 of a mile ahead, plays a similar psychological game with commuters as does a Mercedes Benz dealer just beyond. Driving this section of I-35 is a potentially expensive proposition.

345.95 (0.4) Although the interstate industry along I-35 is all relatively new, there have already been some casualties. The J. C. Penney Outlet Stores, on the right at Seventy-fifth Street, has taken over a building left vacant by GEM (Government Employment Mart). GEM was a local pioneer in the discount retailing of general merchandise. Originally, customers were restricted to the category indicated by its name, but as competition developed from well-organized national chains such as K-Mart and Venture, GEM opened its doors to all comers in an attempt to maintain volume. Even this was not enough, however, and the company went bankrupt about fourteen years ago.

346.35 (0.4) A consumer service center of Kodak is on the right.

346.4 (0.05) *Georgetown.* Northeast Johnson County has achieved a national reputation as an upper-middle-class and upper-class suburban area. It contains virtually no slums and very little moderate-income housing. Leawood, four miles to the southeast, typifies American upper-middle-class suburbia, and Mission Hills, the same distance to the northeast, is an area of mansions that is practically unmatched in its spatial extent. Georgetown, on the right, is part of the local residential glitter; it is almost the only example visible from I-35.

Georgetown is a luxury apartment complex that strives to imitate the understated elegance of the English or Virginia landed gentry by copying wholesale certain architectural features and place names. Note the extensive use of brick, the row-house design, and details such as ivy-covered walls and trash dumps made to look like gazebos. Place names include Picadilly Circus, Oxford Court, and Monticello. Georgetown is a creation of the J. C. Nichols Company, the developer that almost single-handedly was responsible for creating Johnson County's current suburban image (see discussion at mile 8.4).

346.95 (0.55) The AT&T plant on the left is typical of the light industry that is often associated with interstate-highway locations.

347.15 (0.2) Just beyond the Mercedes Benz dealership the highway descends into the valley of Turkey Creek, a stream that it continues to parallel for the next seven miles. The descent is accompanied by an abrupt change in landscape; a cultural one along with the physical. Industry persists, but its character changes from the pristine facilities of AT&T and Kodak to older buildings that deal in heavier and/or bulkier products. These latter firms are here because of the Frisco Railroad, which follows the Turkey Creek route into Kansas City.

347.45 (0.3) The Sixty-third Street exit leads eastward to the Country Club Plaza, J. C. Nichols's pioneer shopping center.

348.2 (0.75) Downtown Merriam, an old railroad stop that has long since become a suburb, is just off I-35 at the Johnson Drive exit. A mile to the west one can see the water tower of Shawnee, a more recent addition to suburbia. Despite their proximity, both towns are old. Shawnee was founded in 1857; Merriam came ten years later when the Frisco was built.

348.45 (0.25) The noise and congestion associated with the railroad-industry complex in Turkey Creek valley make the area undesirable for many types of activities and land use. The site is ideal, however, for certain low-intensity land users who need to be close to population centers. Two examples occur on the left: a school-bus facility and a junkyard.

349.15 (0.7) Turkey Creek passes from the left to the right side of the road. For the next several miles the interstate stays close to the beautiful wooded creek bluffs on the right side. Their serenity makes it difficult to believe that a bustling city lies just above.

349.95 (0.8) The I-635 exit leads northward to the Fairfax Industrial District and to Kansas City International Airport (see mile 10.2).

350.55 (0.6) Enter Wyandotte County.

351.25 (0.7) Two more examples of low-intensity land uses: a maintenance station of the Kansas Highway Commission on the left and Sandifer's Motors (a salvage yard) on the right.

351.45 (0.2) Cross Eighteenth Street Expressway, a main artery linking Wyandotte and Johnson Counties.

351.95 (0.5) Straight ahead is the skyline of downtown Kansas City, Missouri.

352.65 (0.7) *Rosedale.* Southwest Boulevard, which exits here, parallels I-35 for the remainder of the distance to downtown Kansas City; until recently it was a principal traffic artery. It was built through the initiative of the citizens of Rosedale, the community that occupies Turkey Creek valley for the next mile or so.

Although it is now a part of Kansas City, Kansas, Rosedale has always maintained considerable independence. Partly this is because of its isolation both within the Turkey Creek bluffs and across the Kansas River from Kansas City proper. Its independence also evolved because of its local industry. Rosedale serves as a terminal for the Frisco Railroad and thus contains grain elevators, mills, and railroad shops and yards. A variety of these is visible just ahead.

352.95 (0.3) Observe the older Rosedale housing area that was bisected by interstate construction.

353.65 (0.7) Cross Seventh Street Trafficway. Downtown Kansas City, Kansas, is three miles north on this route.

354.65 (1.0) Enter Missouri. Ahead in the distance and to the right is the broadcasting tower of KCTV. The large structure near it is the BMA (Business Man's Assurance) building.

» *Mile 355.65 (1.0) Keep to the left as several traffic arteries from the south merge onto I-35.*

355.75 (0.1) *The Kansas City Business Island.* Note that I-35 is suspended above an east-west trending valley for the next quarter mile. This valley has long been important in the development of Kansas City, because it provides a transportation and industrial corridor around the southern edge of the central business district. When combined with the valleys of Turkey Creek, the Kansas River, and the Missouri River, this lowland makes the downtown area a commercial island, efficiently linked to the outside world by railroad-filled valleys (see map). The position is somewhat analogous to New York's Manhattan Island, with rail transportation substituted for water transportation.

Immediately on the right is Union Station, the traditional hub for local railroad activity, and to its right is the city's general post office. Surrounding these is a wide variety of warehouses and other industry, making this area a secondary business focus of the city. Just beyond Union Station the Crown Center development sits atop the valley bluff. This massive conglomeration of hotels, offices, and commercial stores is the creation of Joyce Hall and Hallmark Cards; it reinforces the importance of this area for Kansas City's economy.

On the map this valley appears as an eastward extension of the general course of the Kansas River. It is probable that the river once occupied this channel, perhaps in glacial times.

» *Mile 356.15 (0.4) Note signs for the junction of Interstates 35 and 70 ahead. Keep left, following the directions toward I-70 and U.S. 24.*

356.35 (0.2) A Kansas City landmark is visible ahead, the gold dome of the Cathedral of the Immaculate Conception.

356.65 (0.3) Downtown Kansas City, Missouri, is immediately on the right.

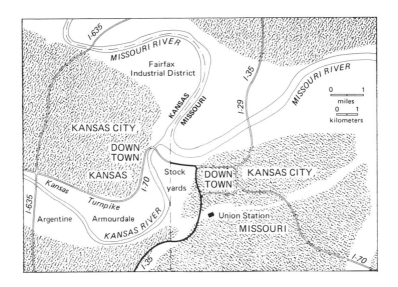

The Kansas City "island"

356.75 (0.1) *Quality Hill.* The highway now leaves the upland island of the city and descends to the Missouri River valley and its industrial district. Just ahead, on the high bluff that appears on the right, is the area known as Quality Hill. This was once Kansas City's most prestigious residential address, but later it degenerated because it was too close to downtown business congestion. More recently the area has been revived by the building of a series of new apartment complexes and the establishment of the offices of the American Hereford Association. The latter's statue of a bull perched high atop a tower overlooking the river bottoms is an appropriate symbol of the agricultural and transportation underpinnings of the Kansas City economy.

The view from the Quality Hill bluff is spectacular, and numerous overlooks have been provided in West Terrace Park. To reach the area, turn east on I-70 ahead, exit south on Broadway, and turn back west on any of the downtown streets.

» *Mile 357.2 (0.45) Merge into the left lane of traffic.*

» *Mile 357.3 (0.1) Turn left onto the Intercity Viaduct and follow the signs to I-70 West and Kansas.*

The Missouri River is directly ahead as you begin the turn, and across the water is Municipal Airport. This used to be the main terminal for the Kansas City area. It was close to the downtown area but it lacked room for the expansion necessary to accommodate the longer runways of modern aircraft. The new airport is fifteen miles north of the city, and Municipal Airport is now used for private planes and as a shopping area.

358.2 (0.9) The Kansas state line again—the end of the tour.

NOTES

1. William P. Bracke, *Wheat Country* (New York: Duell, Sloan & Pearce, 1950), p. 273.
2. For a full discussion of the Strawberry Hill neighborhood see Joseph T. Manzo, "Sequent Occupance in Kansas City, Kansas: A Historical Geography of Strawberry Hill," *Kansas History* 4 (Spring 1981): 20–29. A beautiful series of paintings of the neighborhood by a native is *Images of Strawberry Hill: Works by Marijana*, ed. Jennie Chinn (Topeka: Kansas State Historical Society, 1985).
3. Kansas City (Kans.) Planning Department, "Tax Alternatives to the Property Tax in Kansas City, Kansas," Report no. 1973-6, Feb. 1973 (mimeographed), p. 21.
4. Joseph H. McDowell, *Building a City: A Detailed History of Kansas City, Kansas* (Kansas City, Kans.: Kansas City Kansan, 1970), p. 62.
5. The quotation is from a sign placed in the window of the vacant Helzberg's store at the corner of Seventh and Minnesota during the mid 1970s.
6. See Pamela West's essay "The Rise and Fall of the American Porch," *Landscape* 20 (Spring 1976): 42–47.
7. Alan Farley, "Annals of Quindaro: A Kansas Ghost Town," *Kansas Historical Quarterly* 22 (1956): 305–20.
8. For more on the Exodusters see Glen Schoendemann, "Wyandotte and the First 'Exodusters' of 1879," *Kansas Historical Quarterly* 26 (1960): 223–49; and Nell Irvin Painter, *Exodusters: Black Migration to Kansas after Reconstruction*, paperback ed. (Lawrence: University Press of Kansas, 1986).
9. *Kansas Business News* 8, no. 7 (Oct. 1987): 8–26.
10. McDowell, *Building a City*, p. 26.
11. Ibid., p. 46.

12. The size of this firm was almost unbelievable. In the late 1850s it reportedly had $2 million invested in stock, and it employed six thousand teamsters.

13. For more information on the city rivalries at this time see Frank S. Popplewell, "St. Joseph, Missouri, as a Center of the Cattle Trade," *Missouri Historical Review* 32 (1938): 443–57; James C. Malin, *Grassland Historical Studies*, vol. 1: *Geology and Geography* (Lawrence, Kansas: privately printed, 1950); George L. Anderson, "Atchison, 1865–1886, Divided and Uncertain," *Kansas Historical Quarterly* 35 (1969): 30–45; David G. Taylor, "Boom Town Leavenworth: The Failure of the Dream," ibid., 38 (1972): 389–415; and especially, Charles N. Glaab, *Kansas City and the Railroads* (Madison: Wisconsin State Historical Society, 1962).

14. Two such schools in Kansas have closed recently, the College of Emporia in Emporia (1973) and St. John's College in Winfield (1986).

15. Federal Writers' Project, *A Guide to Leavenworth, Kansas* (Leavenworth: Leavenworth Chronicle, 1940, for the Works Progress Administration, State of Kansas), p. 16.

16. Leavenworth was wealthy enough in the 1930s, for example, to help the Federal Writers Program by subscribing to the local guidebook cited in note 15.

17. The seminal work on voluntary regions is Wilbur Zelinsky's *The Cultural Geography of the United States* (Englewood Cliffs, N.J.: Prentice-Hall, 1973), pp. 134–39.

18. Horace Greeley, *An Overland Journey from New York to San Francisco* (New York: C. M. Saxton, Barker & Co., 1860), pp. 50–51.

19. See Karl B. Raitz, *The Kentucky Bluegrass: A Regional Profile and Guide*, Studies in Geography no. 14 (Chapel Hill: University of North Carolina, Department of Geography, 1980), p. 132.

20. Greeley, *Overland Journey*, pp. 50–51.

21. The classic description of the demoralizing effect of the prairie is O. E. Rolvaag's *Giants in the Earth* (New York: Harper & Brothers, 1927).

22. For more information on the significance of covered bridges see Fred Kniffen, "The American Covered Bridge," *Geographical Review* 41 (1951): 114–23.

23. The Springdale Quakers have now abandoned several of the traditional ways. Plain language is no longer heard, and a sign proclaims the meeting house to be a "church."

24. A third factor is a thin loess mantle that was laid down over much of western Kansas during glacial times. For a readable survey of land-form history in Kansas see Rex C. Buchanan, ed., *Kansas Geology* (Lawrence: University Press of Kansas, 1984).

25. An interesting survey of barn types in the West is Richard Francaviglia's "Western American Barns: Architectural Form and Climatic Considerations," *Yearbook of the Association of Pacific Coast Geographers* 34 (1972): 153-60.

26. Barns have not received the serious study that they deserve, but a start has been made by John Fraser Hart in his *The Look of the Land* (Englewood Cliffs, N.J.: Prentice-Hall, 1975), pp. 123-36. See also Allen G. Noble, *Wood, Brick and Stone*, vol. 2: *Barns and Farm Structures* (Amherst: University of Massachusetts Press, 1984), and the magnificently illustrated book by Eric Arthur and Dudley Witney, *The Barn: A Vanishing Landmark in North America* (Greenwich, Conn.: New York Graphic Society, 1972). For a nineteenth-century view see Byron Halstead, *Barn Plans and Outbuildings* (New York: Orange Judd Co., 1881).

27. An excellent portrayal of haying activities and modern farm life in general is Verlyn Klinkenborg's *Making Hay* (New York: Random House, 1986). A growing collection of rural artifacts can be found at the National Agricultural Hall of Fame in Bonner Springs, Kansas. It is easily accessible via Interstate 70.

28. For a detailed map of the till in Jefferson County see John Winslow, *Geohydrology of Jefferson County, Northeastern Kansas*, bulletin 202, pt. 4 (Lawrence: State Geological Survey of Kansas, 1972), plate 1.

29. For amplification of this and related themes see Kevin P. Condon, "The Cultural Geography of Jefferson County, Kansas" (Master's thesis, Department of Geography, University of Kansas, 1975).

30. The distribution and significance of courthouse squares is discussed by Edward Price in "The Central Courthouse Square in the American County Seat," *Geographical Review* 58 (1968): 29-60.

31. The best statement of this theory is Philip Wells, "Scarp Woodlands, Transported Grassland Soils, and Concept of Grassland Climate in the Great Plains Region," *Science* 148 (1965): 246–49.

32. The case against big dams is eloquently expressed by Walter M. Kollmorgen in "And Deliver Us from Big Dams," *Land Economics* 30 (1954): 333–46.

33. Another force favoring the dams may be America's general obsession with technology and large-scale projects. Skyscrapers and dams are perhaps made more gigantic than necessary just so we can impress ourselves with our ability; see Jean Gottman, "Why the Skyscraper?" *Geographical Review* 56 (1966): 190–212.

34. *Topeka Capital-Journal*, 29 Apr. 1962.

35. The source for these data—and an intriguing book in its own right—is John Rydjord's *Kansas Place-Names* (Norman: University of Oklahoma Press, 1973).

36. The map is properly one of *place* names, rather than simple town names, for it includes the names of a Pennsylvania county (Westmoreland), a New York college (Vassar), and a state (Michigan Valley).

37. The classic study on American folk architecture is Fred B. Kniffen's "Folk Housing: Key to Diffusion," *Annals of the Association of American Geographers* 55 (1965): 549–77. This has been reprinted, together with other relevant studies, in Dell Upton and John Michael Vlach, eds., *Common Places: Readings in American Vernacular Architecture* (Athens: University of Georgia Press, 1986).

38. Many "I" houses in Kansas are known to have been built originally of logs and then covered over with clapboards in later years. One example is south of Wamego, at mile 191.6.

39. Churches serve the same social function, but at the present time, school activities probably draw a larger percentage of most small-town populations than do the churches, especially of those people middle-aged and younger who normally are most active in community development. For more on the role of the school in small-town Kansas society see Roger Barker and Herbert Wright, *Midwest and Its Children* (White Plains, N.Y.: Row, Peterson & Co., 1955).

40. There are four variant spellings of the word *Potawatomi*. The

Kansas county is *Pottawatomie,* the Iowa county is *Pottawattamie,* some Indians use *Pottawatomi,* but most scholars and tribal members prefer *Potawatomi.*

41. Robert John, "Aging in a Native American Community: Service Needs and Support Networks among Prairie Band Potawatomi Elders" (Ph.D. diss., Department of Sociology, University of Kansas, 1986), pp. 195–97.

42. For more on Potawatomi society see James A. Clifton, *The Prairie People: Continuity and Change in Potawatomi Indian Culture: 1665–1965* (Lawrence: Regents Press of Kansas, 1977).

43. C. Hoy Steele, "American Indians and Urban Life: A Community Study" (Ph.D. diss., Department of American Studies, University of Kansas, 1972), p. 93. This excellent study examines the Potawatomis in Topeka.

44. James A. Clifton, "Sociocultural Dynamics of the Prairie Potawatomi Drum Cult," *Plains Anthropologist* 14 (May 1969): 85–93, references on p. 92; see also Robert L. Bee, "Potawatomi Peyotism: The Influence of Traditional Patterns," *Southwestern Journal of Anthropology* 22 (1966): 194–205.

45. Murray L. Wax, quoted by Steele, "American Indians," pp. 28–29.

46. The reservation Catholic church, St. Mary of the Snows, is located four miles north and two and one-half miles west of Shipshee.

47. J. Neale Carman and Karl Pond, "The Replacement of the Indian Languages of Kansas by English," *Transactions of the Kansas Academy of Science* 58 (1955): 131–50.

48. Jen-hu Chang, *Climate and Agriculture* (Chicago: Aldine Publishing Co., 1968), pp. 238–41.

49. Protection of the graves from prowling animals has also been offered as a rationale for the grave houses; see Ruth Landes, *The Prairie Potawatomi: Tradition and Ritual in the Twentieth Century* (Madison: University of Wisconsin Press, 1970), pp. 254–55.

50. Ibid., p. 24.

51. Ruth Landes, "Potawatomi Culture, 1936–1958" (ms., Kansas Collection, University of Kansas Libraries), p. 13.

52. Kansas abounds in rural ethnic communities, as the state was settled during the height of the great emigration from Western Europe. An excellent guide to the Kansas scene is J. Neale Car-

man's work of love *Foreign Language Units of Kansas*, 3 vols. (Lawrence: University of Kansas Press, 1962–74).

53. Ibid., 1:273.

54. The Moravians used to have their own church 2.5 miles south and 1 mile west of here, but the congregation was disbanded in the 1940s, and the building was razed in 1953.

55. A good, although brief, survey of Kansas physical geography is Frank W. Wilson's *Kansas Landscapes: A Geologic Diary* (Lawrence: Kansas Geological Survey, 1978). The best treatment remains Walter H. Schoewe's "The Geography of Kansas, Part II: Physical Geography," *Transactions of the Kansas Academy of Science* 52 (1949): 261–333.

56. *Kansas Business News* 7, no. 6 (May 1986): 49.

57. This map is adapted from Henry V. Beck, "Geology and Ground-Water Resources of Kansas River Valley between Wamego and Topeka Vicinity," bulletin 135, State Geological Survey of Kansas, 1956. Bulletin 96, pt. 5, and bulletin 130, pt. 1, include maps of the Kaw terraces for the Lawrence-Topeka and Kansas City–Lawrence areas, respectively.

58. The severe flood of June 1951 did inundate Newman Terrace, adding some 5 mm. of new material to it.

59. Good introductions to the history and character of Flint Hills ranching are James C. Malin, "An Introduction to the History of the Bluestem-Pasture Region of Kansas," *Kansas Historical Quarterly* 11 (1942): 1–22; and Walter M. Kollmorgen and David S. Simonett, "Grazing Operations in the Flint Hills–Bluestem Pastures of Chase County, Kansas," *Annals of the Association of American Geographers* 55 (1965): 260–90.

60. Kollmorgen and Simonett, "Grazing Operations," p. 290.

61. For a penetrating yet sympathetic look at the history of small midwestern towns see Louis Atherton's *Main Street on the Middle Border* (Bloomington: Indiana University Press, 1954).

62. The significance of this unobtrusive element in the landscape is explored by James F. Hoy in *The Cattle Guard: Its History and Lore* (Lawrence: University Press of Kansas, 1982).

63. An excellent guide to prairie vegetation is *Pasture and Range Plants*, originally published in 1965 by the Phillips Petroleum Company of Bartlesville, Oklahoma. Bartlesville is in the big-pasture country of Oklahoma, and the family of the late Phillips executive K. S. ("Boots") Adams owns a large ranch there.

64. The relationship between railroads and town founding in the Great Plains is a fascinating subject; see John C. Hudson, *Plains Country Towns* (Minneapolis: University of Minnesota Press, 1985).

65. Francaviglia, "Western American Barns," pp. 153–60.

66. *Lawrence* (Kans.) *Journal-World*, 27 Nov. 1987.

67. An excellent guide to the trail has been written by Marc Simmons, *Following the Santa Fe Trail: A Guide for Modern Travelers*, rev. ed. (Santa Fe, N.Mex.: Ancient City Press, 1986).

68. For more information on Kansas images see James R. Shortridge, "Vernacular Regions in Kansas," *American Studies* 21 (Spring 1980): 73–94, and "Cowboy, Yeoman, Pawn, and Hick: Myth and Contradiction in Great Plains Life," *Focus* 35 (Oct. 1985): 22–27. More-general issues are explored by Peter Gould and Rodney White in *Mental Maps* (Baltimore, Md.: Penguin Books, 1974).

69. This idea is more fully developed by J. B. Jackson in "Metamorphosis," *Annals of the Association of American Geographers* 62 (1972): 155–58.

70. An excellent account of the Osage County coal industry is D. Lane Hartsock's "Coal Mining in Osage County, Kansas: Resource Development in an Economically Marginal Area" (Master's thesis, Department of Geography, University of Kansas, 1969); see also his "The Impact of the Railroads on Coal Mining in Osage County, 1868–1910," *Kansas Historical Quarterly* 37 (1971): 429–40.

71. Dennis Holzman, "U.S. Homebuilders: Ignoring Solar," *Technology Review* 87 (Jan. 1974): 69–70; Roger Pollack, "Solar Power: The Promise Fades," *Progressive* 48 (Sept. 1984): 32–35.

72. Richard A. Burk, "A History of Scranton, Kansas," in *Scranton Centennial: 1872–1972* (n.p., 1972), p. 5.

73. See Lisa Gubernick, "Small Towns, Big Money," *Forbes*, 17 Nov. 1986, pp. 50, 52. Other locations for Casey's in the tour area include nearby Burlingame and Carbondale, Oskaloosa, Ozawkie, Silver Lake, and, somewhat uncharacteristically, Leavenworth.

74. David Wolford, owner of Comin-Tek, Inc., which publishes the programming magazine *Satellite Orbit*, as quoted in Alex B. Block, "An Eye on the Sky," *Forbes*, 5 Nov. 1984, pp. 196, 198–99, quotation on p. 198. A good survey of the industry's

development is David Owen's "Satellite Television," *Atlantic Monthly*, June 1985, pp. 45–62.

75. The outlook for Kansas entrepreneurs is discussed in *Kansas Business News* 8, no. 5 (Aug. 1987): 7.

76. Carbondale *Carbondalian*, 15 Mar. 1887.

77. Albert D. Richardson, *Beyond the Mississippi* (Hartford, Conn.: American Publishing Co., 1867), p. 37.

78. Terry Humphrey, executive director of the Kansas Manufactured Housing Institute, quoted in *Kansas Business News* 6, no. 8 (July 1985): 36.

79. Three excellent guidebooks, on completely different scales from this one, coincide with this section of the route: see Gregory M. Franzwa, *The Oregon Trail Revisited*, 2d ed. (Gerald, Mo.: Patrice Press, 1978); George R. Stewart, *U.S. 40: Cross Section of the United States of America* (Boston, Mass.: Houghton Mifflin Co., 1953); and Thomas R. Vale and Geraldine R. Vale, *U.S. 40 Today: Thirty Years of Landscape Change in America* (Madison: University of Wisconsin Press, 1983).

80. The name comes from the bow, or "U" shaped piece of wood, placed under and around the neck of an ox as a kind of collar; its upper ends were inserted in the bar of a yoke.

81. E. C. Becker, "Kansas Lake Where Daniel Boone Trapped," *Outdoor Life* 19 (1907): 379–81. Another old and prominent Kaw Valley oxbow lake gives its name to Silver Lake, Kansas.

82. Two recent explorations of the topic are Richard Horwitz's *The Strip: An American Place* (Lincoln: University of Nebraska Press, 1985) and Chester H. Liebs's *From Main Street to Miracle Mile: American Roadside Architecture* (Boston: Little, Brown & Co., 1985).

83. Because most drained land is indistinguishable from other farmland, people are generally unaware of how much of the United States is underlain by clay tiles. The acreage is considerably larger than that in irrigation. For a good case study see Leslie Hewes and Phillip Frandson, "Occupying the Wet Prairie: The Role of Artificial Drainage in Story County, Iowa," *Annals of the Association of American Geographers* 42 (1952): 24–50.

84. Charles L. Wood, "Fencing in Five Kansas Counties between 1875 and 1895" (Master's thesis, Department of History,

University of Kansas, 1968), p. 54, quoting a letter to the editor in the *Atchison* (Kans.) *Daily Champion*, 30 June 1883.

85. The transpiration rationale for increasing rainfall is faulty in that it ignores the large scale of atmospheric dynamics. Air masses that are over Kansas on one day will typically be found five hundred miles farther eastward on the next day. For more on rain-making attempts on the plains see Walter M. Kollmorgen and Johanna Kollmorgen, "Landscape Meteorology in the Plains Area," *Annals of the Association of American Geographers* 63 (1973): 424–41.

86. Wood, "Fencing in Five Kansas Counties," p. 28, quoting an editorial in the *Atchison* (Kans.) *Daily Champion*, 16 Mar. 1880.

87. U.S. Department of Agriculture, *Bulletin 321* (12 Jan. 1916), p. 31.

88. The authoritative book on the subject is T. Lindsay Baker's *A Field Guide to American Windmills* (Norman: University of Oklahoma Press, 1986).

89. The old bell from the academy has been incorporated into a monument located in front of the meeting house. The development of the Hesper neighborhood has been traced by S. Lindley Stanley, "A History of the Quaker Settlement at Hesper, Kansas" (Master's thesis, Department of History, Kansas State Teachers College–Pittsburg, 1937).

90. The plant's design and purpose attracted national attention when it was first opened; see Paul W. Kearney, "Hell's a Poppin' in Kansas," *Reader's Digest*, Apr. 1945, pp. 35–37.

91. *Lawrence* (Kans.) *Journal-World*, 22 July 1942.

92. Ibid., 23 Sept. 1942.

93. A brief history has been written by Floyd Talley, "Sunflower Then (1942) and Now (1972)" (mimeographed, 1972).

94. Dot Ashlock-Longstieth, *DeSoto, Kansas is 100 Years Old, 1857–1957* (n.p., n.d.).

95. The other four streets are Kickapoo, Shawnee, Delaware, and Wyandotte. For a similar naming process see the discussion at Leavenworth, mile 40.5.

96. Familiar "kill" examples include the Catskill Mountains of New York and the Schuylkill River at Philadelphia. "Rio Grande River" and "Sierra Nevada Mountains" are other redundancies of the Kill Creek type.

97. *Lawrence* (Kans.) *Journal-World*, 23 Dec. 1987.
98. Tax rates are relative, of course. A given rate may seem quite high to a farmer who has large acreages yet be low for a manufacturing plant.
99. Robert Irving, *Amenity Agriculture*, British Columbia Geographical ser. no. 11 (Vancouver: Tantalus Publishing Co., 1966), p. 75. The number of horses on farms declined so much after the 1930s that the U.S. Census Bureau stopped collecting data about them in 1959. This was just about the time when urban horse ownership began to reach impressive numbers.
100. See the discussion of this term at mile 39.4.
101. Examples are Deer Run, Meadow Lane, Bittersweet Drive, Pebble Lane, and Bridle Dale.
102. A good introduction to the general topic is William K. Stevens's "Beyond the Mall: Suburbs Evolving into 'Outer Cities,'" *New York Times*, 8 Nov. 1987, sec. 4, p. 5.

SOURCES FOR FURTHER READING

The following books and other references are recommended for those who wish to learn more about the Kansas countryside and the art of landscape reading in general.

MAPS

The 7.5-minute topographic maps published by the U.S. Geological Survey are the beginning point for any detailed study of Kansas geography. Each map covers an area about eight by seven miles and contains a wealth of information not only on vegetation and land forms but also on cultural features such as houses, barns, roads, and place names. These maps are available in large libraries, at some bookstores, and from the Kansas Geological Survey in Lawrence. County-level maps are useful for slightly more generalized information. Road maps at this scale are available from the Kansas State Highway Commission in Topeka, and the U.S. Geological Survey is in the process of completing a series of county topographic maps. Geologic maps for most counties have been published by the Kansas Geological Survey, but some are out of print.

Socolofsky, Homer E., and Huber Self. *Historical Atlas of Kansas*. Norman: University of Oklahoma Press, 1972.

PHYSICAL GEOGRAPHY

Buchanan, Rex C., ed. *Kansas Geology: An Introduction to Landscapes, Rocks, Minerals, and Fossils*. Lawrence: University Press of Kansas, 1984.

Collins, Joseph T., ed. *Natural Kansas*. Lawrence: University Press of Kansas, 1985.

Madson, John. *Where the Sky Began: Land of the Tallgrass Prairie*. Boston: Houghton Mifflin Co., 1982.

Schoewe, Walter H. "The Geography of Kansas, Part II: Physical Geography." *Transactions of the Kansas Academy of Science* 52 (1949): 261–333.

CULTURE STUDIES

Details of Kansas local history and geography are fugitive. Many relevant studies appear in *Kansas History*, the journal of the Kansas State Historical Society, as well as in its predecessors, the *Kansas Historical Quarterly* and the *Kansas Historical Collections*. Various county and town histories contain good information, too, but the manuscript "clippings file," maintained for each county by the staff of the state historical society, is perhaps the most useful single source.

Bader, Robert S. *Hayseeds, Moralizers, and Methodists: The Twentieth-Century Image of Kansas*. Lawrence: University Press of Kansas, 1988.

Carman, J. Neale. *Foreign Language Units of Kansas*. 3 vols. Lawrence: University of Kansas Press, 1962–74.

Davis, Kenneth S. *Kansas: A History*. New York: W. W. Norton & Co., 1976.

Leland, Lorrin, ed. *The Kansas Experience in Poetry*. Lawrence: University of Kansas, Division of Continuing Education, 1978.

Rydjord, John. *Kansas Place-Names*. Norman: University of Oklahoma Press, 1973.

Schmeckebier, Lawrence E. *John Steuart Curry's Pageant of America*. New York: American Artists Group, 1943.

Shortridge, James R. "Cowboy, Yeoman, Pawn, and Hick: Myth and Contradiction in Great Plains Life." *Focus* 35 (Oct. 1985): 22–27.
_____. "Vernacular Regions in Kansas." *American Studies* 21 (Spring 1980): 73–94.

Webb, Walter P. *The Great Plains*. Boston: Ginn, 1931.

GUIDEBOOKS

Two excellent guides exist to other parts of the country at a scale similar to this Kaw Valley study. They are listed immediately below. Other citations are to works of broader scope that include aspects of the Kansas scene.

Raitz, Karl B. *The Kentucky Bluegrass: A Regional Profile and Guide*. Studies in Geography no. 14. Chapel Hill: University of North Carolina, Department of Geography, 1980.

Swain, Harry, and Cotton Mather. *St. Croix Border Country*. Prescott, Wis.: Trimbelle Press, 1968.

Buchanan, Rex C., and James R. McCauley. *Roadside Kansas: A Traveler's Guide to Its Geology and Landmarks*. Lawrence: University Press of Kansas, 1987.

Fitzgerald, Daniel C. *Ghost Towns of Kansas: A Traveler's Guide*. Lawrence: University Press of Kansas, 1988.

Franzwa, Gregory M. *The Oregon Trail Revisited*. 2d ed. Gerald, Mo.: Patrice Press, 1978.

Simmons, Marc. *Following the Santa Fe Trail: A Guide for Modern Travelers*. Rev. ed. Santa Fe, N.Mex.: Ancient City Press, 1986.

Stewart, George R. *U.S. 40: Cross Section of the United States of America*. Boston: Houghton Mifflin, 1953.

Vale, Thomas R., and Geraldine R. Vale. *U.S. 40 Today: Thirty Years of Landscape Change in America*. Madison: University of Wisconsin Press, 1983.

WPA Guide to 1930s Kansas, The. Reprint. Lawrence: University Press of Kansas, 1984.

INTERPRETATION OF THE LANDSCAPE

John Brinckerhoff Jackson has inspired many to search for meaning in commonplace American landscapes. The journal he founded, *Landscape*, is an excellent, very readable magazine. Jackson's essays have been collected several times, most recently as *Discovering the Vernacular Landscape* (New Haven, Conn.: Yale University Press, 1984).

Meinig, Donald W., ed. *The Interpretation of Ordinary Landscapes: Geographical Essays*. New York: Oxford University Press, 1979.

Stilgoe, John R. *Common Landscapes of America, 1580–1845*. New Haven, Conn.: Yale University Press, 1982.

_____. *Metropolitan Corridor: Railroads and the American Scene*. New Haven, Conn.: Yale University Press, 1983.

Upton, Dell, and John Michael Vlach, eds. *Common Places: Readings in American Vernacular Architecture*. Athens: University of Georgia Press, 1986.

INDEX